ML
1741
N49
1914A

Newmarch, Rosa Harriet (Jeaffreson) 1857–1940.

The Russian opera, by Rosa Newmarch. New York, E. P. Dutton & company ₁1914₎

xv p., 2 l., 403 p. front., plates (1 double) ports. 19½ cm.

Reprint ed., Westport, Conn., Greenwood Press, 1972.

1. Opera, Russian—Hist. & crit.   I. Title.

14—30799

Library of Congress   ML1741.N49

₁a18a1₎

THE
RUSSIAN
OPERA

FEODOR IVANOVICH SHALIAPIN

THE
RUSSIAN OPERA

BY
R O S A
NEWMARCH

GREENWOOD PRESS, PUBLISHERS
WESTPORT, CONNECTICUT

The Library of Congress has catalogued this publication as follows:

Library of Congress Cataloging in Publication Data

Newmarch, Rosa Harriet (Jeaffreson) 1857-1940.
   The Russian opera.

   Reprint of the 1914 ed.
   1. Opera, Russian--History and criticism.
ML1741.N49   1972   782.1'0947   72-109807
ISBN 0-8371-4298-9

Originally published in 1914
by E. P. Dutton & Company, New York

First Greenwood Reprinting 1972

Library of Congress Catalogue Card Number 72-109807

ISBN 0-8371-4298-9

Printed in the United States of America

TO

FEODOR IVANOVICH SHALIAPIN

IN MEMORY OF OUR OLD FRIEND

VLADIMIR VASSILIEVICH STASSOV

PREFACE

ETWEEN January 19th, 1900, and April 4th, 1905, I read before the Musical Association of London five papers dealing with the Development of National Opera in Russia, covering a period from the first performance of Glinka's *A Life for the Tsar* in 1836, to the production of Rimsky-Korsakov's opera *The Tsar's Bride*, in 1899. These lectures were illustrated by the following artists : the late Mrs. Henry J. Wood, Miss Grainger Kerr, Mr. Seth Hughes, Mr. Robert Maitland ; Sir (Mr.) Henry J. Wood and Mr. Richard Epstein at the piano. While using these lectures as the scaffolding of my present book, I have added a considerable amount of new material, amassed during ten years unremitting research into my subject. The additions concern chiefly the earlier phases of Russian music, and the operas that have appeared since 1900. The volume also contains some account of the foundation of the nationalist school of composers

under the leadership of Balakirev. It has been
my privilege to meet and converse with most of
the members of this circle. I give also a few
details about the literary champion of " the
Invincible Band," Vladimir Stassov, under whose
guidance I first studied the history of Russian
music. With all modesty I believe I may claim
to have been a pioneer worker in this field.
When in 1895 I published my translation (from
the French edition of M. Habets) of Stassov's
book on Borodin, and followed it up in 1897 by
a series of articles—the fruits of my first visit to
Russia—in that short-lived weekly *The Musician*,
the literature of the subject was by no means
copious, even in Russia itself ; while the daily
increasing public in Western Europe who were
anxious to learn something about the remarkable
galaxy of composers newly arisen in the east,
based their knowledge and opinions almost
entirely upon César Cui's pamphlet *La Musique
en Russie*, an interesting, but in many respects
misleading, statement of the phenomenon; or
upon the views propagated by Rubinstein and
his followers, wherefrom they learnt that the
Russians, though musically gifted, were only
represented by incapable amateurs.

Happily for its own enjoyment, the world

has grown wiser. The last few years have witnessed the vindication of Moussorgsky's genius in France and England ; a consummation devoutly wished, but hardly anticipated, by those who had been convinced from the beginning of the nobility and sincerity of spirit and motive which entitles his two finished operas to be regarded as masterpieces. During Sir Joseph Beecham's season of Russian Opera at Drury Lane last year, Rimsky-Korsakov's early music-drama *Ivan the Terrible* (" The Maid of Pskov ") made a profound impression, with Shaliapin in the part of the tyrant Tsar. In the forthcoming season it is Borodin's turn to be introduced to the British public, and I confidently predict the success of his lyric opera *Prince Igor*. So, one by one, these Russians, " eaters of tallow candles, Polar bears, too long consumers of foreign products, are admitted in their turn in the character of producers." [1]

In view of the extended interest now felt in Russian opera, drama and ballet, it has been thought worth while to offer to the public this outline of the development of a genuine national opera, from the history of which we have much to learn in this country, both as regards the

[1] Letter from Borodin to Countess Mercy-Argenteau.

things to be attempted and those to be shunned. Too much technical analysis has been intentionally avoided in this volume. The musician can supply this deficiency by the study of the scores mentioned in the book, which, dating from Glinka's time, have nearly all been published and are therefore accessible to the student ; the average opera-goer will be glad to gain a general view of the subject, unencumbered by the monotonous terminology of musical analysis.

CONTENTS

CHAPTER I

THE DAWN OF MUSIC IN RUSSIA

CHAPTER II

THE RUSSIAN OPERA PRIOR TO GLINKA

CHAPTER III

MICHAEL IVANOVICH GLINKA

CONTENTS

CONTENTS

CHAPTER VIII
BALAKIREV AND HIS DISCIPLES

CHAPTER IX
PERSONAL MEMORIES OF BALAKIREV'S CIRCLE

CHAPTER X
MOUSSORGSKY

CHAPTER XI
BORODIN AND CUI

CHAPTER XII

RIMSKY-KORSAKOV

CHAPTER XIII

TCHAIKOVSKY

CONTENTS

CHAPTER XIV

CONCLUSION

ILLUSTRATIONS

THE
RUSSIAN
OPERA

THE RUSSIAN OPERA

CHAPTER I

THE DAWN OF MUSIC IN RUSSIA

THE early history of the development of the national music, like that of most popular movements in Russia, has its aspects of oppression and conflict with authority. On the one hand we see a strong natural impulse moving irresistibly towards fulfilment ; on the other, a policy of repression amounting at moments to active persecution. That the close of the nineteenth century has witnessed the triumph of Russian music at home and abroad proves how strong was the innate capacity of this people, and how deep their love of this art, since otherwise they could never have finally overcome every hindrance to its development. That from primitive times the Slavs were easily inspired and moved by music, and that they practised it in very early phases of their civilisation, their early historians are all agreed. In the legend of " Sadko, the Rich Merchant " (one of the *byline* of the Novgorodian

Cycle) the hero, a kind of Russian Orpheus, who suffers the fate of Jonah, makes the Sea-king dance to the sound of his *gusslee*, and only stays his hand when the wild gyrations of the marine deity have created such a storm on earth that all the ships on the ocean above are in danger of being wrecked.   In the " Epic of the Army of Igor," when the minstrel Boyan sings, he draws " the grey wolf over the fields, and the blue-black eagle from the clouds."   In peace and war, music was the joy of the primitive Slavs.   In the sixth century the Wends told the Emperor in Constantinople that music was their greatest pleasure, and that on their travels they never carried arms but musical instruments which they made themselves.   Pro-copius, the Byzantine historian, describing a night attack made by the Greeks, A.D. 592, upon the camp of the Slavs, says that the latter were so completely absorbed in the delights of singing that they had forgotten to take any pre-cautionary measures, and were oblivious of the enemy's approach.   Early in their history, the Russian Slavs used a considerable number of musical instruments : the *gusslee*, a kind of horizontal harp, furnished with seven or eight strings, and the *svirel*, a reed pipe (chalumet), being the most primitive.   Soon, however, we read of the *goudok*, a species of fiddle with three strings, played with a bow ; the *dombra*,

an instrument of the guitar family, the forerunner of the now fashionable *balalaïka*, the
strings of which were vibrated with the fingers ;
and the *bandoura*, or *kobza*, of the Malo-
Russians, which had from eight to twenty
strings. Among the primitive wind instruments were the *sourna*, a shrill pipe of Eastern
origin, and the *doudka*, the bagpipe, or corne-
muse. The drum, the tambourine, and the
cymbals were the instruments of percussion
chiefly in use.

Berezovsky makes a convenient division of
the history of Russian music into four great
periods. The first, within its limits, was purely
national. It included all the most ancient folk-
songs and *byline*, or metrical legends ; it saw
the rise and fall of the *Skomorokhi*, the minstrels
who were both the composers and preservers
of these old epics and songs. This period
reached its highest development in the reign
of Vladimir, " The Red Sun," first Christian
prince of Russia, about A.D. 988. The second
period, which Berezovsky describes as already
falling away from the purely national ideal,
dates from the establishment of Christianity
in Russia, at the close of the tenth century,
when the folk music lost much of its independence and fell under Byzantine influence. Russian music entered upon its third period about
the middle of the eighteenth century ; national

songs now regained some of their former importance, but its progress was checked because the
tastes of Western Europe were already paramount in the country. Italian music had
reached the capital and long held the field.
The first twenty years of the nineteenth century
witnessed a passionate revival of interest in
the national music, and when, in 1836, Glinka
created *A Life for the Tsar,* he inaugurated
a fourth period in the history of national art, the
limits of which have yet to be ultimately defined.

Of the first, the primitive period in Russian
music, there are few records beyond the allusions
to the love of minstrelsy which we find in the
earliest known songs and legends of the Russian
Slavs. When we reach the second period, at
which the national music entered upon a struggle
with the spiritual authorities, we begin to
realise from the intolerance of the clerical
attitude how deeply the art must have already
laid hold upon the spirit of the people. Whether
from a desire to be faithful to oriental asceticism,
and to the austere spirit which animated the
Church during the first centuries which followed
the birth of Christ, or because of the need to
keep a nation so recently converted, and still
so deeply impregnated with paganism, fenced
off from all contaminating influences, the
Church soon waged relentless war upon every
description of profane recreation. The Orthodox

clergy were not only opposed to music, but to every form of secular art. Moreover the folk-songs were of pagan origin ; therefore, just as the priests of to-day still look askance at the songs and legends of the Brittany peasants which perpetuate the memory of heathen customs, so the Byzantine monks of the eleventh century, and onwards, denounced the national songs of Russia as being hostile to the spirit of Christianity. Songs, dances, and spectacular amusements were all condemned. Even at the weddings of the Tsars, as late as the seventeenth century, dancing and singing were rigorously excluded, only fanfares of trumpets, with the music of flutes and drums, and fireworks, being permitted. Professor Milioukhov, in his "Sketch for a History of Russian Culture," quotes one of the austere moralists of mediæval times who condemns mirth as a snare of the evil one ; " laughter does not edify or save us ; on the contrary it is the ruin of edification. Laughter displeases the Holy Spirit and drives out virtue, because it makes men forget death and eternal punishment. Lord, put mirth away from me ; give me rather tears and lamentations." So persistent and effectual was the repression of all secular enjoyments that one monkish chronicler was able to remark with evident satisfaction that, for the time being, " there was silence in all the land of Russia."

Under these conditions the primitive music had little chance of development. Driven from the centres of dawning civilisation, it took refuge in forest settlements and remote villages. With it fled the bards and the mummers, the gleemen—those " merry lads " as the Russians called them—so dear to the hearts of the people. These musicians were originally of two classes : minstrels and *gusslee* players (harpists), such as the famous Skald, Bayan ; and the *Skomorokhi*, or mummers, who sang and juggled for the diversion of the people. In course of time we find allusions to several subdivisions in the band of *Skomorokhi*, all of which may now be said to have their modern equivalents in Russia. There was the *Skomorokh-pievets*, or singer of the mythical or heroic songs, who afterwards became absorbed into the ranks of the poets with the rise of a school of poetry at the close of the sixteenth century ; the *Skomorokh-goudets*, who played for dancing, and was afterwards transformed into the orchestral player, exchanging his *gusslee* or *dombra* for some more modern western instrument ; the *Skomorokh-plyassoun*, the dancer, now incorporated in the corps-de-ballet ; and the *Skomorokh-gloumosslovets*, the buffoon or entertainer, who eventually became merged in the actor.

Monkish persecution could not entirely stamp out the love of music in the land. To attain that end it would have been necessary to uproot the very soul of the nation. Despite the fulminations of the clergy, the nobles still secretly cherished and patronised their singers, who beguiled the tedium of the long winters in their *poteshni palati*. These dependents of the aristocracy were the first actors known to the Russians. At the same time such fanatical teaching could not fail to alter in some degree the temper of a people wholly uneducated and prone to superstition. The status of the minstrels gradually declined. They ceased to be " welcome guests " in hut and hall, and the *Skomorokhi* degenerated into companies of roving thieves, numbering often from fifty to a hundred, who compelled the peasants to supply them with food, as they moved from place to place, driven onward by their clerical denunciators. By way of compromise, the gleemen now appear to have invented a curious class of song which they called " spiritual," in which pagan and Christian sentiments were mingled in a strange and unedifying jumble. The pure delight of singing having been condemned as a sin, and practised more or less *sub rosa*, the standard of songs became very much corrupted. The degeneracy of music and kindred forms of recreation was most probably the outcome of this intolerant persecution. But though they had helped to bring about this state of affairs, there was no doubt something to be said for the attitude of the clergy, if we may believe the testimony of western travellers in Russia in the sixteenth century. The minstrels in the service of the richer nobles deteriorated as a class, and claimed their right to give entertainments in towns and villages, which were often of scandalous coarseness and profanity. The same may be said of the puppet-shows (*Koukolnaya teatr*), of somewhat later date, the abominable performances of which shocked the traveller Adam Olearius when he accompanied the ambassador sent by Frederick Duke of Holstein to the Great Duke of Muscovy in 1634 and 1636. The long struggle between spiritual authority and the popular craving for secular recreation continued until the reign of Alexis Mikhaïlovich (1645-1676).

In a measure the Church was successful in turning the thoughts of the people from worldly amusements to the spiritual drama enacted within her doors. During these long dark centuries, when Russia had neither universities nor schools, nor any legitimate means of recreation, the people found a dramatic sensation in the elaborate and impressive ritual of the Orthodox Church. Patouillet, in his book " Le Théâtre de Mœurs Russes," says : " the iconostasis, decorated with paintings, erected between the altar and the faithful, resembles, with its three doors, an antique proscenium. The 'imperial' door, reserved for the officiating priest, and formerly for the Emperor, recalls by its name, if not by its destination, the 'royal' entrance of the Greek theatre. Thus there is, as it were, a double scene being enacted, one which takes place before the eyes of the congregation, the other hidden from them during certain portions of the ritual, particularly at the moment of the 'Holy Mysteries' (the Consecration of the elements). These alternations of publicity and mystery; the celebrant reappearing and disappearing; the deacon, who goes in and out at the side doors and stands upon the *Ambon*, like a kind of λογεῖον, to declare the divine word to the assembled Christians, dialoguing sometimes with them, sometimes with the officiating priest; the double choir of singers, arranged even in this day on each side of the iconostasis, and finally the attitude of the faithful themselves—rather that of a crowd of spectators than of participants—all these details formed a spectacle full of dramatic interest in times of simple faith."

On certain religious festivals, allegorical representations, such as the Washing of the Feet and the Entrance of Christ into Jerusalem, were enacted in public places. The early marriage service of the Orthodox Church, with its pompous religious ceremonial and social

customs, such as the pretended lamentations
of the bride, and the choruses of the young
girls, held distinctly dramatic elements. In
these ecclesiastical ceremonies and social usages
may be traced the first germs of the Russian
drama.

In Western Russia we find the school drama
(Shkolnaya-drama) established in the ecclesiastical Academy of Kiev as early as the close
of the fifteenth century. The students used
to recite the events of the Nativity in public
places and illustrate their words by the help
of the *Vertep*, a kind of portable retable on which
were arranged figures representing the Birth
of Christ. The Passion of Our Lord was represented in the same way, and the recital was
interspersed with choral singing, and not in-
frequently with interludes of a secular or comic
nature. This form of drama had found its
way into Russia from Poland. In 1588 Giles
Fletcher, Queen Elizabeth's ambassador to
Russia, gives an account of a representation
in Moscow, which reminds us of the Scoppio
del Carro, the Easter ceremony at Florence,
when a mechanical dove carrying the " Pazzi
fire," lit from the sacred flint brought back
from the Holy Sepulchre, is set rushing along a
wire from the altar to the car, hung about with
fireworks, which stands outside the great West
Door of the Duomo. When the bird comes in

contact with the car the pyrotechnical display is ignited, and if all goes without a hitch the vintage and harvest will prosper.

Says Fletcher: "The weeke before the Nativitie of Christ every bishop in his cathedral church setteth forth a shew of the three children in the oven.[1] Where the Angell is made to come flying from the roof of the church, with great admiration of the lookers-on, and many terrible flashes of fire are made with rosen and gun-powder by the Chaldeans (as they call them), that run about the town all the twelve days, disguised in their plaiers coats, and make much good sport for the honour of the bishop's pageant. At the Mosko, the emperour himselfe and the empress never faile to be at it, though it be but the same matter plaid every yeere, without any new invention at all."

Dr. Giles Fletcher was a member of the family so well-known in the history of English literature; he was the uncle of John Fletcher, the dramatist, and the father of Phineas Fletcher, the author of the poem "The Purple Island." How naïve and almost barbarous must this Russian mystery play have seemed to the Englishman who had probably witnessed some of the innumerable comedies, tragi-comedies, farces, and tragedies which were then enacted

[1] The show refers to a legend of St. Nicholas, Bishop of Myra, the saint held in most honour by the Russians.

at home in the universities, the Inns of Court, and elsewhere ; and who may very likely already have frequented the theatre in Blackfriars or Shoreditch, and seen the plays of Marlowe and Greene, although as yet hardly anything of Shakespeare !

Ivan the Terrible (1533-1584), who first sent for printers from Germany and published the earliest Russian book (containing the Acts of the Apostles and the Epistles) in 1564, did nothing towards the secular education of his Court or of the people. Nor was there much progress in this respect in the reign of Boris Godounov (1598-1605). Secular dramatic art continued to be discouraged by the Church, without any patronage being accorded to it in high places until the reign of Alexis Mikhaïlovich. This prince, who may justly be called the founder of a national theatre in Russia, showed a real interest in the fine arts. He summoned a few musicians to Moscow, who taught the Russians the use of instruments hitherto unused by them. This encouragement of music at his Court provoked a final outburst of clerical intolerance. In 1649, by order of the Patriarch Joseph, all the musical instruments in the city of Moscow were confiscated and burnt in the open market place. Those belonging to the Tsar's private band were spared, perhaps from a fear of offending their royal patron, but more probably because their owners, being Germans, were welcome to go to perdition in their own way.

When we come to the middle of the seventeenth century and the advent of the enlightened Alexis Mikhaïlovich, the history of Russian drama, so closely associated with that of its opera, assumes a more definite outline. This prince married Natalia Naryshkin, the adopted daughter of the Boyard Artamon Matveiev. Matveiev's wife was of Scottish origin—her maiden name was Hamilton—so that the outlook of this household was probably somewhat cosmopolitan. The Tsaritsa Natalia was early interested in the theatre; partly perhaps because she had heard of it from her adopted parents, but most probably her taste was stimulated by witnessing one of the performances which were given from time to time among the foreigners in the German quarter of Moscow. Lord Carlisle, in his " Relation of Three Embassies from His Majesty Charles II. to the Great Duke of Moscovy," makes mention of one of these performances in 1664. He says : " Our Musique-master composed a Handsome Comedie in Prose, which was acted in our house."

Travelled nobles and ambassadors also told of the great enjoyment derived from the theatre in Western Europe. Likhatchev, who was sent

to Florence in 1658, wrote with naïve enthusiasm
of an opera which he had seen there ; but he
seems to have been more impressed by the scenic
effects, which included a moving sea filled with
fish, and a vanishing palace, than by the music
which accompanied these wonders. Potemkin,
who represented the Tsar at the Court of the
Grand Monarque, saw Molière's company in
" Amphitryon," in 1668, and doubtless communicated his impressions to his sovereign.
But before this date, as early as 1660, Alexis
Mikhaïlovich had given orders to an Englishman in his service to engage for him " Master
Glassblowers, Master Engravers and Master
Makers of comedies." It was long, however,
before Russia actually attained to the possession
of this last class of workers. Finally, incited
by his wife's tastes, by the representations of
his more polished nobles, and not a little by
personal inclinations, Alexis issued an *Oukaz*,
on May 15th, 1672, ordering Count Von-Staden
to recruit in Courland all kinds " of good master
workmen, together with very excellent skilled
trumpeters, and masters who would know how
to organise plays." Unfortunately the reputation of Russia as a dwelling-place was not attractive. Doubtless the inhabitants of Eastern
Europe still spoke with bated breath of the
insane cruelties of Ivan the Terrible which
had taken place a hundred years earlier. At

any rate the Courlanders showed no great anxiety to take service under the Tsar, and Staden returned from his mission to Riga and other towns, in December, 1672, with only " one trumpeter " and " four musicians." Nevertheless the *Oukaz* itself is an important landmark in the cultural evolution of Russia, marking, according to Tikhonraviev, the end of her long term of secular isolation as regards the drama. These five imported musicians formed the nucleus of what was to expand one day into the orchestra of the Imperial Opera.

Alexis Mikhaïlovich was evidently impatient to see some kind of drama enacted at his Court ; for in June of the same year, without waiting for " the masters who would know how to organise plays," he determined to celebrate the birthday of his son Peter—later to be known as Peter the Great—with a theatrical performance. The Tsar therefore commissioned Yagan (otherwise Johann) Gottfried Gregory, one of the protestant pastors residing in the German quarter of Moscow, to write a play, or " act " as it is described in the Tsar's edict, dealing with the Biblical subject of Esther. As a temporary theatre, a room was specially arranged at Preobrajensky, a village on the outskirts of Moscow which now forms part of the city. Red and green hangings, carpets and tapestries of various sorts were lent from the Tsar's household to decorate the walls and the seats of honour ; the bulk of the audience, however, had to content themselves with bare wooden benches. The scenery was painted by a Dutchman named Peter Inglis, who received the pompous title of " Master-Perspective-Maker." The Boyard Matveiev, the Tsaritsa's adoptive father, took an active interest in the organisation of this primitive theatre, and was appointed about this time, " Director of the Tsar's Entertainments," being in fact the forerunner of the later " Intendant " or Director of the Imperial Opera. Pastor Gregory, aided by one or two teachers in the German school, wrote the text of a "tragi-comedy" entitled *The Acts of Artaxerxes.* Gregory, who had been educated at the University of Jena, probably selected just such a subject as he had been accustomed to see presented in German theatres in his early youth. Although he had long resided in Moscow he does not seem to have acquired complete command of the Russian language, which was then far from being the subtle and beautiful medium of expression which it has since become. The tragi-comedy was written in a strange mixture of Russian and German, and we read that he had the assistance of two translators from the Chancellery of Ambassadors. A company numbering sixty-four untrained actors was placed at his service ; they were drawn from among the children of foreign residents and from the better class of tradesfolk. Music evidently played an important part in the performance ; the orchestra consisting of Germans, and of servants from Matveiev's household who played on " organs, viols and other instruments." The organist of the German church, Simon Gutovsky, was among the musicians. A chorus also took part in the play, consisting of the choir of the Court Chapel, described as " the Imperial Singing-Deacons."

The actual performance of *The Acts of Artaxerxes* took place on October 17th, 1672 (O.S.), and is said to have lasted ten hours, making demands upon the endurance of the audience which puts Wagnerian enthusiasts completely to shame. The Tsar watched the spectacle with unflagging attention and afterwards generously rewarded those who had taken part in the performance. The attitude of the clergy had so far changed that the Tsar's chaplain, the Protopope Savinov, undertook to set at rest his master's last scruples of conscience by pointing to the example of the Greek emperors and other potentates.

Gaining courage, and also a growing taste for this somewhat severe form of recreation, Alexis went on to establish a more permanent theatrical company. In the following year (1673) Pastor Gregory was commanded to

instruct twenty-six young men, some drawn
from the clerks of the Chancellery of State,
others from the lower orders of the merchants
or tradespeople, who were henceforth to be
known as " the Comedians of His Majesty the
Tsar." At first the audience consisted only
of the favoured intimate circle of the Tsar, and
apparently no ladies were present ; but after
a time the Tsaritsa and the Tsarevnas were
permitted to witness the performance from the
seclusion of a Royal Box protected by a substantial *grille.* The theatre was soon transferred from Preobrajensky to the Poteshny
Dvorets in the Kremlin.

The Acts of Artaxerxes was followed by a series
of pieces, nearly all of a highly edifying nature,
written or arranged by Gregory and others :
*Tobias, The Chaste Joseph, Adam and Eve,
Orpheus and Eurydice* (with couplets and choruses) and *How Judith cut off the head of Holofernes.* The libretto of the last-named play
is still in existence, and gives us some idea
of the patient endurance of primitive theatre-
goers in Russia. It is in seven acts, subdivided
into twenty-nine scenes, with a prologue and an
interlude between the third and fourth acts ;
the characters number sixty-three ; all the
female parts were acted by youths. The libretto
is constructed more or less on the plan of the
German comedies of the period, but what gives

the piece a special importance in the history of Russian opera is the fact that it contains arias and choruses linked with the action of the piece, such as the Song of the Kings, in which they bewail their sad fate when taken captive by Holofernes, a soldier's Drinking Song, a Love-Song sung by Vagav at Judith's feast, and a Jewish Song of Victory, the words of which are paraphrased from Biblical sources. The author is supposed, without much foundation in fact, to have been Simeon Polotsky, of whom we shall hear later. The piece was probably translated from German sources. A custom was then started, which prevailed for a considerable time in Russia, of confiding the translation of plays to the clerks in the Chancellery of the Ambassadors, which department answered in some measure to our Foreign Office. The composer of the music is unknown, but Cheshikin, in his " History of Russian Opera," considers himself fully justified in describing it as the *first Russian opera*. Two hundred years later Serov composed a popular opera on the subject of Judith, an account of which will be found on page 150.

All the Russian operas of the eighteenth century follow this style of drama, or comedy, with some musical numbers interpolated ; it is the type of opera which is known in Germany as the *Singspiel*. As *Judith* represents the prototype of many succeeding Russian operas, a few details concerning it will not be out of place here. The work is preserved in manuscript in the Imperial Public Library. It is evident that the dramatic action was strongly supported by the music ; for instance, to quote only one scenic direction in the piece, " Seloum beats the drum and cries aloud," alarm is here expressed by the aid of trumpets and drums. The action develops very slowly, and the heroine does not appear until the fourth act. In Act I. Nebuchadnezzar and his great men take counsel about the invasion of Judea ; the king summons Holofernes and appoints him leader of his army. In Act II. the sufferings of the Jews are depicted ; and the embassy to Holofernes from the Asiatic kings. Act III. is concerned with the speech which the God-fearing man Achior delivers in honour of Israel, in the presence of Holofernes ; and with the wrath of the leader who orders the punishment of Achior. Act IV. contains a conversation between Judith and her handmaiden Arboya about the miserable plight of Judea. In Act V. occurs the Lament of Israel : Judith persuades the people not to capitulate to Holofernes and prays God to come to their rescue. Act VI., Judith's Farewell to the Jewish Elders, and her departure for the camp of Holofernes ; she slays Holofernes and the Jews return to

TSAR ALEXIS MIKHAILOVICH

Bethulia. The whole work concludes with Israel's Song of Victory. Side by side with these dramatic scenes are interpolated comic interludes in the characteristic German style of the seventeenth century. The language contains many Germanisms and South Russian locutions, as though the translator had been a Malo-Russian. The piece is certainly tedious and contains much sententious moralising, with a reflection of sentiment which seems to belong peculiarly to the Orthodox Church. The pious tone of the work was indispensable at that period, and it was not until the Tsar's patronage of the drama became more assured that Pastor Gregory ventured on the production of a secular play founded on a distant echo of Marlowe's " Tamerlane the Great " (1586), written on the same lines as *Judith*, and containing also musical numbers.

Besides pieces of the nature of the Singspiel, Patouillet tells us that there were ballets at the Court of Alexis Mikhaïlovich. School dramas were in vogue at the Ecclesiastical Academy (of Zaikonospasskaya), for which Simeon Polotsky, and later on Daniel Touptalo (afterwards canonised as Saint Dimitri of Rostov), wrote sacred plays. Polotsky, educated at the Academy of Kiev, joined the Ecclesiastical School of Moscow, in 1660, as professor of Latin. He adapted, or wrote, *St. Alexis, Nebuchadnezzar,*

The Golden Calf, and the Three Children who were not consumed in the Fiery Furnace, and *The Prodigal Son.* The last-named play was undoubtedly performed before the Court, and was reprinted in 1685 with a number of plates showing the costumes of the actors and spectators.

Dimitri of Rostov, who was also a student at Kiev, composed a series of Mystery Plays with rhymed verse. *The Prodigal Son,* by Simeon Polotsky, says Patouillet, " had interludes which have not been preserved, and in Dimitri of Rostov's *Nativity,* the scene of the Adoration of the Shepherds was long in favour on account of a certain naïve folk-style of diction." None of these plays can be claimed as literature, but they are interesting as marking the transition from sacred to secular drama, and in some of them there was a faint reflection of contemporary manners. But this was not a spontaneous or popular movement ; it was merely a Court ordinance. The clerks and artisans who were trained as actors often took part in these spectacles against the wish of their parents, who were only partly reconciled by the Tsar's example to seeing their sons adopt what they had long been taught to regard as a disorderly and irreligious career. Because the movement had no roots in the life of the people it could not flourish healthily. When Alexis

died in 1670, the " Chamber of Comedians "
was closed, Matveiev was exiled, and there was
a reaction in favour of asceticism.

But the impetus had been given, and henceforth the drama was never to be entirely banished
from Russian life. Some of the westernised
Boyards now maintained private theatres—
just as their ancestors had maintained the bards
and the companies of *Skomorokhi*—in which were
played pieces based upon current events or upon
folk legends ; while the School Drama long
continued to be given within the walls of the
Ecclesiastical Academy of Zaikonospasskaya.
Thus the foundations of Russian dramatic art,
including also the first steps towards the opera
and the ballet, were laid before the last decade
of the seventeenth century.

The advent of Peter the Great to the throne
was not on the whole favourable to music. The
fine arts made no special appeal to the utilitarian
mind of this monarch. Music had now ceased
to be regarded as one of the seven deadly sins,
but suffered almost a worse fate, since in the
inrush of novel cosmopolitan ideas and customs
the national songs seem for a time to have been
completely forgotten. With the drama things
advanced more quickly. Peter the Great, who
conceived his mission in life to be the more or
less forcible union of Russia with Western
Europe, realised the importance of the theatre

as a subordinate means to this end. During
his travels abroad he had observed the influence
exercised by the drama upon the social life
of other countries. In 1697 he was present
at a performance of the ballet " Cupidon," at
Amsterdam, and in Vienna and London he
heard Italian opera, which was just coming
into vogue in this country, and waxed enthusiastic over the singing of our prima donna Cross.
During his sojourn in Vienna he took part
himself, attired in the costume of a Friesland
peasant, in a pastoral pageant (*Wirthschaft*)
given at the Court. Thus the idea of reorganis-
ing the " Comedians' Chamber " founded by
his father was suggested to him. As Alexis
had formerly sent Von-Staden to find foreign
actors for Russia, so Peter now employed a
Slovak, named Splavsky, a captain in the Russian
army, on a similar mission. The Boyard Golo-
vin was also charged with the erection of a
suitable building near to the Kremlin. After
two journeys, Splavsky succeeded in bringing
back to Russia a German troupe collected by an
entrepreneur in Dantzig, Johann Christian Kunst.
At first the actors were as unwilling to come
as were those of a previous generation, having
heard bad accounts of the country from a
certain Scottish adventurer, Gordon, who had
been connected with a puppet-show, and who
seems to have been a bad character and to have

been punished with the knout for murder.
Finally, in April, 1702, Kunst signed a contract
by which his principal comedians undertook for
the yearly sum of about 4,200 roubles in the
present currency " to make it their duty like
faithful servants to entertain and cheer His
Majesty the Tsar by all sorts of inventions and
diversions, and to this end to keep always
sober, vigilant and in readiness." Kunst's
company consisted of himself, designated
" Director of the Comedians of His Majesty
the Tsar," his wife Anna, and seven actors.
Hardly had he settled in Moscow before he
complained that Splavsky had hastened his
departure from Germany before he had had
time or opportunity to engage good comedians
skilled in " singing-plays." The actors played
in German, but a certain number of clerks
in the Chancellery of the Embassies were
sent to Kunst to be taught the repertory in
Russian. It was not until 1703 that the first
public theatre in Russia, a wooden building,
was erected near the Kremlin in Moscow.
Meanwhile the plays were given at the residence
of General Franz Lefort, in the German quarter
of the city. Here, on the occasion of the state
entry of Peter into Moscow, Kunst performed
Alexander and Darius, followed by *The
Cruelty of Nero*, a comedy in seven acts,
Le Médecin malgré lui, and *Mahomet and*

Zulima, a comedy interspersed with songs and dances. The new theatre was a genuine attempt on the part of the Tsar Peter to bring this form of entertainment within reach of a larger public than the privileged circle invited to witness the plays given at the Court of Alexis. For the country and period, the installation was on quite a sumptuous scale. There were seats at four prices : ten, six, five and three kopecks. In 1704 there were two performances in the week which usually lasted about five hours, from five to ten p.m. Peter the Great gave orders in 1705 that the pieces should be given alternately in Russian and German, and that at the performance of the plays " the musicians were to play on divers instruments." Russians of all ranks, and foreigners, were bidden to attend " as they pleased, quite freely, having nothing to fear." On the days of performance the gates leading into the Kremlin, the Kitaï-gorod and the Bieli-gorod were left open till a later hour in order to facilitate the passage of theatre-goers. From the outset Kunst demanded facilities for the mounting of opera, and also an orchestra. Seven musicians were engaged by special contract in Hamburg and an agent was commissioned " to purchase little boys in Berlin with oboes and pipes." By this time a few Russian magnates had started private bands in imitation of those maintained by some of the nobility in Germany. Prince Gregory Oginsky contributed four musicians from his private band for the royal service in Moscow. To the director of the musicians from Hamburg, Sienkhext, twelve Russian singers were handed over to be taught the oboe. We learn nothing as to the organisation of a company of singers, because in all probability, in accordance with the custom of those days, the actors were also expected to be singers.

In the comedy of *Scipio Africanus*, and *The Fall of Sophonisba, The Numidian Queen*, an adaptation from Loenstein's tragedy *Sophonisba* (1666), short airs and other incidental music formed part of the play. Music also played a subordinate part in an adaptation of Cicconini's tragic opera *Il tradimento per l'honore, overo il vendicatore pentito* (Bologna, 1664), and in an adaptation of Molière's *Don Juan*. These and other pieces from the repertory of the day were culled from various European sources, but almost invariably passed into the Russian through the intermediary of the German language. The work continued to be carried on in the Chancellery of the Embassies, where alone could be found men with some knowledge of foreign tongues. The translations were perfunctory and inaccurate, and there is no literary vitality whatever in the productions of this period, unless it is found in the interludes of a somewhat coarse humour which found more favour with the uncultivated public than did the pieces themselves. Simeon Smirnov was the first Russian who wrote farcical interludes of this kind, which were almost as rough and scandalous as the plays of the *Skomorokhi* of earlier centuries. It cannot be proved that in the time of Peter the Great an opera in the sense of a drama in which music preponderated was ever put upon the stage, but it is an undoubted fact, according to Cheshikin, that there exists the manuscript of a libretto for an opera on the subject of Daphne. It seems to be the echo of what had taken place in Florence at least a hundred years previously, when translations of the book of " Daphne," composed by Caccini and Peri in 1594, gradually made their way into various parts of Europe. In 1635 we hear of its being given in Warsaw in the original Italian, and two or three years later it was translated into Polish, running through three editions ; from one of these it was put into Russian early in the eighteenth century by an anonymous author. The manuscript of the translation exists in the Imperial Public Library, under one of the usual voluminous titles of the period, *Daphnis pursued by the love of Apollo is changed into a laurel bush,* or *the Act of Apollo and the fair Daphne; how Apollo conquered the evil snake Python and was himself overcome by little Cupid.*

It bears the signature of one Dimitri Ilyinski, graduate of the Slaviano-Latin Academy of Moscow, who appears to have been merely the copyist, not the author, and the date "St. Petersburg, 1715." The pupils of this Academy kept alive for some time the traditions of the "School Drama" side by side with the official theatre subsidised by the state. The plays continued to consist chiefly of Biblical episodes, and were usually so framed as to be a defence of the Orthodox Church. They were given periodically and were bare of all reference to contemporary life. Side by side with these we may place the allegorical and panegyrical plays performed by the medical students of the great hospital in Moscow. Crude as were the productions of these two institutions they represent, however, the more spontaneous movement of the national life rather than the purely imported literary wares of the official theatre.

Kunst died in 1703, and was succeeded by Otto Fürst, whose Russian name was Artemiem. He was a fair Russian scholar, and in a short time the company became accustomed to playing in the vernacular. But it cannot be said that this tentative national theatre was truly a success. It was a hothouse plant, tended and kept alive by royal favour, and when the Tsar removed his Court to St. Petersburg it gradually failed more and more to hold the

attention of the public. The theatre in the
Red Square was demolished before 1707. Fürst's
company, however, continued to give performances at Preobrajensky, the residence of the
Tsarevna Natalia Alexseievna, youngest sister
of Peter the Great, and later on at the palace of
the Tsaritsa Prascovya Feodorovna at Ismailov.
The private theatre of this palace was never
closed during the life of the widowed Tsaritsa,
who died in 1723. Her eldest daughter, the
Duchess of Mecklenburg, was fond of all sorts
of gaiety ; while her second daughter, the
Duchess of Courland, afterwards the Empress
Anne of Russia, who often visited her mother
at Ismailov, was also a lover of the theatre.
The ladies in waiting joined Fürst's pupils
in the performance of plays, while the Duchess
of Mecklenburg frequently acted as stage manager. The entrance was free, and although
the places were chiefly reserved for the courtiers,
the public seems to have been admitted somewhat indiscriminately, if we can believe the
account of the page in waiting, Bergholds, who
says that once his tobacco was stolen from his
pocket and that two of his companions complained of losing their silk handkerchiefs.

About 1770 a theatrical company, consisting
entirely of native actors and actresses, was
established in St. Petersburg under the patronage of the Tsarevna Natalia Alexseievna, who

herself wrote two plays for them to perform. This princess did all in her power to second the efforts of Peter the Great to popularise the drama. In 1720 the Tsar sent Yagoujinsky to Vienna to raise a company of actors who could speak Czech, thinking that they would learn Russian more quickly than the Germans, but the mission was not successful. In 1723 a German company, under the direction of Mann, visited the new capital and gave performances in their own tongue. They were patronised by the Empress Catherine I. At that time the Duke of Holstein, who afterwards married the Tsarevna Anne, was visiting St. Petersburg, and the Court seem to have frequently attended the theatre ; but there is no definite record of Mann's company giving performances of opera. A new theatre was inaugurated in St. Petersburg in 1725, the year of Peter the Great's death.

CHAPTER II

THE history of Russian music enters upon a new period with the succession of the Empress Anne. The national melodies now began to be timidly cultivated, but the inauguration of a native school of music was still a very remote prospect, because the influence of Western Europe was now becoming paramount in Russian society. Italian music had just reached the capital, and there, as in England, it held the field against all rivals for many years to come.

Soon after her coronation, in 1732, the pleasure-loving Empress Anne organised private theatricals in her Winter Palace and wrote to Bishop Theofane Prokovich, asking him to supply her with three church singers. The piece given was a "school drama" entitled *The Act of Joseph*, and in its mounting and composition, a famous pupil of the Slaviano-Latin Academy took part, Vassily Cyrillovich **Trediakovsky**, poet and grammarian, and one of the first creators of the literary language of Russia. The rest of the actors consisted of the singers lent by the Bishop and of pupils selected from the Cadet Corps, among them Peter and Carl, sons of Anne's favourite, Biron. Some of the actors' parts are still in existence, with descriptions of their costumes, and details as to the requirements of the piece, which seem to show that the entire Biblical story of Joseph was presented, and that some allegorical personages such as Chastity, Splendour, Humility, and Envy, were introduced into the play. Splendour was attired in a red cloth garment, slashed and trimmed with silver braid ; Chastity was in white without ornaments, crowned with a laurel wreath and carrying a sheaf of lilies. Besides Jacob, Joseph, and his Brethren, there were parts for King Pharaoh and two of his senators, Wise Men, slaves, attendants, and an executioner, who, we read, was clad in a short tunic of red linen and wore a yellow cap with a feather.

These old-fashioned, edifying plays soon bored the Empress Anne. Italian actors appeared at the Court and gave amusing comedies, occasionally containing musical interludes. The Empress employed Trediakovsky to translate the pieces that were played before her ; for she was no Italian scholar. The new form of entertainment was so much to her liking that she determined to establish a permanent Italian company in St. Petersburg, and was the first to open a theatre in Russia exclusively for opera. This brings upon the scene a personality inseparably linked with the history of Russian opera : Francesco Araja, who is the first palpable embodiment of operatic music in Russia, for all his predecessors who composed for the plays of Kunst and Fürst have remained anonymous.

Araja was born at Naples in 1700. His first opera, *Berenice*, was given at the Court of Tuscany in 1730 ; his second, *Amore per Regnante*, was produced soon afterwards in Rome. This seemed to have attracted the attention of the Russian ambassador to Italy, and in 1735 the composer was invited to St. Petersburg as director of the new Italian opera company. The performances took place in the Winter Palace during the winter, and in the summer in the Theatre of the Summer Garden. It is possible that Araja's first season opened with a performance of one of his own works with Russian text. Trediakovsky's translation of *La Forza dell' Amore e dell' Odio* is described as " a drama for music performed at the New Theatre, by command of Her Imperial Highness Anna Johannovna, Autocrat of all the Russias. Published in St. Petersburg by the Imperial Academy of Science." It is not impossible that this comparatively unimportant work actually led to Trediakovsky's great literary innovation : the replacing of syllabic verse by tonic accent.

It is significant that his book on this subject came out in the same year, and Cheshikin thinks that the study of the Italian opera of the eighteenth century, with its correct versification, may have suggested to him the theories which he sets forth in it. The same opera was given two years later in Italian under the title of *Abizare*. Other operas by Araja given in the Russian language are *Seleucus* (1744), *Mithriadates* (1747), *Eudocia Crowned, or Theodosia II.* (1751), and *Dido Forsaken*, the libretto by Metastasio (1758) ; the last named was given in Moscow the following year, and was apparently the first of Araja's works to be heard in the old capital.

The Empress Elizabeth succeeded her cousin Anne in 1741, and Araja continued to be Court Capellmeister. Like Peter the Great, Elizabeth was anxious to popularise the drama in Russia. She showed a taste for Gallic art, and established a company which gave French comedies and tragedies alternately with Araja's opera company. Elizabeth urged her ladies in waiting to attend every performance, and occasionally announced that the upper classes among the merchants might be present on certain nights " provided they were properly dressed."[1]

Russian opera made a decided step in advance

[1] Gorbounov. "A Sketch for the History of Russian Opera " (in Russian).

when in 1751 Araja composed music to a purely
Russian text. The subject, *La Clemenza di
Tito*, which Mozart subsequently treated in
1791, had nothing in common with the national
life, but the libretto was the work of F. G.
Volkov, and the effect was quite homogeneous,
for all the singers sang in the vernacular instead
of some using the Russian and some the Italian
language as was formerly done. This tasteless
custom did not wholly die out until well into
the nineteenth century, but it became less and
less general. Thus in 1755 we hear of Araja's
Cephalus and Procius being confided entirely
to singers of Russian birth. The book of this
opera was by Soumarakov, based on materials
borrowed from the " Metamorphoses " of Ovid.
The work is said to have been published in 1764,
and is claimed by some to be the earliest piece
of music printed in Russia. J. B. Jurgenson,
head of the famous firm of music publishers in
Moscow, who has diligently collected the Russian
musical publications of the eighteenth century,
states that he has never found any of Araja's
operas printed with music type. The fact that
music was printed in Russia before the reign
of Catherine II. still needs verification. The
scenery of *Cephalus* was painted by Valeriani,
who bore one of the high sounding titles which
it was customary to bestow at the Court of
Russia—being distinguished as " First Historical

Painter, Professor of Perspective (scene painting) and Theatrical Engineer at the Imperial Court of Russia." Among the singers who took part in the performance were Elizabeth Bielogradsky, daughter of a famous lute player, Count Razoumovsky, and Gravrilo Martsenkovich, known as Gravriloushko. The success of the opera was brilliant, and the Empress presented the composer with a fine sable coat as a mark of her gratification. In 1755, Araja, having amassed considerable wealth, returned to Italy and spent the remaining years of his life at Bologna.

Music under the Empress Elizabeth became a fashionable craze. Every great landowner started his private band or choir. About this time, the influence of the Empress's favourite, Razoumovsky, made itself felt in favour of Russian melodies. By this time, too, a few talented native musicians had been trained either in the Court Chapel or in some of the private orchestras established by the aristocracy ; but the influx of foreigners into Russia threatened to swamp the frail craft of native talent which had just been launched with pride upon the social sea. The majority of these foreigners were mediocrities who found it easier to impose upon the unsophisticated Russians than to make a living in their own country ; but the names of Sarti, Paisiello, and Cimarosa stand out as glorious exceptions among this crowd of third and fourth rate composers.

To Feodor Grigorievich Volkov, whose name has been already mentioned as the author of the first genuine Russian libretto, has been also accorded the honour of producing the first Russian opera boasting some pretensions to the national style. Volkov was born at Kostroma, in 1729, the son of a merchant. On his father's death and his mother's re-marriage his home was transferred to Yaroslav. Here he received his early education from a German pastor in the service of Biron, Duke of Courland, then in banishment at Yaroslav. During a visit to St. Petersburg in 1746, Volkov was so captivated by his first impressions of Italian opera that he determined to start a theatrical company of his own in Yaroslav. He gathered together a few enthusiastic amateurs and began by giving performances in his own home. The attempt was so successful that the fame of his entertainments reached the Empress Elisabeth, and the young actors were summoned to her Court in 1752, where they gave a private performance of a " comedy " with musical interludes entitled *The Sinner's Repentance,* by Dimitri, metropolitan of Rostov. One result of this production was that the Empress resolved to continue the education of two members of the company, one of whom, Ivan Dmitrievsky, became the

most famous Russian actor of his day. In
1759 Volkov was sent to Moscow to establish
a "Court theatre" there. The festivities with
which the coronation of Catherine II. was
celebrated in the old capital included a sumptuous masquerade entitled *Minerva Triumphant*,
arranged by Volkov, in which choral music
played a part. While engaged in organising
the procession, Volkov caught a severe chill
from which he never recovered, and died in April
1763. He was an amateur of music and made
use of it in the entertainments which he produced ; but there seem to be grave doubts
as to whether he was capable of composing
music to the first Russian comic opera, *Taniousha
or The Fortunate Meeting*, said to have been produced in November 1756. Gorbounov thinks
it highly improbable that such an opera ever
existed,[1] because Volkov's biographer, Rodi-
slavsky, had no better foundation for assuming
its composition and production than some old
handbills belonging to the actor Nossov, which
seem to have existed only in the imagination of
their collector. The assertion that *Taniousha*
was the first Russian national opera must
therefore be accepted with reserve.

Evstignei Platovich Fomin was born August
5th 1741 (O.S.), in St. Petersburg. He was a

[1] Gorbounov. "A Sketch for the History of Russian
Opera."

pupil of the Imperial Academy of Arts, and in view of his promising musical talent was sent to study in Italy, where he entered for a time the Academy of Music at Bologna, and made rapid progress. He began his musical career in Moscow in 1770, but appears to have migrated to St. Petersburg before the death of Catherine II. He was commissioned to compose the music for a libretto from the pen of the Empress herself, entitled *Boeslavich, the Novgorodian Hero.* Catherine not being quite confident as to Fomin's powers submitted the score to Martini. The result appears to have been satisfactory. In 1797 Fomin was employed at the Imperial Theatres as musical coach and *répétiteur ;* he was also expected to teach singing to the younger artists of both sexes in the Schools, and to accompany in the orchestra for the French and Italian operas. For these duties he received an annual sum of 720 roubles. Fomin died in St. Petersburg in April, 1800. He wrote a considerable number of operas, including *Aniouta* (1772), the libretto by M. V. Popov ; *The Good Maiden* (*Dobraya Devka*), libretto by Matinsky (1777) ; *Regeneration* (*Pereiojdenia*), (1777)[1] ; in January 1779 his *Wizard-Miller* (*Melnik-Koldoun*) an opera in three acts, the libretto by Ablessimov, was produced for the first time, and proved one

---

[1] Some authorities believe that the music, as well as the text of this opera, was written by Matinsky.

of the most successful operas of the eighteenth century ; a one-act opera, the book by Nikolaiev, entitled *The Tutor Professor, or Love's Persuasive Eloquence*, was given in Moscow ; and in 1786 *Boeslavich*, in five acts, the text by Catherine II., was mounted at the Hermitage Palace ; *The Wizard, The Fortune Teller and The Matchmaker*, in three acts, dates from 1791. In 1800 appeared two operas, *The Americans*, the libretto by Kloushin, and *Chlorida and Milon*, the words of which were furnished by the well-known writer Kapnist. As far as is known, Fomin composed ten operas and also wrote music to a melodrama entitled *Orpheus*.[1] It is probable, however, that Fomin really produced many more musical works for the stage, for it has been proved that he occasionally took an assumed name for fear of his work proving a failure. Of his voluminous output only three works need be discussed here.

Aniouta owed some of its success to Popov's libretto, which was a mild protest against the feudal aristocracy. The peasant Miron sings in the first act some naïve verses in which he bewails the hard fate of the peasant ; " Ah, how tired I am," he says. " Why are we peasants not nobles ? Then, we might crunch sugar all day long, lie warm a'top of the stove

[1] Karatagyn gives a list of twenty-six operas in the preface to Jurgenson's edition of *The Miller*.

and ride in our carriages." If we put aside
the idea that Volkov's *Taniousha* was the first
opera written by a Russian composer, then this
honour must be rendered to Fomin's *Aniouta*.

Contemporary proof of the immense success
of *The Miller* (*Melnik-Koldoun*) is not wanting.
The Dramatic Dictionary for 1787 informs us
that it was played twenty-seven nights running
and that the theatre was always full. Not only
were the Russians pleased with it, but it interested the foreigners at Court. The most obvious
proof of its popularity may be found in the
numerous inferior imitations which followed in
its wake.

The libretto of *The Miller*, like that of *Aniouta*,
was tinged by a cautious liberalism. Here it
is not a peasant, but a peasant proprietor,
who " tills and toils and from the peasants
collects the rent," who plays the principal rôle.
The part of the Miller was admirably acted by
Kroutitsky (1754-83), who, after the first performance, was called to the Empress's box
and presented with a gold watch. But undoubtedly Fomin's music helped the success of the
opera. The work has been reissued with an
interesting preface by P. Karatagyn (Jurgenson,
Moscow), so that it is easily accessible to those
who are interested in the early history of
Russian opera. The music is somewhat amateurish and lacking in technical resource.

Fomin does not venture upon a chorus, although there are occasionally couplets with choral refrains ; lyric follows lyric, and the duets are really alternating solos with a few phrases in thirds at the close of the verses. But the public in Russia in the eighteenth century was not very critical, and took delight in the novel sensation of hearing folk-songs on the stage. In the second act the heroine Aniouta sings a pretty melody based on a familiar folk-tune which awakened great enthusiasm among the audience. The songs and their words stand so close to the original folk-tunes that no doubt they carried away all the occupants of the pit and the cheap places ; while, for the more exacting portion of the audience, the rôle of the Miller was written in the conventional style of the *opera buffa*. This judicious combination pleased all tastes.

We find far greater evidences of technical capacity in Fomin's opera *The Americans*, composed some thirteen years later. In the second act there is a fairly developed love-duet between Gusman and Zimara ; the quartets and choruses, though brief, are freer and more expressive ; there is greater variety of modulation, and altogether the work shows some reflection of Mozart's influence, and faintly foreshadows a more modern school to come. The libretto is extremely naïve, the Americans being in reality the indigenous inhabitants, the Red Indians ; but there is nothing in the music allotted to them which differentiates them from the Spanish characters in the opera. The advance, however, in the music as compared with that of his earlier operas proves that Fomin must have possessed real and vital talent. Yet it is by *The Miller* that he will live in the memory of the Russian people, thanks to his use of the folk-tunes. To quote from Karatagyn's preface to this work : " Fomin has indisputably the right to be called our first national composer. Before the production of *The Miller*, opera in Russia had been entirely in the hands of travelling Italian *maestri*. Galuppi, Sarti, Paisiello, Cimarosa, Salieri, Martini, and others ruled despotically over the Court orchestra and singers. Only Italian music was allowed to have an existence and Russian composers could not make their way at all except under the patronage of the Italians." This sometimes led to tragic results, as in the case of Berezovsky, whose efforts to free himself from the tutelage of Sarti cost him the patronage of the great Potemkin and drove him to a pitch of despair which ended in suicide. Too much weight, however, must not be attached to this resentment against the Italian influence, so loudly expressed in Russia and elsewhere. The Italians only reigned supreme in the lands of their musical conquest so long as there existed no national composer strong enough to compete with them. Fomin's success clearly proves that as soon as a native musician appeared upon the scene who could give the people of their own, in a style that was not too elevated for their immature tastes, he had not to complain of any lack of enthusiasm.

It is to be regretted that none of his contemporaries thought it worth while to write his biography, but at that time Russian literature was purely aristocratic, and Fomin, though somewhat of a hero, was of the people—a serf.

Contemporary history is equally silent as regards Michael Matinsky, who died in the second decade of the nineteenth century. He, too, was a serf, born on the estate of Count Yagjinsky and sent by his master to study music in Italy. He composed several operas, the most successful of which was *The Gostinny Dvor in St. Petersburg*, a work that eventually travelled to Moscow. In his youth Matinsky is said to have played in Count Razoumovsky's private band. In addition to his musical activity he held the post of professor of geometry in the Smolny Institute in St. Petersburg.

Vassily Paskievich was chamber-musician to the Empress Catherine II. In 1763 he was engaged, first as violinist, and then as composer, at the theatres in St. Petersburg ; he also conducted the orchestra at the state balls. Some of his songs, which are sentimental, but pleasingly national in colour, are still popular in Russia.   He is said to have written seven operas in all.   The first of these, *Love brings Trouble*, was produced at the Hermitage Theatre in 1772.   Some years later he was commissioned to set to music a libretto written by the Empress Catherine herself.   The subject of this opera is taken from the tale of *Tsarevich Feveï*, a panegyric upon the good son of a Siberian king who was patriotic and brave—in fact possessed of all the virtues.   In her choice of subject the Empress seems to have been influenced by her indulgent affection for her favourite grandchild, the future Alexander I.   Prince Feveï does nothing to distinguish himself, but most of the characters in the opera go into ecstasies over his charms and qualities, and it is obvious that in this libretto Catherine wished to pay a flattering compliment to her grandson.   There are moments in the music which must have appealed to the Russian public, especially an aria " Ah, thou, my little father," sung in the style of an old village dame.   Other numbers in the opera have the same rather sickly-sweet flavour that prevails in Paskievich's songs.   The redeeming feature of the opera was probably its Kalmuc element, which must have imparted a certain humour and oriental character to both words and music. In one place the text runs something like this : " Among the Kalmuc folk we eat kaimak, souliak, tourmak, smoke tabac(co) and drink koumiss," and the ring of these unfamiliar words may have afforded some diversion to the audiences of those days.[1]

But however dull the subject of *Feveï* may appear to modern opera-goers, that of Paskievich's third opera, *Fedoul and Her Children*, must surely take the prize for ineptitude even among Russian operas of the eighteenth century. Fedoul, a widow, announces to her fifteen grown-up children her intention of getting married again to a young widower ; at first the family not unnaturally grumble at the prospect of a stepfather, but having been scandalised by the marriage with the prince in the first act, they solemnly sing his praises in the finale of the last.

In co-operation with Sarti and Canobbio, Paskievich composed the music to another book by the Empress Catherine, entitled *The Early Reign of Oleg*, produced at the Hermitage Theatre, St. Petersburg, September, 1794. Paskievich's share of this work seems to have been the choruses, which give a touch of national sentiment to the opera. Here he uses themes that have now become familiar to us in the works

[1] A History of Russian Opera (*Istoriya Russ. Operï*), Jurgenson, St. Petersburg, 1905.

of later Russian musicians, such as the *Slavsia* in honour of the Tsar, and the Little Russian theme "The Crane" (*Jouravel*), which Tchaikovsky employed in his Second Symphony. The orchestral accompaniments sometimes consist of variations upon the theme, a form much favoured by Russian musicians of a more modern school. Other operas by Paskievich are *The Two Antons* (1804) and *The Miser* (1811). Paskievich had not as strong a talent as Fomin, but we must give him credit, if not for originating, at least for carrying still further the use of the folksong in Russian opera.

In a book which is intended to give a general survey of the history of Russian opera to English readers, it is hardly necessary to enter into details about such composers as Vanjour, Bulant, Br.ks, A. Plestcheiev, Nicholas Pomorsky, the German, Hermann Raupach, Canobbio, Kerzelli, Troinni, Staubinger, and other musicians, Russian and foreign, who played more or less useful minor parts in the musical life of St. Petersburg and Moscow during the second half of the eighteenth century.

Three Italians and two Russians, however, besides those already mentioned, stand out more prominently from the ranks and deserve to be mentioned here.

Vincente Martin (Martin y Solar), of Spanish descent, born about 1754, migrated in his boyhood to Italy, where he was known as *lo Spagnulo*. He wrote an opera, *Iphigenia in Aulis*, for the carnival in Florence in 1781, and having won some reputation as a composer in Italy, went to Vienna in 1785. Here his success was immense, so much so that his opera *Una Cosa Rara* was a serious rival to Mozart's "Nozze di Figaro." A year later Mozart paid Martin the compliment of introducing a fragment of *Una Cosa Rara* into the finale of the second act of "Don Juan." Martin went to St. Petersburg in 1788, at the invitation of the Italian opera company. During his stay in Russia eight of his operas were given in the vernacular, including *Dianino*, an *opera d'occasion*, the text by Catherine the Great ; *La Cosa Rara*, translated by Dmitrievsky ; *Fedoul and her Children*, in which he co-operated with the native composer Paskievich ; *A Village Festival*, the libretto by V. Maikov, and a comic opera in one act, *Good Luke, or Here's my day*, the words by Kobyakov. The fact that he wrote so frequently to Russian texts entitles him to a place in the history of Russian opera. Martin was held in great honour in the capital, and the Emperor Paul I. made him a Privy Councillor. This did not prevent him, however, from suffering from the fickleness of fashion, for in 1808 the Italians were replaced by a French opera company and Martin lost his occupation. He continued, however, to live in Russia, teaching at the Smolny monastery and in the aristocratic families of St. Petersburg, where he died in May, 1810.

Among the foreigners who visited Russia in the time of Catherine the Great, none was more distinguished than Guiseppe Sarti.   Born at Faenza in December, 1729, celebrated as a composer of opera by the time he was twenty-four, he was appointed in 1753 Director of the Italian opera, and Court Capellmeister to Frederick V. of Denmark.   He lived in Copenhagen, with one interval of three years, until the summer of 1775, when he returned to Italy and subsequently became Maestro di Capella of the cathedral of Milan.   Here he spent nine years of extraordinary activity composing fifteen operas, besides cantatas, masses and motets. In 1784 Catherine the Great tempted him to visit St. Petersburg, and constituted him her Court-composer.   His opera *Armida* was received with great enthusiasm in the Russian capital in 1786.   It was sung in Italian, for it was not until 1790 that Sarti took part in the composition of an opera written to a Russian libretto.   This was the *Early Rule of Oleg*, the book from the pen of the Empress herself, in which he co-operated with Paskievich.   He also composed a *Te Deum* in celebration of the fall of Ochakov before the army of Potemkin ; this was for double chorus, its triumphal effect being enhanced by drums and salvos of artillery ; a procedure which no doubt set a precedent for Tchaikovsky when he came to write his occasional Overture "1812." Many honours fell to Sarti's lot during the eighteen years he lived in Russia, among others the membership of the Academy of Science. The intrigues of the Italian singer Todi obliged him to retire for a time to a country estate belonging to Potemkin in the Ukraine ; but he was eventually reinstated in Catherine's good graces. After the Empress's death he determined to return to Italy, but stayed for a time in Berlin, where he died in 1802.

Giovanni Paesiello (1741-1816) was another famous Italian whom Catherine invited to St. Petersburg in 1776, where he remained as " Inspector of the Italian operas both serious and buffa " until 1784. Not one of the series of operas which he wrote during his sojourn in St. Petersburg was composed to a Russian libretto or sung in the Russian tongue. His *Barber of Seville*, written during the time when he was living in St. Petersburg, afterwards became so popular with the Italians that when Rossini ventured to make use of the same subject the public regarded it as a kind of sacrilege. Paesiello's influence on Russian opera was practically nil.

The generous offers of Catherine the Great drew Baldassare Galuppi (1706-1785) to St. Petersburg in 1765. One can but admire the spirit of these eighteenth-century Italian musicians—many of them being well advanced in years—who were willing to leave the sunny skies of Italy for the " Boreal clime " of St. Petersburg. Galuppi acted as the Director of the Imperial Court Chapel for three years, and was the first foreigner to compose music to a text in the ecclesiastical Slavonic, and to introduce the motet (the Russian name for which is "concert") into the service of the Orthodox Church. His operas, *Il Ré Pastore*, *Didone*, and *Iphigenia in Taurida*, the last named being composed expressly for the St. Petersburg opera, were all given during his sojourn in the capital, but there is no record to prove that any one of these works was sung in Russian.

Maxim Sozontovich Berezovsky[1] (1745-1777) studied at the School of Divinity at Kiev, whence, having a remarkably fine voice, he passed into the Imperial Court Chapel. In 1765 he was sent at the Government expense to study under the famous Padre Martini at Bologna. His studies were brilliant, and he returned to St. Peters-

---

[1] He must not be confounded with V. V. Berezovsky, whose "Russian Music" (Rousskaya Muzyka : Kritiko-istorichesky Ocherk) appeared in 1898.

burg full of hope and ambition, only to find himself unequal to coping with the intrigues of the Italian musicians at Court. Discouraged and disappointed, his mind gave way, and he committed suicide at the age of thirty-two. He left a few sacred compositions (*a capella*) which showed the highest promise. While in Italy he composed an opera to an Italian libretto entitled *Demofonti* which was performed with success at Bologna and Livorno.

Dmitri Stepanovich Bortniansky, born in 1751, also began his career as a chorister in the Court Choir, where he attracted the attention of Galuppi, who considered his talents well worth cultivation. When Galuppi returned to Italy in 1768, Bortniansky was permitted to join him the following year in Venice, where he remained until 1779. He was then recalled to Russia and filled various important posts connected with the Imperial Court Choir. He is now best known as a composer of sacred music, some of his compositions being still used in the services of the Orthodox Church. Although somewhat mellifluous and decidedly Italianised in feeling, his church music is not lacking in beauty. He wrote four operas, two to Italian and two to French texts. The titles of the Italian operas are as follows : *Alcide, Azioni teatrale postea in musica da Demetrio Bortnianski, 1778, in Venezia* ; and *Quinto Fabio, drama per musica rappresentata nel ducal teatro di Modena, il carnavale dell' anno* 1779. The French comic opera *Le Faucon* was composed for the entertainment of the Tsarevich Paul Petrovich and his Court at Gatchina (1786) ; while *Le Fils Rival* was produced at the private theatre at Pavlovsk in 1787, also for the Tsarevich Paul and his wife Maria Feodorovna.

Throughout the preceding chapters I have used the word " opera " as a convenient general term for the works reviewed in them ; but although a few such works composed by Italians, or under strong Italian influences, might be accurately described as melodic opera, the nearer they approach to this type the less they contain of the Russian national style. For the most part, however, these productions of the eighteenth century were in the nature of vaudevilles : plays with couplets and other incidental music inserted, in which, as Cheshikin points out, the verses were often rather spoken than sung ; consequently the form was more declamatory than melodic. Serov, in a sweeping criticism of the music of this period, says that it was for the most part commissioned from the pack of needy Italians who hung about the Court in the various capacities of *maîtres d'hôtel*, wig-makers, costumiers, and confectioners. This, as we have seen, is somewhat exaggerated, since Italy sent some of her best men to the Court of Catherine II. But even admitting that a large proportion of the musicians who visited Russia were less than second-rate, yet beneath this tawdry and superficial foreign disguise the pulse of national music beat faintly and irregularly. If some purely Italian tunes joined to Russian words made their way into various spheres of society, and came to be accepted by the unobservant as genuine national melodies, on the other hand some true folk-songs found their way into semi-Italian operas and awoke the popular enthusiasm, as we have witnessed in the works of Fomin and Paskievich. In one respect the attitude of the Russian public in the eighteenth century towards imported opera differed from our own. All that was most successful in Western Europe was brought in course of time to St. Petersburg, but a far larger proportion of the foreign operas were translated into the vernacular than was the case in this country.

With regard to the location of opera, the first "opera house" was erected by the Empress Anne in St. Petersburg, but was not used exclusively for opera, French plays and other forms of entertainment being also given there. The building was burnt down in 1749, and the theatrical performances were continued temporarily in the Empress's state apartment. A new, stone-built opera house was opened in St.

Petersburg in 1750, after the accession of the Empress Elizabeth. It was situated near the Anichkov Palace. Catherine the Great added another stone theatre to the capital in 1774, which was known as " The Great Theatre." After damage from fire it was reconstructed and reopened in 1836.[1] Rebuilt again in 1880, it became the home of the Conservatoire and the office of the Imperial Musical Society. Besides these buildings, the Hermitage Theatre, within the walls of the Winter Palace, was often used in the time of Catherine the Great.

In Moscow the Italian *entrepreneur* Locatelli began to solicit the privilege of building a new theatre in 1750. Six years later he was accorded the necessary permission, and the building was opened in January, 1759. But Locatelli was not very successful, and his tenure only lasted three years. Titov managed the Moscow theatre from 1766 to the death of Catherine in 1796. After this the direction passed into the hands of Prince Ouroussov, who in association with a Jew named Medoks[2] proceeded to build a new and luxurious theatre in Petrovsky Street. Prince Ouroussov soon retired, leaving Medoks sole manager. The season began with comic operas such as *The Miller* by Fomin. In 1805

---

[1] The first performance of Glinka's *A Life for the Tsar* took place here in November of that year.
[2] Possibly Madox.

the Petrovsky theatre shared the fate of so many Russian buildings and was destroyed by fire.

Alexander I. succeeded the unfortunate Paul Petrovich, done to death in the Mikhaïlovsky Palace during the night of March 23rd, 1801. With his advent, social sentiment in Russia began to undergo a complete revolution. The Napoleonic wars in Western Europe, in which the Russian troops took part, culminating in the French invasion of 1812, awoke all the latent patriotism of the nation. The craze for everything foreign, so marked under the rule of Catherine II., now gave place to ultra-patriotic enthusiasm. This reaction, strongly reflected in the literature of the time, was not without its influence on musical taste. In Russia, music and literature have always been closely allied, and the works of the great poet Poushkin, of the fabulist Krylov, and the patriotic historian Karamzin, gave a strong impulse and a new tone to the art. At the same time a wave of romanticism passed over Russia. This was partly the echo of Byron's popularity, then at its height in England and abroad ; and partly the outcome of the annexation of the old kingdom of Georgia, in 1801, which turned the attention of Young Russia to the magic beauty and glamour of the Caucasus.

There was now much discussion about national

music, and a great deal was done to encourage
its progress ; but during the first quarter of the
nineteenth century composers had but a superficial idea of the meaning of a national school,
and were satisfied that a Russian subject and a
selection of popular tunes constituted the only
formula necessary for the production of a native
opera.

During his short reign the Emperor Paul had
not contributed to the advancement of music,
but in spite of somewhat unfavourable conditions, an Italian opera company under the
management of Astarito[1] visited St. Petersburg in 1797. Among their number was a
talented young Italian, Catterino Cavos, whose
name is inseparably connected with the musical
history of Russia. Born at Venice in 1776,
the son of the musical director of the celebrated " Fenice " Theatre, it is said that at
fourteen Cavos was the chosen candidate for
the post of organist of St. Mark's Cathedral,
but relinquished his chance in favour of a poor
musician. The story is in accordance with
what we read of his magnanimity in later life.
His gifts were remarkable, and in 1799 he was
appointed Court Capellmeister. In 1803 he
became conductor of the Italian, Russian and
French opera companies. Part of his duties
consisted in composing for all three institutions.

[1] Sometimes written Astaritta,

Light opera and ballet, given by the French company, was then all the fashion in St. Petersburg. Cavos quickly realised the direction and scope of the public taste, and soon began to write operas to romantic and legendary subjects borrowed from Russian history and folk-lore, and endeavoured to give his music a decided touch of national colour. In May, 1804, he made an immense success with his *Roussalka of the Dneiper*, in which he had the co-operation of Davidov. The following year he dispensed with all assistance and produced a four-act opera to a Russian text called *The Invisible Prince*, which found great favour with the public. Henceforth, through over thirty years of unresting creative activity, Cavos continued to work this popular vein. His operas have practically all sunk into oblivion, but the catalogue of their titles is still of some interest to students of Russian opera, because several of his subjects have since been treated and re-vitalised by a more recent generation of native composers. His chief works, given chronologically, are as follows : *Ilya the Hero*, the libretto by Krilov (1806) ; *The Three Hunchback Brothers* (1808) ; *The Cossack Poet* (1812) ; *The Peasants, or the Unexpected Meeting* (1814) ; *Ivan Sousanin* (1815) ; *The Ruins of Babylon* (1818) ; *Dobrinya Nikitich* (1810) ; and *The Bird of Fire* (1822)—the last two in co-operation with Antonolini ;

Svietlana, text by Joukovsky (1822) ; *The Youth of Joan III.* (1822) ; *The Mountains of Piedmont, or The Devil's Bridge* (1825) ; *Miroslava, or the Funeral Pyre* (1827).

The foregoing list does not include any works which Cavos wrote to French or Italian texts, amounting to nearly thirty in all. In *Ilya the Hero* Cavos made his first attempt to produce a national epic opera. Founded on the Legend of Ilya Mouromets, from the Cycle of Kiev, the opera is not lacking in spirit, and evoked great enthusiasm in its day, especially one martial aria, " Victory, victory, Russian hero ! " Cavos was fortunate in having secured as librettist a very capable writer, Prince Shakovsky, who also supplied the text for *Ivan Sousanin*, the most successful of all Cavos's national operas ; although we shall see in the next chapter how completely it was supplanted in the popular favour by Glinka's work dealing with the same subject.

In the spring of 1840 Cavos's health began to fail, and he received leave of absence from his many arduous but lucrative official posts. He became, however, rapidly much worse and had to abandon the idea of a journey. He died in St. Petersburg on April 28th (O.S.). His loss was deeply felt by the Russian artists, to whom, unlike many of his Italian predecessors, he had always shown generous sympathy ;

they paid him a last tribute of respect by singing
Cherubini's *Requiem* at his funeral.

The Russian musician Youry Arnold, who was
well acquainted with Cavos in the later years
of his life, describes him at sixty as a robust
and energetic man, who was at his piano by
9 a.m., rehearsing the soloists till 1 p.m., when
he took the orchestral rehearsals. If by
any chance these ended a little sooner than he
expected, he would occupy himself again with
the soloists. At 5 p.m. he made his report to
the Director of the Imperial Theatres, and then
went home to dine. But he never failed to
appear at the Opera House punctually at
7 o'clock. On evenings when there was no performance he devoted extra time to his soloists.
He worked thus conscientiously and indefatigably year after year. He was not, however,
indifferent to the pleasures of the table and was
something of a *gourmet*. Even in the far-
distant north he managed to obtain consign-
ments of his favourite " *vino nero.*" " He told
me more than once," said Arnold, " that
except with tea, he had never in the whole
course of his life swallowed a mouthful of water :
' *Perchè cosa snaturalle, insoffribile e noce-
vole !* ' "

Cavos was an admirable and painstaking conductor, and his long *régime* must have greatly contributed to the discipline and good organisation

of the opera, both as regards orchestra and
singers.   His own works, as might be expected
from a musician whose whole life was spent in
studying the scores of other composers, were
not highly original.   He wrote well, and with
knowledge, for the voice, and his orchestration
was adequate for that period, but his music
lacks homogeneity, and reminiscences of Mozart,
Cherubini and Méhul mingle with echoes of
the Russian folk-songs in the pages of his operas.
But the public of his day were on the whole
well satisfied with Russian travesties of Italian
and Viennese vaudevilles.   It is true that new
sentiments were beginning to rouse the social
conscience, but the public was still a long way
from desiring idealistic truth, let alone realism,
in its music and literature.   In spite of the one
electrical thrill which Glinka administered to
the public in *A Life for the Tsar*, opera was
destined to be regarded for many years to come
as a pleasing and not too exacting form of
recreation.   The libretto of Cavos's *Ivan Sousanin* shows what society demanded from opera
even as late as 1815 ; for here this tragedy
of unquestioning loyalty to an ideal is made
to end quite happily.   At the moment when the
Poles were about to slay him in the forest,
Sousanin is rescued by a Russian boyard and
his followers, and the hero, robust and jovial,
lives to moralise over the   footlights in the

following couplets, in which he takes leave of
the audience :

> Now let the cruel foe beware,
> And tremble all his days ;
> But let each loyal Russian heart
> Rejoice in songs of praise.

At the same time it must be admitted that
in this opera Cavos sometimes gives an echo
of the genuine national spirit. The types of
Sousanin and his young son Alexis, and of
Masha and her husband, Matthew, are so clearly
outlined, says Cheshikin, that Glinka had only
to give them more relief and finish. The well-
constructed overture, the duet between Masha
and Alexis, and the folk-chorus " Oh, do not
rave wild storm-wind " are all far in advance
of anything to be found in the Russian operas
of the eighteenth century.

Among those who were carried along by the
tide of national feeling which rose steadily in
Russia from 1812 onward was the gifted amateur
Alexis Nicholaevich Verstovsky. Born in 1799,
near Tambov, the son of a country gentleman,
Verstovsky was educated at the Institute of
Engineers, St. Petersburg, where he took piano-
forte lessons from John Field, and later on from
Steibelt. He also learnt some theory from
Brandt and Steiner ; singing from an operatic
artist named Tarquini ; and violin from Böhm
and Maurer. Verstovsky composed his first

vaudeville at nineteen and its success encouraged him to continue on the same lines.   In 1823 he was appointed Director of the Moscow Opera, where he produced a whole series of operettas and vaudevilles, many of which were settings of texts translated from the French.   After a time he became ambitious of writing a serious opera, and in May 1828, he produced his *Pan Tvardovsky*, the libretto by Zagoskin and Aksakov, well known literary men of the day.   The book is founded on an old Polish or Malo-Russian legend, the hero being a kind of Slavonic Faust. The music was influenced by Méhul and Weber, but Verstovsky introduced a gipsy chorus which in itself won immediate popularity for the opera.   Its success, though brilliant, was short-lived.

Pan Tvardovsky was followed by *Vadim, or the Twenty Sleeping Maidens*, based on a poem by Joukovsky, but the work is more of the nature of incidental music to a play than pure opera.

Askold's Tomb, Verstovsky's third opera, by which he attained his greatest fame, will be discussed separately.

Homesickness (*Toska po rodine*), the scene laid in Spain, was a poor work produced for the benefit night of the famous Russian bass O. A. Petrov, the precursor of Shaliapin.

The Boundary Hills, or the Waking Dream,

stands nearest in order of merit to *Askold's Tomb*. The scene is laid in mythical times, and the characters are supernatural beings, such as Domovoi (the House Spirit), Vodyanoi (the Water Sprite) and Liessnoi (the Wood Spirit). The music breathes something of the spirit of Russian folk-song, and a Slumber Song, a Triumphal March, and a very effectively mounted Russian Dance, which the composer subsequently added to the score, were the favourite numbers in this opera.

Verstovsky's last opera *Gromoboi* was based upon the first part of Joukovsky's poem " The Twenty Sleeping Maidens." An oriental dance (*Valakhsky Tanets*) from this work was played at one of the concerts of the Imperial Russian Musical Society, and Serov speaks of it as being quite Eastern in colour, original and attractive as regards melody but poorly harmonised and orchestrated as compared with the *Lezginka* from Glinka's *Russlan and Liudmilla*, the lively character of the dance being very similar.

A few of the composers mentioned in the previous chapter were still working in Russia at the same time as Verstovsky. Of those whose compositions belong more particularly to the first forty years of the nineteenth century, the following are most worthy of notice :

Joseph Antonovich Kozlovsky (1757-1831), of Polish birth, began life as a soldier in Prince

Potemsky's army. The prince's attention having been called to the young man's musical talents, he appointed him director of his private band in St. Petersburg. Kozlovsky afterwards entered the orchestra of the Imperial Opera. He wrote music to Oserov's tragedy *Œdipus in Athens* (1804) ; to *Fingal* (1805), *Deborah*, libretto by Shakovsky (1810), *Œdipus Rex* (1811), and to Kapnist's translation of Racine's *Esther* (1816).

Ludwig Maurer (1789-1878), a famous German violinist, played in the orchestra at Riga in his early days, and after touring abroad and in Russia settled in St. Petersburg about 1820, where he was appointed leader of the orchestra at the French theatre in 1835. Ten years later he returned to Germany and gave many concerts in Western Europe ; but in 1851 he went back to St. Petersburg as Inspector-General of all the State theatrical orchestras. Maurer is best known by his instrumental compositions, especially his Concertos for four violins and orchestra, but he wrote music for several popular vaudevilles with Russian text, and co-operated occasionally with Verstovsky and Alabiev.

The brothers Alexis and Sergius Titov were types of the distinguished amateurs who played such an important part in the musical life of Russia during the first half of the last century. Alexis (d. 1827) was the father of that Nicholas Titov often called " the ancestor of Russian song." He served in the Cavalry Guards and rose to the rank of Major-General. An admirable violinist, he was also a voluminous composer. Stassov gives a list of at least fourteen operas, melodramas, and other musical works for the stage, many of which were written to French words. His younger brother Sergius (b. 1770) is supposed to have supplied music to *The Forced Marriage*, text by Plestcheiev (1789), *La Veillée des Paysans* (1809), *Credulity* (1812), and, in co-operation with Bluhm, *Christmas Festivals of Old* (1813). It is probable that he had a hand in the long list of works attributed to his brother Alexis, and most of the Russian musical historians seem puzzled to decide how to apportion to each of the brothers his due share of creative activity.

A composer belonging to this period is known by name even beyond the Russian frontiers, owing to the great popularity of one of his songs, " The Nightingale." Alexander Alexandrovich Alabiev was born at Moscow, August 4th, 1787[1] (O.S.). He entered the military service and, becoming acquainted with Verstovsky, co-

---

[1] In Grove's Dictionary of Music I give the date of Alabiev's birth as August 30th, 1787, following most of the approved authorities of the day. But more recent investigations have revealed the correct date as August 4th.

operated in several of his vaudevilles. For some breach of discipline Alabiev was exiled for a time to Tobolsk. Inspired by the success of Cavos's semi-national operas, Alabiev attempted a Russian fairy opera entitled *A Moonlight Night or the Domovoï*. The opera was produced in St. Petersburg and Moscow, but did not long hold a place in the repertory of either theatre. He next attempted music to scenes from Poushkin's poem *The Prisoner in the Caucasus*, a naïve work in which the influence of Bellini obscures the faint national and Eastern colour which the atmosphere of the work imperatively demands. Alabiev, after his return from Siberia, settled in Moscow, where he died February 22nd, 1851 (O.S.).

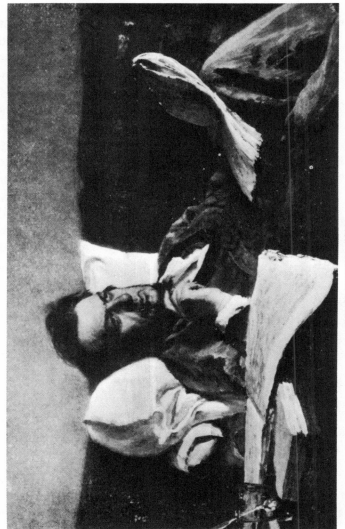

MICHAEL IVANOVICH GLINKA
From a portrait by Repin

CHAPTER III

MICHAEL IVANOVICH GLINKA

IN the preceding chapters I have shown how long and persistently Russian society groped its way towards an ideal expression of nationalism in music. Gifted foreigners, such as Cavos, had tried to catch some faint echo of the folk-song and reproduce it disguised in Italian accents; talented, but poorly equipped, Russian musicians had exploited the music of the people with a certain measure of success, but without sufficient conviction or genius to form the solid basis of a national school. Yet all these strivings and aspirations, these mistaken enthusiasms and immature presentiments, were not wasted. Possibly the sacrifice of many talents is needed before the manifestation of one genius can be fulfilled. When the yearning after a musical Messiah had acquired sufficient force, the right man appeared in the person of Michael Ivanovich Glinka. With his advent we reach the first great climax in the history of Russian music.

It is in accordance with the latent mysticism and the ardour smouldering under the semi-oriental indolence of the Russian temperament that so many of their great men—especially their musicians—seem to have arrived at the consciousness of their vocation through a kind of process of conversion. Moussorgsky, Tchaikovsky, and Rimsky-Korsakov, to mention but one or two examples, all awoke suddenly from a condition of mental sloth or frivolity to the conviction of their artistic mission ; and some of them were prepared to sacrifice social position and an assured livelihood for the sake of a new, ideal career. Glinka was no exception. He, too, heard his divine call and followed it. Lounging in the theatres and concert rooms of Italy, listening to Italian singers and fancying himself " deeply moved " by Bellini's operas, suddenly it flashed upon Glinka, a cultivated amateur, that this was not what he needed to stimulate his inspiration. This race, this art, were alien to him and could never take the place of his own people. This swift sense of remoteness, this sudden change of thought and ideal, constituted the psychological moment in the history of Russian music. Glinka's first impulse was merely to write a better Russian opera than his predecessors ; but this impulse held the germ of the whole evolution of the new Russian School as we know it to-day.

It is rather remarkable that outside the Russian language so little has been written about this germinal genius, who summed up the ardent desires of many generations and begat a great school of national music. The following details of his childhood and early youth are taken from his Autobiographical Notes and now appear for the first time in an English translation.

" I was born on June 2nd (May 20th, O.S.), 1804, in the glow of the summer dawn at the village of Novospasskoï, which belonged to my father, Ivan Nicolaevich Glinka, a retired army captain. . . . Shortly after my birth, my mother, Eugenia Andreievna (*née* Glinka), was obliged to leave my early bringing up to my grandmother who, having taken possession of me, had me transferred to her own room. Here in company with her, a foster mother, and my nurse, I spent the first three or four years of my life, rarely seeing anything of my parents. I was a child of delicate constitution and of nervous tendencies. My grandmother was in her declining years, and almost always ailing, consequently the temperature of her room in which I lived was never less than 20 Réaumur. . . . In spite of this, I was not allowed to take off my pelisse, and night and day I was given tea with cream and quantities of sugar in it, and also cracknels and fancy bread of all kinds. I seldom went into the fresh air, and then only in hot weather. There is no doubt that this early upbringing had a great influence on my physical development and explains my unconquerable affection for warm climates. . . .

" My grandmother spoilt me to an incredible degree and never denied me anything I wanted. In spite of this I was a gentle and well-behaved child, and only indulged in passing fits of peevishness—as indeed I still do when disturbed at one of my favourite occupations. One of my chief amusements was to lie flat on the floor and draw churches and trees with a bit of chalk. I was piously inclined, and church ceremonies, especially at the great festivals, filled me heart and soul with the liveliest poetic enthusiasm. Having learnt to read at a remarkably early age, I often moved my grandmother and her elderly friends to tears by reading the Scriptures aloud to them. My musical proclivities showed themselves at that time in a perfect passion for the sound of bells ; I drank in these harsh sounds, and soon learnt how to imitate them rather cleverly by means of two copper bowls. When I was ill they used to give me a little hand-bell to keep me amused.

" On the death of my grandmother, my way of living underwent some changes. My mother spoilt me rather less, and tried to accustom me to the fresh air ; but her efforts in this direction were not very successful. . . . My musical sense still remained undeveloped and crude. In my eighth year (1812), when we were delivered from the French invasion, I listened with all my old delight to the ringing of the bells, distinguishing the peals of the different churches, and imitating them on my copper bowls.

" Being entirely surrounded by women, and having for playmates only my sister, who was a year younger than myself, and my nurse's little daughter, I was never like other boys of my age ; moreover the passion for study, especially of geography and drawing—and in the latter I had begun to make sensible progress—drew me away from childish pastimes, and I was, from the first, of a quiet and gentle disposition.

" At my father's house we often received many relatives and guests ; this was usually the case on his name-day, or when someone came to stay whom he wished to entertain with special honours. On these occasions he would send for the musicians belonging to my maternal uncle, who lived eight versts away. They often remained with us for several days, and when the dances were over and the guests departed, they used to play all sorts of pieces. I remember once (it was in 1814, or 1815, when I was about ten) they played a quartet by Cruselli ; this music produced in me an inconceivably new and rapturous effect ; after hearing it I remained

all day long in a state of feverish excitement,
lost in inexplicably sweet dreamy emotions, and
the next day at my drawing lesson I was
quite absent-minded. My distracted condition
increased as the lesson proceeded, and my
teacher, remarking that I was drawing very
carelessly, scolded me repeatedly, until finally
guessing what was the matter with me, said
that I now thought of nothing but music.
' What's to be done ? ' I answered : ' music is
the soul of me ! '

" In truth at that time I loved music passionately. My uncle's orchestra was the source of
the liveliest delight to me. When they played
dances, such as écossaises, quadrilles and valses,
I used to snatch up a violin or piccolo and join
in with them, simply alternating between tonic
and dominant. My father was often annoyed
with me because I did not dance, and deserted
our guests ; but at the first opportunity I slipped
back again among the musicians. During
supper they generally played Russian folk-songs
arranged for two flutes, two clarinets, two
horns, and two bassoons ; this poignantly
tender, but for me perfectly satisfactory, combination delighted me (I could hardly endure
shrill sounds, even the lower notes of the horn
when they were not played loud), and perhaps
these songs, heard in my childhood, were the
first cause of my preference in later years for

Russian folk-melodies. About this time we had a governess from St. Petersburg called Barbara Klemmer. She was a girl about twenty, very tall, strict and exacting. She taught us Russian, French, German, geography and music. . . . Although our music lessons, which included reading from notes and the rudiments of the piano, were rather mechanical, yet I made rapid progress with her, and shortly after she came one of the first violins from my uncle's band was employed to teach me the fiddle. Unfortunately he himself did not play quite in tune and held his bow very stiffly, a bad habit which he passed on to me.

" Although I loved music almost unconsciously, yet I remember that at that time I preferred those pieces which were most accessible to my immature musical intelligence. I enjoyed the orchestra most of all, and next to the Russian songs, my favourite items in their repertory were : the Overtures to ' Ma Tante Aurore,' by Boieldieu, to ' Lodoïska,' by Rodolph Kreutzer, and to ' Les Deux Aveugles,' by Méhul. The last two I liked playing on the piano, as well as some of Steibelt's sonatas, especially ' The Storm,' which I played rather neatly."

I have quoted *verbatim* from Glinka's record of his childish impressions, because they undoubtedly influenced his whole after career, and

the nature of his genius was conditioned by
them. Like most of the leading representatives
of Russian music, Glinka was born and spent
the early years of his life in the country, where
he assimilated subconsciously the purer elements
of the national music which had already begun
to be vulgarized, if not completely obliterated,
in the great cities. Saved from the multi-
tudinous distractions of town life, the love of
the folk-music took root in his heart and grew
undisturbed. Had he been brought up in one
of the capitals, taken early, as Russian children
often were, and still are, to the opera and to
concerts, his outlook would have been widened
at the expense of his individuality. Later on,
as we shall see, he was led away from the tracks
of nationality by his enthusiasm for Italian
opera ; but the strong affections of his childhood guided him back instinctively to that way
of art in which he could best turn his gifts to
account. It has been said that Glinka remained
always somewhat narrow in his ideas and
activities ; but it was precisely this exclusive-
ness and concentration that could best serve
Russia at the time when he appeared. In his
letters and Autobiographical Notes, he often
adopts the tone of a genius misunderstood, and
hints that an unkind Providence enjoyed putting
obstacles in his path. It is true that in later
life, after the production of his second opera,

Russlan and Liudmilla, he had some grounds for complaining of the fickleness and mental indolence of the Russian public. But his murmurings against destiny must be discounted by the fact that Glinka, the spoilt and delicate child, grew up into Glinka, the idolised and hypochondriacal man. On the whole his life was certainly favourable to his artistic development.

Stassov, in his fine monograph upon the composer, lays stress on this view of Glinka's career. The history of art, he argues, contains only too many instances of perverted talent ; even strongly gifted natures have succumbed to the ill-judged advice of friends, or to the mistaken promptings of their own nature, so that they have wasted valuable years in the manufacture of works which reached to a certain standard of academic excellence, and even beauty, before they realised their true individual vocation and their supreme powers. Glinka was fortunate in his parents, who never actually opposed his inclinations ; and perhaps he was equally lucky in his teachers, for if they were not of the very highest class they did not at any rate interfere with his natural tendencies, nor impose upon him severe restrictions of routine and method. Another happy circumstance in his early life, so Stassov thinks, was his almost wholly feminine environment.

Glinka's temperament was dual ; on the one hand he possessed a rich imagination, both receptive and creative, and was capable of passionate feeling ; in the other side of his nature we find an element of excessive sensibility, a something rather passive and morbidly sentimental. Women had power to soothe and at the same time to stimulate his temperament. Somewhere in his memoirs, Glinka, speaking of his early manhood, says : " At that time I did not care for the society of my own sex, preferring that of women and girls who appreciated my musical gifts." Stassov considers that these words might be applied to the whole of Glinka's life, for he always seemed most at ease in the company of ladies.

In the autumn of 1817, being then thirteen, he was sent to the newly opened school for the sons of the aristocracy, where he remained until 1822. His schooldays appear to have been happy and profitable. He was industrious and popular alike with the masters and pupils. In the drawing class the laborious copying from the flat, with its tedious cross-hatching and stippling then in vogue, soon disgusted him. Mathematics did not greatly interest him. Dancing and fencing were accomplishments in which he never shone. But he acquired languages with a wonderful ease, taking up Latin, French, German, English and Persian.

In after years he dropped to some extent Persian and English, but became proficient in Italian and Spanish. Geography and zoology both attracted him. That he loved and observed nature is evident from all his writings ; and the one thing in which he resembled other boys was in his affection for birds, rabbits, and other pets. While travelling in the Caucasus in 1823 he tamed and kept wild goats, and sometimes had as many as sixteen caged birds in his room at once, which he would excite to song by playing the violin.

Glinka's parents spared nothing to give their son a good general education, but the idea that they were dealing with a budding musical genius never occurred to them. As he had shown some aptitude for the piano and violin in childhood, he was allowed to continue both these studies while at school in St. Petersburg. He started lessons with the famous Irish composer and pianist John Field, who, being on the eve of his departure for Moscow, was obliged to hand Glinka over to his pupil Obmana. Afterwards he received some instruction from Zeuner, and eventually worked with Carl Meyer, an excellent pianist and teacher, with whom he made rapid progress. At the school concert in 1822, Glinka was the show pupil and played Hummel's A minor Concerto, Meyer accompanying him on a second piano. With the violin he made less progress, although he took lessons from Bohm, a distinguished master and virtuoso who had not, however, so Glinka declared, the gift of imparting his own knowledge to others. Bohm would sigh over his pupil's faulty bowing and remark : " *Messieu Klinka, fous ne chouerez chamais du fiolon.*"

Glinka's repertory at nineteen contained nothing more profound than the virtuoso music of Steibelt, Herz, Hummel and Kalkbrenner. Although Beethoven had already endowed the world with his entire series of sonatas, and was then at the zenith of his fame, his music only began to make headway in Russia some ten years later. As time went on, Glinka heard and met most of the great pianists of his day, and his criticisms of their various styles are unconventional and interesting, but would lead us far away from the subject of Russian opera.

Imperfect as his mastery of the violin appears to have been, it was of more importance to his subsequent career than his fluency as a pianist, because during the vacations at home he was now able to take part in earnest in his uncle's small orchestra. The band generally visited the Glinkas' estate once a fortnight, and sometimes stayed a whole week. Before the general rehearsal, the son of the house would take each member of the orchestra through his part— with the exception of the leaders—and see that they were all note perfect and played in tune. In this way he learnt a good deal about instrumentation and something about the technique of conducting. Their repertory included overtures by Cherubini, Méhul, and Mozart ; and three symphonies, Haydn in B, Mozart in G minor, and Beethoven's second symphony, in D major, the last named being Glinka's special favourite.

In St. Petersburg he began to frequent the opera, which was not then so exclusively given over to Italian music as it was a few years later. Méhul's " Joseph," Cherubini's " Water-Carriers," Isouard's " Gioconda " and Boieldieu's " Le Bonnet Rouge " were among the works which he heard and admired in the early 'twenties.

In 1824 Glinka entered the Government service as a clerk in the Ministry of Ways and Communications. Here he found several amateurs as enthusiastic as himself, and was soon launched in a social circle where his musical gifts were greatly appreciated and he ran the risk of degenerating into a spoilt dilettante. From the beginning to the end of his career Glinka remained an amateur in that higher sense of the word which implies that he merely wrote what he liked and was exempt from the necessity of composing to order for the sake of a livelihood.

He himself has related the circumstances of

his first creative impulse.   In the spring of 1822, when he was about nineteen, he made the acquaintance of a young lady " of fascinating appearance, who played the harp and had also a beautiful voice.   This voice was not to be compared to any musical instrument ; it was just a resonant silvery soprano, and she sang naturally and with extraordinary charm.   Her attractive qualities and her kindness to me (she called me her nephew and I called her aunt) stirred my heart and my imagination."   We see the rest of the picture : a Petersburg drawing room with its semi-French decoration, an amiable grandpapa reposing in his armchair, while Glinka played by the hour and the young lady joined in with her silvery soprano.   So the first compositions were written—" to do her a service and laid at her feet "—variations upon her favourite theme from Weigel's " Swiss Family," an opera then all the vogue, variations for harp and piano on a theme by Mozart and an original Valse in F for piano.   Of these only the variations for harp survive.

At twenty Glinka took singing lessons from the Italian Belloli.   This led to his first essays in song writing, and after one hopeless failure he succeeded in setting some words by Baratynsky, " Do not needlessly torment me."

Henceforth Glinka began to be conscious of his powers, and between 1825 and 1830 he was constantly composing. Although the best of relations existed between himself and his father, he does not seem to have shown him anything of his deeper artistic nature, and Glinka's family accepted his music merely as an agreeable addition to his social qualities. Meanwhile he wrote many of the songs of his first period, and a few isolated dramatic scenas with orchestral accompaniment, including the Chorus on the Death of a Hero, in C minor, and an Aria for baritone, a part of which he used in the finale of the second act of his opera *Russlan and Liudmilla*. He also learnt Italian and received some instruction in theory from Zamboni. In 1829 he published an album containing most of his early compositions.

From time to time Glinka was incapacitated by an affection of the eyes, and his general health was far from satisfactory. He was possessed of a craving to travel in Spain or Italy, and his father's refusal to let him go abroad " hurt me," he says, " to the point of tears." However, a famous doctor having examined him, reported to his father that the young man had " a whole quadrille of ailments " and ought to be sent to a warm climate for at least three years. Glinka left Russia for Italy in 1830, and remained abroad until the spring of 1834.

During his visit to Italy, Glinka wrote regularly and fully to his family, but unfortunately the correspondence was not deemed worthy of preservation, and the letters were destroyed shortly after his return. If we may judge by the communications to his friends sent later in life from Spain, France and Germany, the destruction of these records of his early impressions is a real loss to musical biography.

The two chief objects of Glinka's journey abroad were to improve his physical condition and to perfect his musical studies. As regards his health, he was benefited perhaps but not cured. " All his life," says Stassov, " Glinka was a martyr to doctors and remedies," and his autobiography is full of details concerning his fainting fits and nervous depression, and his bodily sufferings in general. He had, however, sufficient physical and moral strength to work at times with immense energy.

As regards his musical education, Glinka had now begun to realise that his technical equipment did not keep pace with his creative impulse. He felt the need of that theoretical knowledge which Kirnberg says is to the composer what wings are to a bird. He was by no means so completely ignorant of the theory of his art as many of his critics have insinuated. He had already composed music which was quite on a level with much that was popular in his day, and had won some flattering attentions from musical society in St. Petersburg. We must respect the self-criticism which prompted him to put himself to school again at six-and-twenty. But Italy could not give him that deeper and sounder musical culture of which he was in search. In Milan he began to work under Basili, the Director of the Milan Conservatoire, distinguished for having refused a scholarship to Verdi because he showed no aptitude for music. Basili does not seem to have had *la main heureuse* with budding genius ; Glinka found his methods so dry and pedantic that he soon abandoned his lessons as a waste of time. Nevertheless Italy, then and now the Mecca of all aspiring art students, had much to give to the young Russian. He was deeply impressed by the beauty of his surroundings, but, from the practical side, it was in the art of singing and writing for the voice that Glinka made real progress during his sojourn in the South. He had arrived in Italy in company with Ivanov, who became later on the most famous Russian operatic tenor. Glinka's father had persuaded the tenor to accompany his son abroad and had succeeded in getting him two years leave of absence from the Imperial Chapel. The opera season 1830-1831 was unusually brilliant at Milan, and the two friends heard Grisi, Pasta, Rubini, Galli and Orlandi. Their greatest experience came at the end of the season, when Bellini's " La Sonnambula " was mounted for the first time, " Pasta and Rubini singing their very best in order to uphold their favourite *maestro.*" " We, in our box," continues Glinka, " shed torrents of tears—tears of emotion and enthusiasm." But still more important to his appreciation of vocal music was his acquaintance in Naples with Nozzari and Fodor-Mainville. Ivanov studied with both masters, and Glinka was permitted to be present at his lessons. Nozzari had already retired from the stage, but his voice was still in its fullest beauty. His compass was two octaves, from B to B, and his scale so perfect that Glinka says it could only be compared to Field's scale upon the piano. Under the influence of Italian music, he wrote at this time a few piano pieces and two songs to Russian words. His setting of Koslov's " Venetian Night " was merely an echo of his surroundings ; " The Victor," music to Joukovsky's words, showed more promise of originality, and here we find for the first time the use of the plagal cadence which he employed so effectively in *A Life for the Tsar.*

During the third year of his visit, he felt a conviction that he was moving on the wrong track, and that there was a certain insincerity in all that he was attempting. " It cost me some pains to counterfeit the Italian *sentimento brilliante*," he says. " I, a dweller in the North, felt quite differently (from the children of

the sunny South) ; with us, things either
make no impression at all, or they sink deep
into the soul ; it is either a frenzy of joy or
bitter tears." These reflections, joined to an
acute fit of homesickness, led to his decision
to return to Russia. After a few pleasant days
spent in Vienna, he travelled direct to Berlin,
where he hoped to make up some of the defi-
ciencies of his Italian visit with the assistance
of the well-known theorist Siegfried Dehn.

Dehn saw at once that his pupil was gifted
with genius, but impatient of drudgery. He
gave himself the trouble to devise a short cut
to the essentials of musical theory. In five
months he succeeded in giving Glinka a bird's-
eye view of harmony and counterpoint, fugue
and instrumentation ; the whole course being
concentrated into four small exercise books.
" There is no doubt," writes Glinka, " that I
owe more to Dehn than to any of my masters.
He not only put my musical knowledge into
order but also my ideas on art in general, and
after his lessons I no longer groped my way
along, but worked with the full consciousness
of what I was doing."

While studying with Dehn, he still found time
for composition, and it is noticeable that what
he wrote at this time is by no means Germanised
music. Two songs, " The Rustling Oak," words
by Joukovsky, and Delvig's poem, " Say not

that love has fled," the Variations for piano on Alabiev's " Nightingale," and outlines of the melody for the Orphan's Song " When they slew my mother," afterwards used in a *Life for the Tsar*, besides a sketch for one of the chief themes in the overture of the opera, all tend to prove that he was now deeply preoccupied with the expression of national sentiment in music.

In April 1834 his profitable studies with Dehn were cut short by the death of his father, which necessitated his immediate return to Russia. Stassov sums up the results of this period abroad in the words : " Glinka left us a *dilettante* and returned a *maestro*."

CHAPTER IV

GLINKA'S OPERAS

THE idea of composing a national opera now began to take definite shape in Glinka's mind. In the winter of 1834-1835, the poet Joukovsky was living in the Winter Palace at St. Petersburg as tutor to the young Tsarevich, afterwards Alexander II. The weekly gatherings which he held there were frequented by Poushkin, Gogol, Odoievsky, Prince Vyazemsky—in short, by all the higher *intelligentsia* of the capital. Here Glinka, the fame of whose songs sufficed to procure him the entrée to this select society, was always welcome. When he confided to Joukovsky his wish to create a purely Russian opera, the poet took up the idea with ardour and suggested the subject of Ivan Sousanin, which, as we have seen, had already been treated by Cavos. At first Joukovsky offered to write the text of the work and actually supplied verses for the famous trio in the last act : " Not to me, unhappy one, the storm wind brought his last sign." But his many occupations made it impossible for him to keep pace with Glinka's creative activity once his imagination had been fired. Consequently the libretto had to be handed over to Baron Rozen, a Russianised German, secretary to the young Tzarevich. Rozen could hardly have been a whole-hearted patriot ; certainly he was no poet. The words of the opera leave much to be desired, but we must make allowances for the fact that Glinka, in his impatience, sometimes expected the librettist to supply words to ready-made music. The opera was first called *Ivan Sousanin.* Among Glinka's papers was found the original plan for the work : " *Ivan Sousanin,* a native tragi-heroic opera, in five acts or sections. Actors : Ivan Sousanin (Bass), the chief character ; Antonida, his daughter (Soprano), tender and graceful ; Alexis (afterwards Bogdan) Sobinin, her affianced husband (tenor), a brave man ; Andrew (afterwards Vanya), an orphan boy of thirteen or fourteen (alto), a simple-hearted character."

While at work upon the opera in 1835, Glinka married. This, the fulfilment of a long-cherished wish, brought him great happiness. Soon after his marriage he wrote to his mother, " my heart is once more hopeful, I can feel and pray, rejoice and weep—my music is re-awakened ; I cannot find words to express my gratitude to Providence for this bliss." In this beatific state of mind he threw himself into the completion of his task. During the summer he took the two acts of the libretto which were then ready into the country with him. While travelling by carriage he composed the chorus in 5-4 measure: " Spring waters flow o'er the fields," the idea of which had suddenly occurred to him. Although a nervous man, he seems to have been able to work without having recourse to the strictly guarded padded-room kind of isolation necessary to so many creative geniuses. " Every morning," he says in his autobiography, " I sat at a table in the big sitting-room of our house at Novospasskoï, which was our favourite apartment ; my mother, my sister and my wife— in fact the whole family—were busy there, and the more they laughed and talked and bustled about, the quicker my work went." All through the winter, which was spent in St. Petersburg, he was busy with the opera. " The scene where Sousanin leads the Poles astray in the forest, I read aloud while composing, and entered so completely into the situation of my hero that I used to feel my hair standing on end and cold shivers down my back." During Lent, 1836, a trial rehearsal of the first act was given at the house of Prince Youssipov, with the assistance of his private orchestra. Glinka, satisfied with the results, then made some efforts to get his opera put on the stage, but at first he met with

blank refusals from the Direction of the Imperial
Theatres.   His cause was helped by the generous
spirit of Cavos, who refused to see in Glinka
a rival in the sphere of patriotic opera, and was
ready to accept his work. Even then the
Director of the Opera, Gedeonov, demanded
from Glinka a written undertaking not to claim
any fee for the rights of public performance.
Glinka, who was not dependent upon music for
a livelihood, submitted to this injustice. The
rehearsals were then begun under the super-
vision of Cavos. The Emperor Nicholas I.
attended one of the rehearsals at the great
Opera House and expressed his satisfaction,
and also his willingness to accept the dedication
of the opera. It was then that it received the
title by which it has since become famous,
Glinka having previously changed the name
of *Ivan Sousanin* to that of *Death for the
Tsar*.

The first performance took place on November
27th (O.S.), 1836, in the presence of the Emperor
and the Court. " The first act was well
received," wrote Glinka, " the trio being loudly
and heartily applauded. The first scene in
which the Poles appear (a ballroom in Warsaw)
was passed over in complete silence, and I went
on the stage deeply wounded by the attitude
of the public." It seems, however, that the
silence of the audience proceeded from a certain

timidity as to how they ought to receive the appearance of these magnificent, swaggering Poles in the presence of the Emperor, the Polish insurrection of 1830-1831 being still painfully fresh in the public memory. The rest of the opera was performed amid a scene of unparalleled enthusiasm. The acting of the Russian chorus seems to have been even more realistic in those days than it is now. " In the fourth act," to quote the composer himself, " the representatives of the Polish soldiers in the scene in the forest, fell upon Petrov (the famous bass who created the part of Sousanin) with such fury that they broke his arm, and he was obliged to defend himself from their attacks in good earnest." After the performance, Glinka was summoned to the Emperor's box to receive his compliments, and soon afterwards he was presented with a ring, worth 4,000 roubles, and offered the post of Capellmeister to the Imperial Chapel.

Some account of the story of *A Life for the Tsar* will be of interest to those who have not yet seen the opera, for the passionate idealism of the subject still appeals to every patriotic Russian. The action takes place at one of the most stirring periods of Russian history, the Russo-Polish war of 1633, just after the boy-king Michael Feodorovich—first of the present Romanov line—had been elected to the throne.

Glinka himself sketched out the plot, which runs as follows : The Poles, who have been supporting the claims of their own candidate for the Russian throne, form a conspiracy against the life of the young Romanov. A Polish army corps is despatched to Moscow, ostensibly on a peaceful embassy, but in reality to carry out this sinister design. On the march, they enter the hut of a loyal peasant, Ivan Sousanin, and compel his services as a guide. Sousanin, who suspects their treachery, forms a heroic resolve. He secretly sends his adopted son, the orphan Vanya, to warn the Tsar of his danger ; while, in order to gain time, he misleads the Poles in the depths of the forest and falls a victim to their vengeance when they discover the trick which has been played upon them.

Whether the story be true or not—and modern historians deny its authenticity[1]—Ivan Sousanin will always remain the typical embodiment of the loyalty of the Russian peasant to his Tsar, a sentiment which has hitherto resisted most of the agitations which have affected the upper and middle classes of Russian society.

The music of *A Life for the Tsar* was an

---

[1] Soloveiv asserts that Sousanin did not save the Tsar from the Poles but from the Russian Cossacks who had become demoralised during the long interregnum.

immense advance on anything that had been previously attempted by a Russian composer. Already the overture—though not one of Glinka's best symphonic efforts—shows many novel orchestral effects, which grew out of the fundamental material of his music, the folk-songs of Great Russia. Generally speaking, his tendency is to keep his orchestra within modest limits. Although he knew something of the orchestration of Berlioz, it is Beethoven rather than the French musician that Glinka takes as his model. " I do not care," he says, " to make use of every luxury." Under this category he places trombones, double bassoons, bass drum, English horn, piccolo and even the harp. To the wind instruments he applies the term " orchestral colour," while he speaks of the strings as " orchestral motion." With regard to the strings, he thought that " the more these instruments interlace their parts, the nearer they approach to their natural character and the better they fulfil their part in the orchestra." It is remarkable that Glinka usually gives free play to the various individual groups of instruments, and that his orchestration is far less conventional and limited than that of most operatic composers of his time. The thematic material of *A Life for the Tsar* is partly drawn from national sources, not so much directly, as modelled on the folk-song pattern. The crude folk-stuff is treated in a very different way to that which prevailed in the early national operas. Glinka does not interpolate a whole popular song—often harmonised in a very ordinary manner—into his opera, in the naïve style of Fomin in his *Aniouta* or *The Miller*. With Glinka the material passes through the melting pot of his genius, and flows out again in the form of a plastic national idiom with which, as he himself expresses it, " his fellow-countrymen could not fail to feel completely at home." Here are one or two instances in which the folk-song element is recognisable in *A Life for the Tsar*. In the first act, where Sousanin in his recitative says it is no time to be dreaming of marriage feasts, occurs a phrase which Glinka overheard sung by a cab-driver[1]; the familiar folk-song " Down by Mother Volga," disguised in binary rhythm, serves as accompaniment to Sousanin's words in the forest scene " I give ye answer," and " Thither have I led ye," where its gloomy character is in keeping with the situation ; the recitative sung by Sobinin in the first act, " Greeting, Mother Moscow," is also based upon a folk-tune. But Glinka has also melodies of

---

[1] This fragment of a familiar melody drew down on Glinka the criticism of an aristocratic amateur that the music of *A Life for the Tsar* was fit for coachmen and serfs, and provoked Glinka's sarcastic retort : " What matter, since the servants are better than their masters."

his own invention which are profoundly national in character. As Alfred Bruneau remarks : " By means of a harmony or a simple orchestral touch he can give to an air which is apparently as Italian as possible a penetrating perfume of Russian nationality." An example of this is to be found in Antonida's aria " I gaze upon the empty fields " (Act I). The treatment of his themes is also in accordance with national tradition ; thus in the patriotic chorus in the first Act. " In the storm and threatening tempest," we have an introduction for male chorus, led by a precentor (Zapievets), a special feature of the folk-singing of Great Russia. Another chorus has a pizzicato accompaniment in imitation of the national instrument, the Balalaika, to the tone of which we have grown fairly familiar in England during the last few years. Many of Glinka's themes are built upon the mediæval church modes which lie at the foundation of the majority of the national songs.

For instance, the Peasants' chorus, " We go to our work in the woods," is written in the hypo-dorian mode ; the Song of the Rowers is in the Æolian mode, which is identical with " the natural minor," which was the favourite tonality of Glinka's predecessors. The strange beauty of the *Slavsia* lies in the use of the mixolydian mode, and its simple harmonisation.

The introduction to the opera is treated contrapuntally, in the style of the folk-singing with its cantus firmus (*zapievkoya*) and its imitations (*podgolossky*).

Glinka wrote the rôle of Sousanin for a bass. He has, indeed, been reproached with giving preference for the bass at the expense of the tenor parts, and other Russian composers have followed his example. But when we bear in mind that Russia produces some of the most wonderful bass voices in the world the preference seems natural enough, and even assumes a certain national significance. Upon Sousanin's part centres the chief interest of the opera and it is convincingly realised and consistently Russian throughout. His opening phrases, in the Phrygian mode, seem to delineate his individuality in a few clear broad touches. Serov is disposed to claim for Glinka the definite and conscious use of a *leitmotif* which closely knits the patriotism of his hero with the personality of the Tsar. Towards the close of the first act, Sousanin sings a phrase to the words taken from the old Russian *Slavsia* or Song of Glory. Making a careful analysis of the score, Serov asserts that traces of this motive may be found in many of Sousanin's recitatives and arias, tending to the fusion of the musical and poetical ideas. Serov, an enthusiastic Wagnerian student, seems to see *leitmotifs* in most unsuspected places and is inclined, we think, to exaggerate their presence in *A Life for the Tsar*. But there are certainly moments in the opera in which Glinka seems to have recourse consciously to this phrase of the *Slavsia* as befitting the dramatic situation. Thus in the quartet in the third act, "God love the Tsar," the melody of the *Slavsia* may be recognised in the harmonic progression of the instrumental basses given in 3-4 instead of 4-4 ; the treatment here is interesting, because, as Cheshikin points out, it is in the antiphonal style of the Orthodox Church, the vocal quartets singing " God love the Tsar," while the string quartet replies with " Glory, glory, our Russian Tsar." Again in another solemn moment in the opera the phrase from the *Slavsia* stands out still more clearly. When the Poles command Sousanin to lead them instantly to the Tsar's abode, the hero answers in words which rise far above the ordinary level of the libretto :

" O high and bright our Tsar's abode,
Protected by the power of God,
All Russia guards it day and night,
While on its walls, in raiment white,
The angels, heaven's winged sentries, wait
To keep all traitors from the gate."

These words are sung by Sousanin to a majestic cantilena in a flowing 6-4 measure, while the orchestra accompany in march rhythm with the *Slavsia*, which, in spite of being somewhat veiled by the change of rhythm and the vocal melody, may be quite easily identified.

Two great scenes are allotted to Sousanin. The first occurs when the Poles insist on his acting as their guide and he resolves to lay down his life for the Tsar. Here the orchestra plays an important part, suggesting the agitations which rend the soul of the hero ; now it reflects his super-human courage, and again those inevitable, but passing, fears and regrets without which his deed would lose half its heroism. The alternating rhythms—Sousanin sings in 2-4 and the Poles 3-4—are effectively managed. Sousanin's second great moment occurs when the Poles, worn out with hunger and fatigue, fall asleep round their camp fire and the peasant-hero, watching for the tardy winter sunrise which will bring death to him and safety to the young Tsar, sings in a mood of intense exaltation the aria " Thou comest Dawn, for the last time mine eyes shall look on thee ! " a touching and natural outburst of emotion that never fails to stir a Russian audience to its emotional depths, although some of the national composers have since reached higher levels, judged from a purely musical standpoint.

In *A Life for the Tsar* Glinka conceived the idea, interesting in itself, of contrasting the characters of the two nations by means of their national music. To this end he devotes the whole of the second act entirely to the Poles. Here it seems to me that he is far less successful than with any other portion of the work. Some critics have supposed that the composer really wished to give an impression of the Poles as a superficial people literally dancing and revelling through life, and possessed of no deeper feelings to be expressed in music. But Glinka was too intelligent a man to take such naïve views of national character. It seems more probable that not being supersaturated with Polish as he was with Russian folk-music, he found it difficult to indicate the personality of the Pole in anything but conventional dance rhythms. This passes well enough in the second act, where the scene is laid at a brilliant festival in the Polish capital, and the ballroom dances which follow constitute the ballet of the opera. But in other parts of the work, as, for instance, when the Polish soldiers burst into Sousanin's cottage and order him to act as their guide, the strains of a stately polonaise seem distinctly out of place ; and again, when they have lost their way in the forest and their situation is extremely precarious, they express their alarm and suspicion in mazurka rhythm. The polonaise, cracoviak, the valse in 6-8 time and the mazurka and finale which form the ballet are somewhat ordinary in character, but presented with a charm and piquancy of orchestration which has made them extremely popular. The representative theme of the Poles, a phrase from the polonaise, hardly suggests the part they play in the opera—their evil designs upon Moscow and the young Michael Feodorovich, about which they sing in the succeeding chorus. But others seem to find this music more impressive, for, says M. Camille Bellaigue, " even when restricted to strictly national forms and formulas, the Russian genius has a tendency to enlarge them. In the polonaise and especially in the sombre and sinister mazurka in *A Life for the Tsar* Glinka obtains from local rhythms an intimate dramatic emotion. . . . He raises and generalises, and from the music of a race makes the music of humanity."

In the last act of *A Life for the Tsar* Glinka has concentrated the ardent patriotism and the profound human sympathy which is not only a feature of his music but common to the whole school of which he is the prototype. The curtain rises upon a street in Moscow, the people are hurrying to the Kremlin to acclaim the young Tsar, and as they go they sing that beautiful hymn-march " Glory, glory, Holy Russia," a superb representation of the patriotic ideal.

In contrast to the gladness of the crowd, Glinka shows us the unfortunate children of Ivan Sousanin, the lad Vanya, Antonida, and her betrothed, Sobinin. Some of the people stop to ask the cause of their sadness, and in reply they sing the touching trio which describes the fate of Sousanin. Then the scene changes to the Red Square under the walls of the Kremlin, and all individual sentiment is merged in a flood of loftier emotion. The close of the act is the apotheosis of the Tsar and of the spirit of loyalty. Here on the threshold of the Kremlin Michael Feodorovich pauses to salute the dead body of the peasant-hero. Once again the great crowd takes up the Slavsia or Glory motive, and amid the pealing of the bells the opera ends with a triumphant chorus which seems to sum up the whole character of the Russian people. " Every element of national beauty, " says M. Camille Bellaigue," is pressed into the service here. The people, their ruler and God himself are present. Not one degree in all the sacred hierarchy is lacking ; not one feature of the ideal, not one ray from the apotheosis of the fatherland."

With all its weaknesses and its occasional lapses into Italian phraseology, *A Life for the Tsar* still remains a patriotic and popular opera, comparable only in these respects with some of the later works which it engendered, or, among contemporary operas, with Weber's *Der Frei-schütz.*

With the unparalleled success of *A Life for the Tsar,* Glinka reached the meridian of his fame and power. He followed up the opera by some of his finest songs, contained in the collection entitled " Farewell to St. Peters-burg," and by the beautiful incidental music to Koukolnik's tragedy *Prince Kholmsky,* of which Tchaikovsky, by no means an indulgent critic of his great predecessor, says : " Glinka here shows himself to be one of the greatest symphonic composers of his day. Many touches in *Prince Kholmsky* recall the brush of Beet-hoven. There is the same moderation in the means employed, and in the total absence of all striving after mere external effects ; the same sober beauty and clear exposition of ideas that are not laboured but inspired ; the same plasticity of form and mould. Finally there is the same inimitable instrumentation, so remote from all that is affected or far-fetched. . . . Every entr'acte which follows the over-ture is a little picture drawn by a master-hand. These are symphonic marvels which would suffice a second-rate composer for a whole series of long symphonies."

The idea of a second national opera began to occupy Glinka's mind very soon after the pro-duction of *A Life for the Tsar.* It was his intention to ask Poushkin to furnish him with a libretto based upon his epic poem "Russlan and Liudmilla." The co-operation of Russia's greatest poet with her leading musical genius should have been productive of great results. Unhappily the plan was frustrated by the tragic death of Poushkin, who was shot in a duel in 1837. Glinka, however, did not renounce the subject to which he had been attracted, and sketched out the plot and even some musical numbers, falling as before into the fatal mistake of expecting his librettist to supply words to music already written. The text for *Russlan and Liudmilla* was supplied by Bakhtourin, but several of Glinka's friends added a brick here and there to the structure, with very patchy results. The introduction and finale were sketched out in 1839, but the composer, partly on account of failing health, did not work steadily at the opera until the winter of 1841. The score was actually completed by April 1842, when he submitted it on approval to Gedeonov. This time Glinka met with no difficulties from the Director of the Imperial Opera; the work was accepted at once and the date of the first production fixed in the following November.

The subject of *Russlan and Liudmilla*, though equally national, has not the poignant human interest that thrills us in *A Life for the Tsar*.

The story belongs to a remote and legendary period in Russian history, and the characters are to a great extent fantastic and mythical. It had none of those qualities which in the first opera made for an immediate popular success in every stratum of Russian society. The days are now long past when the musical world of Russia was split into two hostile camps, the one led by Serov, who pronounced *Russlan* to be the last aberration of a lamentably warped genius ; the other by Stassov, who saw in it the mature expression of Glinka's inspiration. At the same time Stassov was quite alive to the weaknesses and impossible scenic moments of the libretto, faults which are doubtless the reason why seventy years have not sufficed to win popularity for the work, although the lapse of time has strengthened the conviction of all students of Russian opera as to the actual musical superiority of *Russlan and Liudmilla* over *A Life for the Tsar*.

The story of the opera runs as follows :

In days of old—when the Slavs were still Pagans—Prince Svietozar of Kiev had one beautiful daughter, Liudmilla. The maiden had three suitors, the knights-errant Russlan and Farlaf, and the young Tatar prince, Ratmir. Liudmilla's love was bestowed upon Russlan, and Prince Svietozar prepares to celebrate their marriage. Meanwhile the wicked wizard

Chernomor has fallen desperately in love with Liudmilla. At the wedding feast he carries off the bride by means of his magic arts. Prince Svietozar sends the three knights to rescue his daughter and promises to give her to the one who succeeds in the quest. The knights meet with many adventures by the way. Farlaf seeks the help of the sorceress Naina, who agrees to save him from the rivalry of Ratmir, by luring the ardent young Oriental aside from his quest. Russlan takes council with the benevolent wizard Finn, who tells him how to acquire a magic sword with which to deliver his bride from the hands of Chernomor. Russlan saves Liudmilla, but on their homeward journey to Kiev they are intercepted by Farlaf, who casts them both into a magic slumber. Leaving Russlan by the wayside, Farlaf carries the heroine back to her father's house, where he passes himself off as her deliverer and claims her for his bride. Russlan awakes and arrives in time to denounce his treachery, and the opera ends with the marriage of the true lovers, which was interrupted in the first act.

The overture to *Russlan and Liudmilla* is a solid piece of work, sketched on broad lines and having a fantastic colouring quite in keeping with the subject of the opera. The opening subject is national in character, being divided into two strains which lend themselves to contrapuntal treatment.

An introduction follows, consisting of a chorus and two solos for Bayan (tenor), the famous bard of old, who is supposed to relate the legend. This introduction is largely built upon a phrase of eight notes, the characteristic utterance of Bayan when he speaks of the " deeds of long ago."   Afterwards this phrase is repeated in the Dorian mode, and the music acquires an archaic character in conformity with the remote period of the action.

The opera itself may be said to begin with a wedding chorus, followed by a cavatina for Liudmilla in which she takes leave of her father. In writing for his primadonne Glinka seems to have found it difficult to avoid the conventional Italian influence, and this solo, in common with most of the music for Liudmilla, lacks vigour and originality.   Far more interesting from the musical point of view is the chorus in 5-4 measure, an invocation to Lel, the Slavonic God of Love.   At the close of this number a loud clap of thunder is heard and the scene is plunged in darkness, during which the wizard Chernomor carries away the bride.   The consternation of the guests is cleverly depicted over a pedal point for horn on E flat which extends for a hundred and fifty bars.   Prince Svietozar then bids the knights-errant to go in search of his daughter, and with a short chorus imploring the aid of Perun upon their quest the act comes to an end.

The orchestral prelude to the second act is based upon a broad impetuous theme which afterwards appears as the motive of the Giant's head in Act III. The first scene represents a hilly region and the cave of the good wizard Finn. The character of Finn, half humorous and half pathetic, with its peculiar combination of benevolence, vacillation, and pessimistic regret, is essentially Russian. Such characters have been made typical in the novels of Tourgeniev and Tolstoy. Finn relates how, in a vain endeavour to win Naina the sorceress, he has changed himself into a shepherd, a fisherman, and a warrior, and finally into a wizard. In this last character he has succeeded in touching her heart. But now alas, they have awakened to the realisation that there is nothing left to them but regret for lost possibilities fled beyond recall. Glinka expresses all these psychological changes in Finn's famous Ballade which forms the opening number of this act ; but admirable as it is, critics have some ground for their reproach that its great length delays the action of the plot. Russlan, having listened to Finn's love-story, receives from him the sword with which he is to attack the Giant's Head. In the next scene Farlaf meets the elderly but once beautiful Naina, and the two sing a

humorous duet. Farlaf's chief air, a rondo
in opera-bouffe style, is rather ordinary, but
Naina's music is a successful piece of character-
painting. The last scene of the second act is
one of the most fantastic in this fantastic
opera. The stage is enveloped in mist. Russlan
enters and sings his aria, of which the opening
recitative is the strongest part, the *Allegro*
section, which Glinka has written in sonata-
form, being somewhat diffuse. While he is singing, the mist slowly disperses, and the rising moon
reveals the lonely steppe and shines upon the
bleached bones which strew an ancient battle-
field. Russlan now sees with horror the apparition of the Giant's Head. This in its turn sees
Russlan, and threatens the audacious knight
who has ventured upon the haunted field. But
Russlan overcomes the monster head with the
magic sword, as directed by Finn. In order
to give weight to the Giant's voice Glinka has
supplemented the part by a small male chorus
which sings from within the head.

The prelude to the third act is generally
omitted, and is not in fact printed in the pianoforte score of the opera. The opening number,
a Persian chorus for female voices, "The Night
lies heavy on the fields," is full of grace and
oriental languor. The subject of the chorus
is a genuine Persian melody and the variations
which form the accompaniment add greatly

to the beauty of these pages. The chorus is followed by an aria for Gorislava (soprano), Ratmir's former love, whom he has deserted for Liudmilla. This air with its clarinet obbligato is one of the most popular solos in the opera. In answer to Gorislava's appeal, Ratmir appears upon the scene and sings a charming nocturne accompanied by *cor anglais*. The part of the young oriental lover is usually taken by a woman (contralto). For this number Glinka makes use of a little Tatar air which Ferdinand David afterwards introduced, transposed into the major, in his symphonic poem " Le Désert." It is a beautiful piece of landscape painting which makes us feel the peculiar sadness of the twilight in Russia as it falls on the vast spaces of the Steppes. A French critic has said that it might have been written by an oriental Handel. The scene described as the seduction of Ratmir consists of a ballet in rococo style entitled " Naina's magic dance." Then follows a duet for Gorislava and Ratmir, after which the maidens of the harem surround Ratmir and screen Gorislava from him. Afterwards the enchanted palace created by Naina to ensnare Ratmir suddenly vanishes and we see the open plain once more. The act concludes with a quartet in which Russlan and Finn take part with the two oriental lovers.

The entr'acte preceding the fourth act consists

of a march movement (*Marcia allegro risoluto*). The curtain then rises upon Chernomor's enchanted garden, where Liudmilla languishes in captivity. An oriental ballet then follows, but this is preceded by the March of the Wizard Chernomor. This quaint march which personifies the invisible monster is full of imagination, although it tells its tale so simply that it takes us back to the fairyland of childhood. The first of the Eastern dances (*allegretto quasi andante*) is based upon a Turkish song in 6-8 measure. Afterwards follows the Danse Arabesque and finally a Lezginka, an immensely spirited dance built upon another of the Tatar melodies which were given to Glinka by the famous painter Aivazovsky. A chorus of naiads and a chorus of flowers also form part of the ballet, which is considered one of Glinka's *chefs d'œuvre*. While the chorus is being sung we see in the distance an aerial combat between Russlan and Chernomor, and throughout the whole of the movement the wizard's *leitmotif* is prominent in the music. Russlan, having overcome Chernomor, wakes Liudmilla from the magic sleep into which she has been cast by his spells.

The first scene of the last act takes place in the Steppes, where Ratmir and Gorislava, now reconciled, have pitched their tent. Russlan's followers break in upon the lovers with the news that Farlaf has treacherously snatched Liudmilla from their master. Then Finn arrives and begs Ratmir to carry to Russlan a magic ring which will restore the princess from her trance. In the second scene the action returns to Prince Svietozar's palace. Liudmilla is still under a spell, and her father, who believes her to be dead, reproaches Farlaf in a fine piece of recitative (Svietozar's music throughout the work is consistently archaic in character). Farlaf declares that Liudmilla is not dead and claims her as his reward. Svietozar is reluctantly about to fulfil his promise, when Russlan arrives with the magic ring and denounces the false knight. The funeral march which had accompanied the Prince's recitative now gives place to the chorus " Love and joy." Liudmilla in her sleep repeats the melody of the chorus in a kind of dreamy ecstasy. Then Russlan awakens her and the opera concludes with a great chorus of thanksgiving and congratulation. Throughout the finale the characteristics of Russian and Eastern music are combined with brilliant effect.

Russlan and Liudmilla was received with indifference by the public and with pronounced hostility by most of the critics. Undoubtedly the weakness of the libretto had much to do with its early failure ; but it is equally true that in this, his second opera, Glinka travelled so far from Italian tradition and carried his use of national colour so much further and with such far greater conviction, that the music became something of an enigma to a public whose enthusiasm was still wholly reserved for the operas of Donizetti, Bellini and Rossini. Looking back from the present condition of Russian opera we can trace the immense influence of *Russlan and Liudmilla* upon the later generation of composers both as regards opera and ballet. It is impossible not to realise that the fantastic Russian ballets of the present day owe much to Glinka's first introduction of Eastern dances into *Russlan and Liudmilla.*

The coldness of the public towards this work, the fruit of his mature conviction, was a keen disappointment to Glinka. He had not the alternative hope of being appreciated abroad, for he had deliberately chosen to appeal to his fellow-countrymen, and when they rejected him he had no heart for further endeavour. His later symphonic works, " Kamarinskaya " and " The Jota Aragonese," show that his gift had by no means deteriorated. Of the former Tchaikovsky has truly said that Glinka has succeeded in concentrating in one short work what a dozen second-rate talents could only have invented with the whole expenditure of their powers. Possibly Glinka would have had more courage

and energy to meet his temporary dethrone-
ment from the hearts of his own people had not
his health been already seriously impaired.
After the production of *Russlan* he lived chiefly
abroad. In his later years he was much attracted to the music of Bach and to the older
polyphonic schools of Italy and Germany.
Always preoccupied with the idea of nationality in music, he made an elaborate study of
Russian church music, but his failing health
did not permit him to carry out the plans which
he had formed in this connection. In April
1856 he left St. Petersburg for the last time and
went to Berlin, where he intended to pursue
these studies with the assistance of Dehn. Here
he lived very quietly for some months, working
twice a week with his old master and going
occasionally to the opera to hear the works
of Gluck and Mozart. In January 1857 he
was taken seriously ill, and passed peacefully
away during the night of February 2nd. In
the following May his remains were brought from
Germany to St. Petersburg and laid in the cemetery of the Alexander Nevsky monastery near
to those of other national poets, Krylov,
Baratinsky and Joukovsky.

Glinka was the first inspired interpreter of
the Russian nationality in music. During
the period which has elapsed since his death
the impress of his genius upon that of his

fellow countrymen has in no way weakened.
For this reason a knowledge of his music is an
indispensable introduction to the appreciation
of the later school of Russian music ; for in his
works and in those of Dargomijsky, we shall
find the key to all that has since been accomplished.

A. S. DARGOMIJSKY

Makowsky, C.G.

CHAPTER V

DARGOMIJSKY

GLINKA, in his memoirs, relates how in the autumn of 1834 he met at a musical party in St. Petersburg, " a little man with a shrill treble voice, who, nevertheless, proved a redoubtable virtuoso when he sat down to the piano." The little man was Alexander Sergeivich Dargomijsky, then about twenty-one years of age, and already much sought after in society as a brilliant pianist and as the composer of agreeable drawing-room songs. Dargomijsky's diary contains a corresponding entry recording this important meeting of two men who were destined to become central points whence started two distinct currents of tendency influencing the whole future development of Russian music. " Similarity of education and a mutual love of music immediately drew us together," wrote Dargomijsky, " and this in spite of the fact that Glinka was ten years my senior." For the remainder of Glinka's life Dargomijsky was his devoted friend and fellow-worker, but never his unquestioning disciple.

Dargomijsky was born, February 2/14, 1813, at a country estate in the government of Toula, whither his parents had fled from their own home near Smolensk before the French invaders in 1812. It is said that Dargomijsky, the future master of declamation, only began to articulate at five years of age. In 1817 his parents migrated to St. Petersburg. They appear to have taken great interest in the musical education of their son ; at six he received his first instruction on the piano, and two years later took up the violin ; while at eleven he had already tried his hand at composition. His education being completed, he entered the Government service, from which, however, he retired altogether in 1843. Thanks to his parents' sympathy with his musical talent, Dargomijsky's training had been above the average and a long course of singing lessons with an excellent master, Tseibikha, no doubt formed the basis of his subsequent success as a composer of vocal music. But at the time of his first meeting with Glinka, both on account of his ignorance of theory and of the narrowness of his general outlook upon music, he can only be regarded as an amateur. One distinguishing feature of his talent seems to have been in evidence even then, for Glinka, after hearing his first song, written to humorous words, declared that if Dargomijsky would turn his attention to comic opera he would certainly surpass all his predecessors in that line. Contact with Glinka's personality effected the same beneficial change in Dargomijsky that Rubinstein's influence brought about in Tchaikovsky some thirty years later ; it changed him from a mere dilettante into a serious musician. " Glinka's example," he wrote in his autobiography, " who was at that time (1834) taking Prince Usipov's band through the first rehearsals of his opera *A Life for the Tsar*, assisted by myself and Capellmeister Johannes, led to my decision to study the theory of music. Glinka handed over to me the five exercise books in which he had worked out Dehn's theoretical system and I copied them in my own hand, and soon assimilated the so-called mysterious wisdom of harmony and counterpoint, because I had been from childhood practically prepared for this initiation and had occupied myself with the study of orchestration." These were the only books of theory ever studied by Dargomijsky, but they served to make him realise the possession of gifts hitherto unsuspected. After this course of self-instruction he felt strong enough to try his hand as an operatic composer, and selected a libretto founded on Victor Hugo's " Notre Dame de Paris." Completed and translated into Russian in 1839, the work, entitled *Esmeralda*, was not accepted by the Direction of the Imperial Opera

until 1847, when it was mounted for the first
time at Moscow. By this time Dargomijsky
had completely outgrown this immature essay.
The light and graceful music pleased the Russian
public, but the success of this half-forgotten
child of his youth gave little satisfaction to the
composer himself. He judged the work in the
following words : " The music is slight and
often trivial—in the style of Halévy and Meyerbeer ; but in the more dramatic scenes there are
already some traces of that language of force
and realism which I have since striven to develop
in my Russian music."

In 1843 Dargomijsky went abroad, and while
in Paris made the acquaintance of Auber,
Meyerbeer, Halévy, and Fétis. The success of
Esmeralda encouraged him to offer to the
Directors of the Imperial Theatre an opera-
ballet entitled *The Triumph of Bacchus*, which
he had originally planned as a cantata ; but the
work was rejected, and only saw the light some
twenty years later, when it was mounted in
Moscow. Dargomijsky's correspondence during
his sojourn abroad is extremely interesting, and
shows that his views on music were greatly
in advance of his time and quite free from the
influences of fashion and convention.

In 1853 we gather from a letter addressed to a
friend that he was attracted to national music.
As a matter of fact the new opera, upon which

he had already started in 1848, was based upon a genuine Russian folk-subject—Poushkin's dramatic poem "The Roussalka" (The Water Sprite). Greatly discouraged by the refusal of the authorities to accept *The Triumph of Bacchus*, Dargomijsky laid aside *The Roussalka* until 1853. During this interval most of his finest songs and declamatory ballads were written, as well as those inimitably humorous songs which, perhaps, only a Russian can fully appreciate. But though he matured slowly, his intellectual and artistic development was serious and profound. Writing to Prince Odoevsky about this time, he says : " The more I study the elements of our national music, the more I discover its many-sidedness. Glinka, who so far has been the first to extend the sphere of our Russian music, has, I consider, only touched one phase of it—the lyrical. In *The Roussalka* I shall endeavour as much as possible to bring out the dramatic and humorous elements of our national music. I shall be glad if I achieve this, even though it may seem a half protest against Glinka." Here we see Dargomijsky not as the disciple, but as the independent worker, although he undoubtedly kept *Russlan and Liudmilla* in view as the model for *The Roussalka*. The work was given for the first time at the Maryinsky Theatre, St. Petersburg, in 1856, but proved too novel in form and treatment to please a public that was still infatuated with Italian opera.

In 1864-1865 Dargomijsky made a second tour in Western Europe, taking with him the scores of *The Roussalka* and of his three Orchestral Fantasias, " Kazachok " (The Cossack), a " Russian Legend," and " The Dance of the Mummers " (Skomorokhi). In Leipzig he made the acquaintance of many prominent musicians, who contented themselves with pronouncing his music " *sehr neu* " and " *ganz interessant*," but made no effort to bring it before the public. In Paris he was equally unable to obtain a hearing ; but in Belgium— always hospitable to Russian musicians—he gave a concert of his own compositions with considerable success. On his way back to Russia he spent a few days in London and ever after spoke of our capital with enthusiastic admiration.

In 1860 Dargomijsky had been appointed director of the St. Petersburg section of the Imperial Russian Musical Society. This brought him in contact with some of the younger contemporary musicians, and after his return from abroad, in 1865, he became closely associated with Balakirev and his circle and took a leading part in the formation of the new national and progressive school of music. By this time he handled that musical language of " force and realism," of which we find the first distinct traces in *The Roussalka,* with ease and convincing eloquence. For his fourth opera he now selected the subject of *The Stone Guest* (Don Juan) ; not the version by Da Ponte which had been immortalised by Mozart's music, but the poem in which the great Russian poet Poushkin had treated this ubiquitous tale. This work occupied the last years of Dargomijsky's life, and we shall speak of it in detail a little further on. Soon after the composer's return from abroad his health began to fail and the new opera had constantly to be laid aside. From contemporary accounts it seems evident that he did not shut himself away from the world in order to keep alive the flickering flame of life that was left to him, but that on the contrary he liked to be surrounded by the younger generation, to whom he gave out freely of his own richly gifted nature. The composition of *The Stone Guest* was a task fulfilled in the presence of his disciples, reminding us of some of the great painters who worked upon their masterpieces before their pupils' eyes. Dargomijsky died of heart disease in January 1869. On his deathbed he entrusted the unfinished manuscript of *The Stone Guest* to Cui and Rimsky-Korsakov, instructing the latter to carry out the orchestration of it. The composer fixed three thousand roubles (about £330) as the price of his work, but an obsolete law made it illegal for a native composer to receive more than £160 for an opera. At the suggestion of Vladimir Stassov, the sum was raised by private subscription, and *The Stone Guest* was performed in 1872. Of its reception by the public something will be said when we come to the analysis of the work.

We may dismiss *Esmeralda* as being practically of no account in the development of Russian opera ; but the history of *The Roussalka* is important, for this work not only possesses intrinsic qualities that have kept it alive for over half a century, but its whole conception shows that Dargomijsky was already in advance of his time as regards clear-cut musical characterisation and freedom from conventional restraint. In this connection it is interesting to remember that *The Roussalka* preceded Bizet's "Carmen" by some ten or twelve years.

As early as 1843 Dargomijsky had thought of *The Roussalka* as an excellent subject for opera. He avoided Glinka's methods of entrusting his libretto to several hands. In preparing the book he kept as closely as possible to Poushkin's poem, and himself carried out the modifications necessary for musical treatment. It is certain that he had begun the work by September 1848. It was completed in 1855.

As we have already seen, he was aware that

Glinka was not fully in touch with the national character ; there were sides of it which he had entirely ignored in both his operas, because he was temperamentally incapable of reflecting them. Glinka's humour, as Dargomijsky has truthfully said, was not true to Russian life. His strongest tendency was towards a slightly melancholy lyricism, and when he wished to supply some comic relief he borrowed it from cosmopolitan models. The composer of *The Roussalka*, on the other hand, deliberately aimed at bringing out the dramatic, realistic, and humorous elements which he observed in his own race. The result was an opera containing a wonderful variety of interest.

Russian folk-lore teems with references to the *Roussalki*, or water nymphs, who haunt the streams and the still, dark, forest pools, lying in wait for the belated traveller, and of all their innumerable legends none is more racy of the soil than this dramatic poem by Poushkin in which the actual and supernatural worlds are sketched by a master hand. The story of the opera runs as follows :

A young Prince falls in love with Natasha, the Miller's daughter. He pays her such devoted attention that the father hopes in time to see his child become a princess. Natasha returns the Prince's passion, and gives him not only her love but her honour. Circumstances afterwards compel the Prince to marry in his own rank. Deserted in the hour of her need, Natasha in despair drowns herself in the mill-stream. Now, in accordance with Slavonic legends, she becomes a *Roussalka*, seeking always to lure mortals to her watery abode. Misfortune drives the old Miller crazy and the mill falls into ruins. Between the second act, in which the Prince's nuptials are celebrated, and the third, a few years are supposed to elapse. Meanwhile the Prince is not happy in his married life, and is moreover perpetually haunted by the remembrance of his first love and by remorse for her tragic fate. He spends hours near the ruined mill dreaming of the past. One day a little *Roussalka* child appears to him and tells him that she is his daughter, and that she dwells with her mother among the water-sprites. All his old passion is reawakened. He stands on the brink of the water in doubt as to whether to respond to the calls of Natasha and the child, or whether to flee from their malign influence. Even while he hesitates, the crazy Miller appears upon the scene and fulfils dramatic justice by flinging the betrayer of his daughter into the stream. Here we have the elements of an exceedingly dramatic libretto which offers fine opportunities to a psychological musician of Dargomijsky's type. The scene in which the Prince, with caressing grace and tenderness, tries to prepare Natasha for the news of his coming marriage ; her desolation when she hears that they must part ; her bitter disenchantment on learning the truth, and her cry of anguish as she tries to make him realise the full tragedy of her situation—all these emotions, coming in swift succession, are followed by the music with astonishing force and flexibility. Very effective, too, is the scene of the wedding festivities in which the wailing note of the *Roussalka* is heard every time the false lover attempts to kiss his bride—the suggestion of an invisible presence which throws all the guests into consternation. As an example of Dargomijsky's humour, nothing is better than the recitative of the professional marriage-maker, " Why so silent pretty lassies," and the answering chorus of the young girls (in Act II.). As might be expected with a realistic temperament like Dargomijsky's, the music of the *Roussalki* is the least successful part of the work. The sub-aquatic ballet in the last act is rather commonplace ; while Natasha's music, though expressive, has been criticised as being too human and warm-blooded for a soulless watersprite. Undoubtedly the masterpiece of the opera is the musical presentment of the Miller. At first a certain sardonic humour plays about this crafty, calculating old peasant, but afterwards, when disappointed greed and his daughter's disgrace have turned his brain, how subtly the music is made to suggest the cunning of mania in that strange scene in which he babbles of his hidden treasures, " stored safe enough where the fish guard them with one eye ! " With extraordinary power Dargomijsky reproduces his hideous meaningless laugh as he pushes the Prince into the swirling mill-stream. The character of the Miller alone would suffice to prove that the composer possesses dramatic gifts of the highest order.

The Roussalka, first performed at the Maryinsky Theatre in May 1856, met with very little success. The Director of the opera, Glinka's old enemy Gedeonov, having made up his mind that so " unpleasing " a work could have no future, mounted it in the shabbiest style. Moreover, as was usually the case with national opera then—and even at a later date—the interpretation was entrusted to second-rate artists. Dargomijsky, in a letter to his pupil Madame Karmalina, comments bitterly upon this ; unhappily he could not foresee the time, not so far distant, when the great singer Ossip Petrov would electrify the audience with his wonderful impersonation of the Miller ; nor dream that fifty years later Shaliapin would make one of his most legitimate triumphs in this part. The critics met Dargomijsky's innovations without in the least comprehending their drift. Serov-

it was before the days of his opposition to the
national cause—alone appreciated the novelty
and originality shown in the opera ; he placed
it above *A Life for the Tsar* ; but even his
forcible pen could not rouse the public from their
indifference to every new manifestation of art.
Dargomijsky himself perfectly understood the
reason of its unpopularity. In one of his
letters written at this time, he says : " Neither
our amateurs nor our critics recognise my
talents. Their old-fashioned notions cause them
to seek for melody which is merely flattering to the ear. That is not *my* first thought.
I have no intention of indulging them with
music as a plaything. *I want the note to be the
direct equivalent of the word.* I want truth and
realism. This they cannot understand."

Ten years after the first performance of *The
Roussalka*, the public began to reconsider its
verdict. The emancipation of the serfs in
1861 changed the views of society towards the
humble classes, and directed attention towards
all that concerned the past history of the peasan-
try. A new spirit animated the national ideal.
From Poushkin's poetry, with its somewhat
" Olympian " attitude to life, the reading public
turned to the people's poets, Nekrassov and
Nikitin ; while the realism of Gogol was now
beginning to be understood. To these circumstances we may attribute the reaction in favour

of *The Roussalka*, which came as a tardy compensation towards the close of the composer's life.

During the ten years which followed the completion of *The Roussalka*, Dargomijsky was steadily working towards the formulation of new principles in vocal, and especially in dramatic music. We may watch his progress in the series of songs and ballads which he produced at this time. It is, however, in *The Stone Guest* that Dargomijsky carries his theories of operatic reform to a logical conclusion. One of his chief aims, in which he succeeded in interesting the little band of disciples whose work we shall presently review, was the elimination of the artificial and conventional in the accepted forms of Italian opera. Wagner had already experienced the same dissatisfaction, and was solving the question of reform in the light of his own great genius. But the Russian composers could not entirely adopt the Wagnerian theories. Dargomijsky, while rejecting the old arbitrary divisions of opera, split upon the question of the importance which Wagner gave to the orchestra. Later on we shall see how each member of the newly-formed school tried to work out the principles of reformation in his own way, keeping in view the dominant idea that the dramatic interest should be chiefly sustained by the singer, while the orchestra should be regarded as a means of enhancing the interest of the vocal music. Dargomijsky himself was the first to embody these principles in what must be regarded as one of the masterpieces of Russian music—his opera *The Stone Guest*. Early in the 'sixties he had been attracted to Poushkin's fine poem, which has for subject the story of Don Juan, treated, not as we find it in Mozart's opera, by a mere librettist, but with the dramatic force and intensity of a great poet. Dargomijsky was repelled by the idea of mutilating a fine poem ; yet found himself overwhelmed by the difficulties of setting the words precisely as they stood. Later on, however, the illness from which he was suffering seems to have produced in him a condition of rare musical clairvoyance. " I am singing my swan song," he wrote to Madame Karmelina in 1868 ; " I am writing *The Stone Guest*. It is a strange thing : my nervous condition seems to generate one idea after another. I have scarcely any physical strength. . . . It is not I who write, but some unknown power of which I am the instrument. The thought of *The Stone Guest* occupied my attention five years ago when I was in robust health, but then I shrank from the magnitude of the task. Now, ill as I am, I have written three-fourths of the opera in two and a half months. . . . Needless to say the work will not appeal to the many."

" Thank God," comments Stassov, in his energetic language, " that in 1863 Dargomijsky recoiled before so colossal an undertaking, since he was not yet prepared for it. His musical nature was still growing and widening, and he was gradually freeing himself from all stiffness and asperity, from false notions of form, and from the Italian and French influences which sometimes predominate in the works of his early and middle periods. In each new composition Dargomijsky takes a step forward, but in 1866 his preparations were complete. A great musician was ready to undertake a great work. Here was a man who had cast off all musical wrong thinking, whose mind was as developed as his talent, and who found such inward force and greatness of character as inspired him to write this work while he lay in bed, subject to the terrible assaults of a mortal malady."

The Stone Guest, then, is the ultimate expression of that realistic language which Dargomijsky employs in his early cantata *The Triumph of Bacchus*, in *The Roussalka*, and in his best songs. It is applied not to an ordinary ready-made libretto, but to a poem of such excellence that the composer felt it a sacrilege to treat it otherwise than as on an equal footing with the music. This effort to follow with absolute fidelity every word of the book, and to make

the note the representative of the word, led
to the adoption of a new operatic form, and to
the complete abandonment of the traditional soli,
duets, choruses, and concerted pieces. In *The
Stone Guest* the singers employ that *melos*, or
mezzo-recitativo, which is neither melody nor
speech, but the connecting link between the
two. Some will argue, with Serov, that there
is nothing original in these ideas ; they had
already been carried out by Wagner; and that
The Stone Guest does not prove that Dargomijsky
was an innovator but merely that he had the
intelligence to become the earliest of Wagner's
disciples. Nothing could be further from the
truth. By 1866 Dargomijsky had some theoretical knowledge of Wagner's views, but he can
have heard little, if any, of his music. Whether
he was at all influenced by the former, it is
difficult to determine ; but undoubtedly his
efforts to attain to a more natural and realistic
method of expression date from a time when
Wagner and Wagnerism were practically a
sealed book to him. One thing is certain : from
cover to cover of *The Stone Guest* it would be
difficult to find any phrase which is strongly
reminiscent of Wagner's musical style. What
he himself thought of Wagner's music we
may gather from a letter written to Serov in
1856, in which he says : " I have not returned
your score of " Tannhäuser," because I have not

yet had time to go through the whole work.
You are right ; in the scenic disposition there
is much poetry ; in the music, too, he shows us
a new and practical path ; but in his unnatural
melodies and spiciness, although at times his
harmonies are very interesting, there is a sense
of effort—*will und kann nicht !* Truth—above
all truth—but we may demand good taste as
well."

Dargomijsky was no conscious or deliberate
imitator of Wagner. The passion for realistic
expression which possessed him from the first
led him by a parallel but independent path
to a goal somewhat similar to that which was
reached by Wagner. But Dargomijsky adhered
more closely to the way indicated a century
earlier by that great musical reformer Gluck.
In doing this justice to the Russian composer,
a sense of proportion forbids me to draw further
analogies between the two men. Dargomijsky
was a strong and original genius, who would
have found his way to a reformed music drama,
even if Wagner had not existed. Had he been
sustained by a Ludwig of Bavaria, instead of
being opposed by a Gedeonov, he might have
left his country a larger legacy from his abundant inspiration ; but fate and his surroundings
willed that his achievements should be comparatively small. Whereas Wagner, moving on
from strength to strength, from triumph to

triumph, raised up incontestable witnesses to the greatness of his genius.

In *The Stone Guest* Dargomijsky has been successful in welding words and music into an organic whole ; while the music allotted to each individual in the opera seems to fit like a skin. "Poetry, love, passion, arresting tragedy, humour, subtle psychological sense and imaginative treatment of the supernatural,[1] all these qualities," says Stassov, " are combined in this opera." The chief drawback of the work is probably its lack of scenic interest, a fault which inevitably results from the unity of its construction. The music, thoughtful, penetrative, and emotional, is of the kind which loses little by the absence of scenic setting. *The Stone Guest* is essentially an opera which may be studied at the piano. It unites as within a focus many of the dominant ideas and tendencies of the school that proceeded from Glinka and Dargomijsky, and proves that neither nationality of subject nor of melody constitutes nationality of style, and that a tale which bears the stamp and colour of the South may become completely Russian, poetically and musically, when moulded by Russian hands. *The Stone Guest* has never

---

[1] The appearance of the Commandatore is accompanied by a sinister progression as thrilling in its way as that strange and horrible chord with which Richard Strauss leads up to Salome's sacrilegious kiss in the closing scene of this opera.

attained to any considerable measure of popularity in Russia. In spite of Dargomijsky's personal intimacy with his little circle of disciples, in which respect his attitude to his fellow workers was quite different to that of Glinka, the example which he set in *The Stone Guest* eventually found fewer imitators than Glinka's ideal model *A Life for the Tsar*. At the same time in certain particulars, and especially as regards melodic recitative, this work had a decided influence upon a later school of Russian opera. But this is a matter to be discussed in a later chapter.

SEROV

Serov, V. A.

CHAPTER VI

GLINKA and Dargomijsky were to Russian music two vitalising sources, to the power of which had contributed numerous affluent aspirations and activities. They, in their turn, flowed forth in two distinct channels of musical tendency, fertilising two different spheres of musical work. Broadly speaking, they stand respectively for lyrical idealism as opposed to dramatic realism in Russian opera. To draw some parallel between them seems inevitable, since together they make up the sum total of the national character. Their influences, too, are incalculable, for with few exceptions scarcely an opera has been produced by succeeding generations which does not give some sign of its filiation with one or the other of these composers. Glinka had the versatility and spontaneity we are accustomed to associate with the Slav temperament; Dargomijsky had not less imagination but was more reflective. Glinka was not devoid of wit; but Dargomijsky's humour was full flavoured

and racy of the soil. He altogether out-
distanced Glinka as regards expression and
emotional intensity. Glinka's life was not rich
in inward experiences calculated to deepen his
nature, and he had not, like Dargomijsky, that
gift of keen observation which supplies the place
of actual experience. The composer of *The
Stone Guest* was a psychologist, profound and
subtle, who not only observed, but knew how
to express himself with the laconic force of a
man who has no use for the gossip of life.

When Glinka died in 1857, Russian musical
life was already showing symptoms of that
division of aims and ideals which ultimately
led to the formation of two opposing camps :
the one ultra-national, the other more or less
cosmopolitan. In order to understand the
situation of Russian opera at this time, it is
necessary to touch upon the long hostility which
existed between the rising school of young home-
bred musicians, and those who owed their
musical education to foreign sources, and in
whose hands were vested for a considerable
time all academic authority, and most of the
paid posts which enabled a musician to devote
himself wholly to his profession.

While Dargomijsky was working at his last
opera, and gathering round his sick bed that
group of young nationalists soon to be known
by various sobriquets, such as " The Invincible

Band," and " The Mighty Five,"[1] Anton
Rubinstein was also working for the advancement of music in Russia ; but it was the general
aspect of musical education which occupied
his attention, rather than the vindication of the
art as an expression of national temperament.
Up to the middle of the eighteenth century there
had been but two musical elements in Russia,
the creative and the auditory. In the latter
we may include the critics, almost a negligible
quantity in those days. At the close of the
'fifties a third element was added to the situation—the music schools. "The time had come,"
says Stassov, " when the necessity for schools,
conservatoires, incorporated societies, certificates, and all kinds of musical castes and privileges, was being propagated among us. With
these aims in view, the services were engaged
of those who had been brought up to consider
everything excellent which came from abroad,
blind believers in all kinds of traditional prejudices. Since schools and conservatoires existed in Western Europe, we, in Russia, must
have them too. Plenty of amateurs were
found ready to take over the direction of our
new conservatoires. Such enterprise was part
of a genuine, but hasty, patriotism, and the
business was rushed through. It was asserted

[1] Balakirev, Cui, Moussorgsky, Borodin, and Rimsky-
Korsakov.

that music in Russia was then at a very low ebb and that everything must be done to raise the standard of it. With the object of extending the tone and improving the knowledge of music, the Musical Society was founded in 1859, and its principal instrument, the St. Petersburg Conservatoire, in 1862. . . . Not long before the opening of this institution, Rubinstein wrote an article,[1] in which he deplored the musical condition of the country, and said that in Russia 'the art was practised only by amateurs' . . . and this at a time when Bala-kirev, Moussorgsky and Cui had already composed several of their early works and had them performed in public. Were these men really only amateurs? The idea of raising and developing the standard of music was laudable, but was Russia truly in such sore need of that kind of development and elevation when an independent and profoundly national school was already germinating in our midst? In discussing Russian music, the first questions should have been : what have we new in our music ; what is its character ; what are its idiosyncrasies, and what is necessary for its growth and the preservation of its special qualities? But the people who thought to encourage the art in Russia did not, or would not, take this indigenous element into consideration, and from the lofty pinnacle

[1] In *Vek* (The Century). No. I.

of the Western Conservatoire they looked down on our land as a *tabula rasa*, a wild uncultivated soil which must be sown with good seed imported from abroad. . . . In reply to Rubinstein's article I wrote : [1] ' How many academies in Europe are grinding out and distributing certificated students, who occupy themselves more or less with art ? But they cannot turn out artists ; only people all agog to acquire titles, recognised positions, and privileges. Why must this be ? We do not give our literary men certificates and titles, and yet a profoundly national literature has been created and developed in Russia. It should be the same with music. . . . Academic training and artistic progress are not synonymous terms. . . . Germany's noblest musical periods *preceded* the opening of her conservatoires, and her greatest geniuses have all been educated outside the schools. Hitherto all our teachers have been foreigners brought up in the conservatoires abroad. Why then have we cause to complain of the wretched state of musical education in Russia ? Is it likely that the teachers sent out into the world from our future academies will be any better than those hitherto sent to us from abroad ? It is time to cease from this importation of foreign educative influences, and to consider that which will be most truly profitable and

[1] In *Severnoy Pchela* (The Northern Bee).

advantageous for our own race and country. Must we copy that which exists abroad, merely that we may have the satisfaction of boasting a vast array of teachers and classes, of fruitless distributions of prizes and scholarships, of reams of manufactured compositions, and hosts of useless musicians." [1]

I have quoted these extracts from Stassov's writings partly for the sake of the sound common-sense with which he surrounds the burning question of that and later days, and partly because his protest is interesting as echoing the reiterated cry of the ultra-patriotic musical party in this country.

Such protests, however, were few, while the body of public enthusiasm was great ; and Russian enthusiasm, it may be observed, too often takes the externals into higher account than the essentials. Rubinstein found a powerful patroness in the person of the Grand Duchess Helena Pavlovna ; the Imperial Russian Musical Society was founded under the highest social auspices ; and two years later all officialdom presided at the birth of its offshoot, the St. Petersburg Conservatoire. Most of the evils prophesied by Stassov actually happened, and prevailed, at least for a time. But foreign

[1] Reprinted in " Twenty-five Years of Russian Art." The collected works (Sobranie Sochinenie) of Vladimir Stassov. Vol. I.

influences, snobbery, official tyranny and parsimony, the over-crowding of a privileged profession, and mistakes due to the well-intentioned interference of amateurs in high places—these things are but the inevitable stains on the history of most human organisations. What Cheshikin describes as " alienomania," the craze for everything foreign, always one of the weaknesses of Russian society, was undoubtedly fostered to some extent under the early cosmopolitan *régime* of the conservatoire ; but even if it temporarily held back the rising tide of national feeling in music, it was powerless in the end to limit its splendid energy. The thing most feared by the courageous old patriot, Stassov, did not come to pass. The intense fervour of the group known as " The Mighty Band " carried all things before it. Russian music, above all Russian opera, triumphs to-day, both at home and abroad, in proportion to its *amor patriæ*. It is not the diluted cosmopolitan music of the schools, with its familiar echoes of Italy, France and Germany, but the folk-song operas in their simple, forceful and sincere expression of national character that have carried Paris, Milan and London by storm.

The two most prominent representatives of the cosmopolitan and academic tendencies in Russia were Anton Rubinstein and Alexander Serov. Both were senior to any member of the nationalist circle, and their work being in many respects very dissimilar in character to that of the younger composers, I propose to give some account of it in this and the following chapter, before passing on to that later group of workers who made the expression of Russian sentiment the chief feature of their operas.

Alexander Nicholaevich Serov, born in St. Petersburg January 11th, 1820 (O.S.), was one of the first enlightened musical critics in Russia. As a child he received an excellent education. Later on he entered the School of Jurisprudence, where he passed among his comrades as " peculiar," and only made one intimate friend. This youth —a few years his junior—was Vladimir Stassov, destined to become a greater critic than Serov himself. Stassov, in his " Reminiscences of the School of Jurisprudence," has given a most interesting account of this early friendship, which ended in something like open hostility when in later years the two men developed into the leaders of opposing camps. When he left the School of Jurisprudence in 1840, Serov had no definite views as to his future, only a vague dreamy yearning for an artistic career. At his father's desire he accepted a clerkship in a Government office, which left him leisure for his musical pursuits. At that time he was studying the violoncello. Gradually he formed, if not a definite theory of musical criticism, at least strong individual proclivities. He had made some early attempts at composition, which did not amount to much more than improvisation. Reading his letters to Stassov, written at this early period of his career, it is evident that joined to a vast, but vague, ambition was the irritating consciousness of a lack of genuine creative inspiration.

In 1842 Serov became personally acquainted with Glinka, and although he was not at that period a fervent admirer of this master, yet personal contact with him gave the younger man his first impulse towards more serious work. He began to study *A Life for the Tsar* with newly opened eyes, and became enthusiastic over this opera, and over some of Glinka's songs. But when in the autumn of the same year *Russlan and Liudmilla* was performed for the first time, his enthusiasm seems to have received a check. He announced to Stassov his intention of studying this opera more seriously, but his views of it, judging from what he has written on the subject, remain after all very superficial. All that was new and lofty in its intention seems to have passed clean over his head. His criticism is interesting as showing how indifferent he was at that time to the great musical movement which Wagner was leading in Western Europe, and to the equally remarkable activity which Balakirev was directing

in Russia.   He was, indeed, still in a phase of
Meyerbeer worship.

In 1843 Serov began to think of composing
an opera.   He chose the subject of " The Merry
Wives of Windsor," but hardly had he made his
first essays, when his musical schemes were
cut short by his transference from St. Petersburg to the dull provincial town of Simferopol.
Here he made the acquaintance of the revolutionary Bakounin, who had not yet been exiled
to Siberia.   The personality of Bakounin made
a deep impression upon Serov, as it did later
upon Wagner.   Under his influence Serov began
to take an interest in modern German philosophy
and particularly in the doctrines of Hegel.
As his intellect expanded, the quality of his
musical ideas improved.   They showed greater
independence, but it was an acquired originality
rather than innate creative impulse.   He acquired the theory of music with great difficulty,
and being exceedingly anxious to master counterpoint, Stassov introduced him by letter to the
celebrated theorist Hunke, then residing in
St. Petersburg.   Serov corresponded with Hunke,
who gave him some advice, but the drawbacks
of a system of a college by post were only too
obvious to the eager but not very brilliant
pupil, separated by two thousand versts from
his teacher.   At this time he was anxious to
throw up his appointment and devote himself

entirely to music, but his father sternly dis-
countenanced what he called " these frivolous
dreams."

It was through journalism that Serov first
acquired a much desired footing in the
musical world. At the close of the 'forties
musical criticism in Russia had touched its
lowest depths. The two leading men of the
day, Oulibishev and Lenz, possessed undoubted
ability, but had drifted into specialism, the
one as the panegyrist of Mozart, the other of
Beethoven. Moreover both of them published
their works in German. All the other critics
of the leading journals were hardly worthy
of consideration. These were the men whom
Moussorgsky caricatured in his satirical songs
" The Peepshow " and " The Classicist." It
is not surprising, therefore, that Serov's first
articles, which appeared in the " Contemporary"
in 1851, should have created a sensation in the
musical world. We have seen that his literary
equipment was by no means complete, that his
convictions were still fluctuant and unreliable ;
but he was now awake to the movements of the
time, and joined to a cultivated intelligence a
" wit that fells you like a mace." His early
articles dealt with Mozart, Beethoven, Donizetti,
Rossini, Meyerbeer, and Spontini, and in discussing the last-named, he explained and de-
fended the historical ideal of the music-drama.

Considering that at that time Serov was practically ignorant of Wagner's work, the conclusions
which he draws do credit to his foresight and
reflection.

As I am considering Serov rather as a composer than as a critic, I need not dwell at length
upon this side of his work. Yet it is almost
impossible to avoid reference to that long and
bitter conflict which he waged with one whom,
in matters of Russian art and literature, I
must regard as my master. The writings of
Serov, valuable as they were half a century ago,
because they set men thinking, have now all the
weakness of purely subjective criticism. He
was inconstant in his moods, violent in his
prejudices, and too often hasty in his judgments,
and throughout the three weighty volumes
which represent his collected works, there
is no vestige of orderly method, nor of a reasoned
philosophy of criticism. The novelty of his
style, the prestige of his personality, and perhaps we must add the deep ignorance of the
public he addressed, lent a kind of sacerdotal
authority to his utterances. But, like other
sacerdotal divulgations, they did not always
tend to enlightenment and liberty of conscience.
With one hand Serov pointed to the great
musical awakening in Western Europe ; with
the other he sought persistently to blind Russians to the important movement that was

taking place around them. In 1858 Serov returned from a visit to Germany literally hypnotised by Wagner. To quote his own words : " I am now Wagner mad. I play him, study him, read of him, talk of him, write about him, and preach his doctrines. I would suffer at the stake to be his apostle." In this exalted frame of mind he returned to a musical world of which Rubinstein and Balakirev were the poles, which revolved on the axis of nationality. In this working, practical world, busy with the realisation of its own ideals and the solution of its own problems, there was, as yet, no place for Wagnerism. And well it has proved for the development of music in Europe that the Russians chose, at that time, to keep to the high road of musical progress with Liszt and Balakirev, rather than make a rush for the *cul-de-sac* of Wagnerism. Serov had exasperated the old order of critics by his justifiable attacks on their sloth and ignorance ; had shown an ungenerous depreciation of Balakirev and his school, and adopted a very luke-warm attitude towards Rubinstein and the newly-established Musical Society. Consequently, he found himself now in an isolated position. Irritated by a sense of being " sent to Coventry," he attacked with extravagant temper the friend of years in whom, as the champion of nationality, he imagined a new enemy. The long

polemic waged between Serov and Stassov
is sometimes amusing, and always instructive ;
but on the whole I should not recommend it
as light literature.   Serov lays on with bludgeon
and iron-headed mace ; Stassov retaliates with
a   two-edged   sword.   The   combatants   are
not unfairly matched, but Stassov's broader
culture keeps him better armed at all points,
and he represents, to my mind, the nobler
cause.

When Serov the critic felt his hold on the
musical world growing slacker, Serov the composer determined to make one desperate effort
to recover his waning influence.   He was now
over forty years of age, and the great dream
of his life—the creation of an opera—was still
unrealised.   Having acquired the libretto of
Judith, he threw himself into the work of composition with an energy born of desperation.
There is something fine in the spectacle of this
man, who had no longer the confidence and
elasticity of youth, carrying his smarting wounds
out of the literary arena, and replying to the
taunts of his enemies, " show us something
better than we have done," with the significant
words " wait and see." Serov, with his ex-
travagances and cocksureness of opinion, has
never been a sympathetic character to me ;
but I admire him at this juncture.   At first,
the mere technical difficulties of composition

threatened to overwhelm him. The things which should have been learnt at twenty were hard to acquire in middle-life. But with almost superhuman energy and perseverance he conquered his difficulties one by one, and in the spring of 1862 the opera was completed.

Serov had many influential friends in aristocratic circles, notably the Grand Duchess Helena Pavlovna, who remained his generous patroness to the last. On this occasion, thanks to the good offices of Count Adelberg, he had not, like so many of his compatriots, to wait an indefinite period before seeing his opera mounted. In March 1863 Wagner visited St. Petersburg, and Serov submitted to him the score of *Judith*. Wagner was particularly pleased with the orchestration, in which he cannot have failed to see the reflection of his own influence.

The idea of utilising *Judith* as the subject for an opera was suggested to Serov by K. I. Zvantsiev, the translator of some of the Wagnerian operas, after the two friends had witnessed a performance of the tragedy " Giuditta," with Ristori in the leading part. At first Serov intended to compose to an Italian libretto, but afterwards Zvantsiev translated into the vernacular, and partially remodelled, Giustiniani's original text. After a time Zvantsiev, being doubtful of Serov's capacity to carry through the work, left the libretto unfinished, and it was eventually completed by a young amateur, D. Lobanov.

The opera was first performed in St. Petersburg on May 16th, 1862 (O.S.). The part of Judith was sung by Valentina Bianchi, that of Holofernes by Sariotti. The general style of *Judith* recalls that of " Tannhäuser," and of " Lohengrin," with here and there some reminiscences of Meyerbeer. The opera is picturesque and effective, although the musical colouring is somewhat coarse and flashy. Serov excels in showy scenic effects, but we miss the careful attention to detail, and the delicate musical treatment characteristic of Glinka's work, qualities which are carried almost to a defect in some of Rimsky-Korsakov's operas. But the faults which are visible to the critic seemed virtues to the Russian public, and *Judith* enjoyed a popular success rivalling even that of *A Life for the Tsar*. The staging, too, was on a scale of magnificence hitherto unknown in the production of national opera. The subject of Judith and Holofernes is well suited to Serov's opulent and sensational manner. It is said that the scene in the Assyrian camp, where Holofernes is depicted surrounded by all the pomp and luxury of an oriental court, was the composer's great attraction to the subject ; the music to this scene was written by him before all the rest of the opera, and it is considered one of the most successful numbers in the work. The chorus and dances of the Odalisques are full of the languor of Eastern sentiment. The March of Holofernes, the idea of which is probably borrowed from Glinka's March of Chernomor in *Russlan and Liudmilla*, is also exceedingly effective ; for whatever we may think of the quality of that inspiration, which for over twenty years refused to yield material for the making of any important musical work, there is no doubt that Serov had now acquired from the study of Wagner a remarkable power of effective orchestration. Altogether, when we consider the circumstances under which it was created, we can only be surprised to find how little *Judith* smells of the lamp. We can hardly doubt that the work possesses intrinsic charms and qualities, apart from mere external glitter, when we see how it fascinated not only the general public, but many of the young musical generation, of whom Tchaikovsky was one. Although in later years no one saw more clearly the defects and make-shifts of Serov's style, he always spoke of *Judith* as " one of his first loves in music." " A novice of forty-three," he wrote, " presented the public of St. Petersburg with an opera which in every respect must be described as *beautiful*, and shows no indications whatever of being the composer's *first work*. The opera has many

good points.   It is written with unusual warmth
and sometimes rises to great emotional heights.
Serov, who had hitherto been unknown, and
led a very humble life, became suddenly the
hero of the hour, the idol of a certain set, in
fact a celebrity.   This unexpected success turned
his head and he began to regard himself as a
genius.   The childishness with which he sings
his own praises in his letters is quite remarkable.
And Serov had actually proved himself a gifted
composer but not a genius of the first order."
It would be easy to find harsher critics of
Serov's operas than Tchaikovsky, but his opinion
reflects on the whole that of the majority of
those who had felt the fascination of *Judith*
and been disillusioned by the later works.

If *Judith* had remained the solitary and belated
offspring of Serov's slow maturity it is doubtful
whether his reputation would have suffered.
But there is no age at which a naturally vain
man cannot be intoxicated by the fumes of
incense offered in indiscriminate quantities.
The extraordinary popular success of *Judith*
showed Serov the short cut to fame.   The
autumn of the same year which witnessed its
production saw him hard at work upon a second
opera.   The subject of *Rogneda* is borrowed
from an old Russian legend dealing with the
time of Vladimir, " the Glorious Sun," at the
moment of conflict between Christianity and

Slavonic paganism. *Rogneda* was not written
to a ready-made libretto, but, in Serov's own
words, to a text adapted piecemeal "as necessary to the musical situations." It was completed and staged in the autumn of 1865. We
shall look in vain in *Rogneda* for the higher
purpose, the effort at psychological delineation,
the comparative solidity of workmanship which
we find in *Judith*. Nevertheless the work amply
fulfilled its avowed intention to take the public
taste by storm. Once more I will quote
Tchaikovsky, who in his writings has given a
good deal of space to the consideration of
Serov's position in the musical world of Russia.
He says : " The continued success of *Rogneda*,
and the firm place it holds in the Russian
repertory, is due not so much to its intrinsic
beauty as to the subtle calculation of effects
which guided its composer. . . . The public
of all nations are not particularly exacting in
the matter of æsthetics ; they delight in sensational effects and violent contrasts, and are
quite indifferent to deep and original works of
art unless the *mise-en-scène* is highly coloured,
showy, and brilliant. Serov knew how to catch
the crowd ; and if his opera suffers from poverty
of melodic inspiration, want of organic sequence,
weak recitative and declamation, and from
harmony and instrumentation which are crude
and merely decorative in effect—yet what

sensational effects the composer succeeds in piling up ! Mummers who are turned into geese and bears ; real horses and dogs, the touching episode of Ruald's death, the Prince's dream made actually visible to our eyes ; the Chinese gongs made all too audible to our ears, all this—the outcome of a recognised poverty of inspiration—literally crackles with startling effects. Serov, as I have said, had only a mediocre gift, united to great experience, remarkable intellect, and extensive erudition ; therefore it is not surprising to find in *Rogneda* numbers—rare oases in a desert—in which the music is excellent. As to these numbers which are special favourites with the public, as is so frequently the case, their real value proves to be in inverse ratio to the success they have won."

Some idea of the popularity of *Rogneda* may be gathered from the fact that the tickets were subscribed for twenty representations in advance. This success was followed by a pause in Serov's literary and musical activity. He could now speak with his enemies in the gate, and point triumphantly to the children of his imagination. Success, too, seems to have softened his hostility to the national school, for in 1866 he delivered some lectures before the Musical Society upon Glinka and Dargomijsky, which are remarkable not only for clearness of exposition, but for fairness of judgment.

In 1867 Serov began to consider the production of a third opera, and selected one of
Ostrovsky's plays on which he founded a libretto
entitled *The Power of Evil*. Two quotations
from letters written about this time reveal
his intention with regard to the new opera.
" Ten years ago," he says, " I wrote much about
Wagner. Now it is time to act. To embody
the Wagnerian theories in a music-drama written
in Russian, on a Russian subject." And again :
" In this work, besides observing as far as
possible the principles of dramatic truth, I aim
at keeping more closely than has yet been done
to the forms of Russian popular music, as preserved unchanged in our folk-songs. It is
clear that this demands a style which has nothing
in common with the ordinary operatic forms, nor
even with my two former operas." Here we
have Serov's programme very clearly put before
us : the sowing of Wagnerian theories in Russian
soil. But in order that the acclimatisation
may be complete, he adopts the forms of the
folk-songs. He is seeking, in fact, to fuse
Glinka and Wagner, and produce a Russian
music-drama. Serov was a connoisseur of the
Russian folk-songs, but he had not that natural
gift for assimilating the national spirit and
breathing it back into the dry bones of musical
form as Glinka did. In creating this Russo-
Wagnerian work, Serov created something purely

artificial : a hybrid, which could bring forth nothing in its turn. It is characteristic, too, of Serov's short-sighted egotism that we find him constantly referring to this experiment of basing an opera upon the forms of the national music as a purely original idea ; ignoring the fact that Glinka, Dargomijsky and Moussorgsky had all produced similar works, and that the latter had undoubtedly written " music-dramas," which, though not strictly upon Wagnerian lines, were better suited to the genius of the nation.

Ostrovsky's play,[1] upon which *The Power of Evil* is founded, is a strong and gloomy drama of domestic life. A merchant's son abducts a girl from her parents, and has to atone by marrying her. He soon wearies of enforced matrimony and begins to amuse himself away from home. One day while drinking at an inn he sees a beautiful girl and falls desperately in love with her. The neglected wife discovers her husband's infidelity, and murders him in a jealous frenzy. The story sounds as sordid as any of those one-act operas so popular with the modern Italian composers of sensational music-drama. But in the preparation of the libretto Serov had the co-operation of the famous dramatist Ostrovsky, who wrote the first three acts of the book himself. Over the fourth act a

[1] " Accept life as it comes." (*Nie tak iivi kak khochetsya.*)

split occurred between author and composer; the former wished to introduce a supernatural element, recalling the village festival in " Der Freischütz " into the carnival scene ; but Serov shrank from treating a fantastic episode. The book was therefore completed by an obscure writer, Kalashinkev. Thus the lofty literary treatment by which Ostrovsky sought to raise the libretto above the level of a mere " shocker " suffered in the course of its transformation. The action of the play takes place at carnival time, which gives occasion for some lively scenes from national life. The work never attained the same degree of popularity as *Judith* or *Rogneda*. Serov died rather suddenly of heart disease in January 1871, and the orchestration of *The Power of Evil* was completed by one of his most talented pupils, Soloviev.

We have read Tchaikovsky's views upon Serov. Vladimir Stassov, after the lapse of thirty years, wrote in one of his last musical articles as follows : " A fanatical admirer of Meyerbeer, he succeeded nevertheless in catching up all the superficial characteristics of Wagner, from whom he derived his taste for marches, processions, festivals, every sort of ' pomp and circumstance,' every kind of external decoration. But the inner world, the spiritual world, he ignored and never entered ; it interested him not at all. The individualities of his *dramatis personæ* were completely overlooked. They are mere marionettes." His influence on the Russian opera left no lasting traces. His strongest quality was a certain robust dramatic sense which corrected his special tendency to secure effects in the cheapest way, and kept him just on the right side of that line which divides realism from offensive coarseness and bathos.

Two more quotations show an interesting light on Serov. The first is a confession of his musical tastes, written not long before his death : " After Beethoven and Weber, I like Mendelssohn fairly well ; I love Meyerbeer ; I adore Chopin ; I detest Schumann and all his disciples. I am fond of Liszt, with numerous exceptions, and I worship Wagner, especially in his latest works, which I regard as the *ne plus ultra* of the symphonic form to which Beethoven led the way."

The second quotation is Wagner's tribute to the personality of his disciple, and it seems only fair to print it here, since it contradicts almost all the views of Serov as a man which we find in the writings of his contemporaries in Russia. " For me Serov is not dead," says Wagner ; " for me he still lives actually and palpably. Such as he was to me, such he remains and ever will : the noblest and highest-minded of men. His gentleness of soul, his purity of feeling, his serenity, his mind, which reflected all these qualities, made the friendship which he cherished for me one of the gladdest gifts of my life."

CHAPTER VII

ANTON Grigorievich Rubinstein was born November 16/28, 1829, in the village of Vykhvatinets, in the government of Podolia. He was of Jewish descent, his father being, however, a member of the Orthodox Church, while his mother—a Löwenstein—came from Prussian Silesia. Shortly after Anton's birth his parents removed to Moscow, in the neighbourhood of which his father set up a factory for lead pencils and pins. Anton, and his almost equally gifted brother Nicholas, began to learn the piano with their mother, and afterwards the elder boy received instruction from A. Villoins, a well-known teacher in Moscow. At ten years of age Anton made his first public appearance at a summer concert given in the Petrovsky Park, and the following year (1840) he accompanied Villoins to Paris with the intention of entering the Conservatoire. This project was not realised and the boy started upon an extensive tour as a prodigy pianist. In 1843 he was summoned to play to the Court in St. Petersburg, and afterwards gave a series of concerts in that city. The following year he began to study music seriously in Berlin, where his mother took him first to Mendelssohn and, acting on his advice, subsequently placed him under Dehn. The Revolution of 1848 interrupted the ordinary course of life in Berlin. Dehn, as one of the National Guard, had to desert his pupils, shoulder a musket and go on duty as a sentry before some of the public buildings, performing this task with a self-satisfied air, " as though he had just succeeded in solving some contrapuntal problem, such as a canon by retrogression." Rubinstein hastened back to Russia, having all his music confiscated at the frontier, because it was taken for some diplomatic cipher.

Soon after his return, the Grand Duchess Helena Pavlovna appointed Rubinstein her Court pianist and accompanist, a position which he playfully described as that of " musical stoker " to the Court. In April 1852 his first essay in opera, *Dmitri Donskoi* (Dmitri of the Don), the libretto by Count Sollogoub, was given in St. Petersburg, but its reception was disappointing. It was followed, in May 1853, by *Thomouska-Dourachok* (Tom the Fool), which was withdrawn after the third performance at the request of the composer, who seems to have been hurt at the lack of enthusiasm shown for his work.   Two articles from his pen which appeared in the German papers, and are quoted by Youry Arnold in his " Reminiscences," show the bitterness of his feelings at this time.   " No one in his senses," he wrote, " would attempt to compose a Persian, a Malay, or a Japanese opera ; therefore to write an English, French or Russian opera merely argues a want of sanity. Every attempt to create a national musical activity is bound to lead to one result—disaster."

Between the composition of the *Dmitri Donskoi* and *Tom the Fool*, Rubinstein's amazingly active pen had turned out two one-act operas to Russian words : *Hadji-Abrek* and *Sibirskie Okhotniki* (The Siberian Hunters).   But now he laid aside composition for a time and undertook a long concert tour, starting in 1856 and returning to Russia in 1858.   During this tour [1] he visited Nice, where the Empress Alexandra Feodorovna and the Grand Duchess Helena spent the winter of 1856-1857, and it seems probable that this was the occasion on which the idea of the Imperial Russian Musical Society [2] was first mooted, although the final plans may have been postponed until Rubin-

[1] He also visited England, making his appearance at one of the concerts of the Philharmonic Society, in May 1857.

[2] Henceforth alluded to as the I. R. M. S., or the Musical Society.

stein's return to Petersburg in 1858. Little time
was lost in any case, for the society was started
in 1859, and the Moscow branch, under the direction of his brother Nicholas, was founded in 1860.

Piqued by the failure of his Russian operas,
Rubinstein now resolved to compose to German
texts and to try his luck abroad. Profiting
by his reputation as the greatest of living
pianists, he succeeded in getting his *Kinder der
Heide* accepted in Vienna (1861) ; while Dresden
mounted his *Feramors* (based upon Moore's
" Lalla Rookh ") in 1863. Between two concert tours—one in 1867, and the other, with
Wienawski in America, in 1872—Rubinstein
completed a Biblical opera *The Tower of Babel*,
the libretto by Rosenburg. This type of opera
he exploited still further in *The Maccabees*
(Berlin, 1875) and *Paradise Lost*, a concert
performance of which took place in Petersburg
in 1876. Between the completion of these
sacred operas, he returned to a secular and
national subject, drawn from Lermontov's
poem " The Demon," which proved to be the
most popular of his works for the stage. *The
Demon* was produced in St. Petersburg on
January 13th (O.S.), and a more detailed account
of it will follow. *Nero* was brought out in
Hamburg in 1875, and in Berlin in 1879. After
this Rubinstein again reverted to a Russian
libretto, this time based upon Lermontov's

metrical tale *The Merchant Kalashnikov*, but
the opera was unfortunate, being performed
only twice, in 1880 and 1889, and withdrawn
from the repertory on each occasion in consequence of the action of the censor. *The Shulamite*, another Biblical opera, dates from 1880
(Hamburg, 1883), and a comic opera, *Der Papagei*,
was produced in that city in 1884. *Goriousha*, a
Russian opera on the subject of one of Aver-
kiev's novels, was performed at the Maryinsky
Theatre, St. Petersburg, in the autumn of 1889,
when Rubinstein celebrated the fiftieth anniver-
sary of his artistic career.

The famous series of " Historical Concerts,"
begun in Berlin in October, 1885, was concluded in London in May, 1886, after which
Rubinstein returned to St. Petersburg and
resumed his duties as Director of the Conservatoire, a position which he had relinquished
since 1867. During the next few years he
composed the Biblical operas *Moses* (Paris,
1892) and *Christus*, a concert performance of
which was given under his own direction at
Stuttgart, in 1893 ; the first stage performance
following in 1895, at Bremen.

In the winter of 1894 Rubinstein became
seriously ill in Dresden, and, feeling that his
days were numbered, he returned in haste to
his villa at Peterhof. He lingered several
months and died of heart disease in November

1895. " His obsequies were solemnly carried out," says Rimsky-Korsakov.[1] " His coffin was placed in the Ismailovsky Cathedral, and musicians watched by it day and night. Liadov and I were on duty from 2 to 3 a.m. I remember in the dim shadows of the church seeing the black, mourning figure of Maleziomova [2] who came to kneel by the dust of the adored Rubinstein. There was something fantastic about the scene."

With Rubinstein's fame as a pianist, the glamour of which still surrounds his name, with his vast output of instrumental music, good, bad and indifferent, I have no immediate concern. Nor can I linger to pay more than a passing tribute to his generous qualities as a man. His position as a dramatic composer and his influence on the development of Russian opera are all I am expected to indicate here. This need not occupy many pages, since his influence is in inverse ratio to the voluminous outpourings of his pen. Rubinstein's ideal oscillates midway between national and

[1] "The Chronicle of my Musical Life" (Lietopis moi muzykalnoi Jizn), 1844-1906. N. A. Rimsky-Korsakov (Edited by his widow). St. Petersburg, 1909.

[2] Mme. Maleziomova, whom I met in St. Petersburg, was for many years *dame de compagnie,* or chaperon, at Rubinstein's classes at the Conservatoire. She was a devoted friend of the master's, and few people knew more of his fascinating personality or spoke more eloquently of his teaching.

cosmopolitan tendencies. The less people have penetrated into the essential qualities of Russian music, the more they are disposed to regard him as typically Russian ; whereas those who are most sensitive to the vibrations of Russian sentiment will find little in his music to awaken their national sympathies. The glibness with which he spun off music now to Russian, now to German texts, and addressed himself in turn to either public, proves that he felt superficially at ease with both idioms. It suggests also a kind of ready opportunism which is far from admirable. His attack on the national ideal in music, when he failed to impress the public with his *Dmitri Donskoi*, and his rapid change of front when Dargomijsky and the younger school had compelled the public to show some interest in Russian opera, will not easily be forgiven by his compatriots. We have seen how he fluctuated between German and Russian opera, and there is no doubt that this diffusion of his ideals and activities, coupled with a singular lack of self-criticism, is sufficient to account for the fact that of his operas—about nineteen in all[1]—scarcely one has survived him. Let a Russian pass judgment upon Rubinstein's claims to be regarded as a national composer. Cheshikin, who divides his operas into two

[1] Eight Russian and eleven German operas. Six of the latter were secular and five based on Biblical subject.

groups, according as they are written to German or Russian librettos, sums up the general characteristics of the latter as follows :

" Rubinstein's style bears a cosmopolitan stamp. He confused nationality in music with a kind of dry ethnography, and thought the question hardly worth a composer's study. A passage which occurs in his ' Music and its Representatives ' (Moscow, 1891) shows his views on this subject. ' It seems to me,' he writes, ' that the national spirit of a composer's native land must always impregnate his works, even when he lives in a strange land and speaks its language. Look for instance at Handel, Gluck and Mozart. But there is a kind of premeditated nationalism now in vogue. It is very interesting, but to my mind it cannot pretend to awaken universal sympathies, and can merely arouse an ethnographical interest. This is proved by the fact that a melody that will bring tears to the eyes of a Finlander will leave a Spaniard cold ; and that a dance rhythm that would set a Hungarian dancing would not move an Italian.' Rubinstein [comments Cheshikin], is presuming that the whole essence of nationality in music lies not in the structure of melody, or in harmony, but in a dance rhythm. It is not surprising that holding these superficial views his operas based on Russian life are not distinguished for their musical colour, and that he is only unconsciously and instinctively successful when he uses the oriental colouring which is in keeping with his descent. He cultivated the commonly accepted forms of melodic opera which were the fashion in the first half of the nineteenth century. His musical horizon was bounded by Meyerbeer. He held Wagner in something like horror, and kept contemptuous silence about all the Russian composers who followed Glinka. This may be partly explicable on the ground of his principles, which did not admit the claims of declamatory opera ; but it was partly a policy of tit for tat, because Serov and ' the mighty band ' had trounced Rubinstein unsparingly during the 'sixties for his Teutonic tendencies in his double capacity as head of the I. R. M. S. and Director of the Conservatoire. Narrow and conventional forms, especially as regards his arias ; melody as the sole ideal in opera ; an indeterminate cosmopolitan style, and now and again a successful reflection of the oriental spirit—these are the distinguishing characteristics of all Rubinstein's Russian operas from *Dmitri Donskoi* to *Goriousha.*" [1]

It is impossible to speak in detail of all Rubinstein's operas. The published scores are available for those who have time and inclination for

[1] "A History of Russian Opera" (Istoriya Russ. Opera). V. Cheshikin. St. Petersburg, 1905. P. Jurgenson.

so unprofitable a study. Such works as *Hadji-Abrek*, based on Lermontov's metrical tale of bloodshed and horror ; or *Tom the Fool*, which carries us a little further in the direction of nationalism, but remains a mere travesty of Glinka's style ; or *The Tower of Babel ;* or *Nero*, are hardly likely to rise again to the ranks of living operatic works. His first national opera *Dmitri Donskoi*, in five acts, is linked, by the choice of a heroic and historical subject, with such patriotic works as Glinka's *A Life for the Tsar*, Borodin's *Prince Igor* and Rimsky-Korsakov's *Maid of Pskov* ("Ivan the Terrible"); but it never succeeded in gripping the Russian public. The libretto is based on an event often repeated by the contemporary monkish chroniclers who tell how Dmitri, son of Ivan II., won a glorious victory over the Mongolian Khan Mamaï at Kulikovo, in 1380, and freed Russia for the time being from the Tatar yoke. Youry Arnold, comparing Rubinstein's *Dmitri Donskoi* with Dargomijsky's early work *Esmeralda*,[1] finds that, judged by the formal standards of the period, it was in advance of Dargomijsky's opera as regards technique, but, he says, "the realistic emotional expression and unforced lyric inspiration of *Esmeralda* undoubtedly makes

[1] *Dmitri Donskoi* was produced in St. Petersburg in 1852 ; *Esmeralda*, first staged in Moscow in 1847, was brought out in the modern capital in 1853.

a stronger appeal to our sympathies and we recognise more innate talent in its author."

After the failure of *Dmitri Donskoi*, Rubinstein neglected the vernacular for some years and composed only to German texts. But early in the 'seventies the production of a whole series of Russian operas, Dargomijsky's *The Stone Guest*, Serov's *The Powers of Evil*, Cui's *William Ratcliff*, Rimsky-Korsakov's *Maid of Pskov*, and Moussorgsky's *Boris Godounov*, resuscitated the public interest in the national ideal and Rubinstein was obviously anxious not to be excluded from the movement. His comparative failure with purely Russian subjects, and the knowledge that he felt more at ease among Eastern surroundings, may have influenced his choice of a subject in this emergency; but undoubtedly Lermontov's poetry had a strong fascination for him, for *The Demon* was the third opera based upon the works of the Russian Byron. Lermontov's romanticism, and the exquisite lyrical quality of his verse, which almost suggests its own musical setting, may well have appealed to Rubinstein's temperament. The poet Maikov took some part in arranging the text for the opera, but the libretto was actually carried out by Professor Vistakov, who had specialised in the study of Lermontov. When *The Demon* was finished, Rubinstein played it through to " the mighty band " who assembled at Stassov's house to hear this addition to national opera. It would be expecting too much from human nature to look for a wholly favourable verdict from such a court of enquiry, but " the five " picked out for approval precisely the two numbers that have best withstood the test of time, namely, the Dances and the March of the Caravan which forms the Introduction to the third scene of Act III. As a national composer Rubinstein reached his highest level in *The Demon*. The work was presented to the English public, in Italian, at Covent Garden, on June 21, 1881, but as it is unknown to the younger generation some account of its plot and general characteristics will not be out of place here.[1]

The Demon, that " sad and exiled spirit," who is none other than the poet Lermontov himself, thinly veiled in a supernatural disguise, is first introduced to us hovering over the peak of Kazbec, in the Caucasus, gazing in melancholy disenchantment upon the glorious aspects of the world below him—a world which he regards with scornful indifference. The Demon's malady is boredom. He is a mortal with certain " demoniacal " attributes. Like Lermontov, he is filled with vague regrets for

[1] For a fuller analysis of Lermontov's poem see " Poetry and Progress in Russia," by Rosa Newmarch. John Lane, The Bodley Head, London and New York.

wasted youth and yearns to find in a woman's love the refuge from his despair and weariness. From the moment he sees the lovely Circassian, Tamara, dancing with her maidens on the eve of her wedding, the Demon becomes enamoured of her, and the first stirrings of love recall the long-forgotten thought of redemption. Tamara is betrothed to Prince Sinodal, who is slain by Tatar brigands on his way to claim his bride in the castle of her father, Prince Gudal. The malign influence of the Demon brings about this catastrophe. In order to escape from her unholy passion for her mysterious lover, Tamara implores her father to let her enter a convent, where she is supposed to be mourning her lost suitor. But even within these sacred precincts the Demon follows her, although not without some twinges of human remorse. For a moment he hesitates, and is on the point of conquering his sinister desire; then the good impulse passes, and with it the one chance of redemption through unselfish love. He meets Tamara's good angel on the threshold of the convent, and, later on, sees the apparition of the murdered Prince. The Angel does not seem to be a powerful guardian spirit, but rather the weak, tormented soul of Tamara herself. The Demon enters her cell, and there follows the long love duet and his brief hour of triumph. Suddenly the Angel and celestial voices are heard calling

to the unhappy girl : " Tamara, the spirit of
doubt is passing." The nun tears herself from
the arms of her lover and falls dead at the
Angel's feet. The Demon, baffled and furious,
is left gazing upon the corpse of Tamara. In
the end the gates of Paradise are opened to her,
as to Margaret in " Faust," because by its
purity and self-sacrifice her passion works out
its own atonement. But the Demon remains
isolated and despairing, " without hope and
without love."

The poem, with its inward drama of pre-
destined passion, unsatisfied yearning and
possible redemption through love, almost fulfils
the Wagnerian demand for a subject in which
emotion outweighs action ; a subject so purely
lyrical that the drama may be said to be born
of music. Cheshikin draws a close emotional
parallel between *The Demon* and " Tristan and
Isolde " ; but perhaps its spirit might be more
justly compared with the romanticism of " The
Flying Dutchman." Musically it owes nothing
to Wagner. Its treatment is that of pre-
Wagnerian German opera strongly tinged with
orientalism. Rubinstein effectively contrasts
the tender monotonous chromaticism of eastern
music, borrowed from Georgian and Armenian
sources, with the more vigorous melodies based
on Western and diatonic scales, and, in this
respect, his powers of invention were remarkable.

Among the most successful examples of the oriental style are the Georgian Song " We go to bright Aragva," sung by Tamara's girl friends in the second scene of Act I.; the Eastern melody sung in Gudal's castle in Act II. ; the passing of the Caravan, and the Dance for women in the same act. The Demon's arias are quite cosmopolitan in character, and the opening chorus of Evil Spirits and forces of Nature, though effective, are not strikingly original. There is real passion in the great love duet in the last act, with its energetic accompaniment that seems to echo the sound of the wild turbulent river that rushes through the ravine below the convent walls.

The Demon met with many objections from the Director of the Opera and the Censor. The former mistrusted novelties, especially those with the brand of nationality upon them, and was alarmed by the cost of the necessary fantastic setting. The latter would not sanction the lamps and *ikons* in Tamara's cell, and insisted on the Angel being billed as " a Good Genius." The singers proved rebellious, and finally it was decided to produce the work for the first time on January 13th, 1875 (O.S.), on Melnikov's benefit night, he himself singing the title rôle. The other artists, who made up a fine caste, were : Tamara, Mme. Raab ; the Angel, Mme. Kroutikov ; Prince Sinodal, Komessarievich ; Prince Gudal, the veteran Petrov, and the

Nurse, Mme. Shreder. The immediate success
of *The Demon* did much to establish Rubinstein's reputation as a popular composer, and
the opera is still regarded as his best dramatic
work, although many critics give the palm to
The Merchant Kalashnikov, which followed it
about five years later.

As I have already said, the fate of this work,
based on a purely Russian subject, seems to
have been strangely unjust. Twice received
with considerable enthusiasm in St. Petersburg,
it was quashed by the Censor on both occasions
after the first night. The libretto, by Kou-
likov, is founded on Lermontov's " Lay of the
Tsar Ivan Vassilievich (The Terrible), of the
young Oprichnik [1], and the bold merchant
Kalashnikov." The opera is in three acts.
In the first scene, which takes place in the Tsar's
apartments, the Oprichniki are about to celebrate
their religious service. Maliouta enters with
the Tsar's jester Nikitka, and tells them that
the *Zemstvo* has sent a deputation to the Tsar
complaining of their conduct, and that Nikitka
has introduced the delegates at Court. The
Oprichniki fall upon the jester and insist on his

[1] The Oprichniki, a band of hot-headed and dissolute
young nobles who formed the bodyguard of Ivan the
Terrible and were always prepared to carry out his orders.
They carried a dog's head and a broom at their saddle-bow,
to show that they worried the enemies of the Tsar and swept
them from the face of the earth.

buying their forgiveness by telling them a tale.
Nikitka's recital is one of Rubinstein's best
attempts to reproduce the national colour.
Afterwards the Tsar appears, the Oprichniki
don their black cloaks and there follows an
effective number written in strict church style.
The service ended, the Tsar receives the
members of the *Zemstvo*. To this succeeds an
animated scene in which Ivan feasts with his
guards. Observing that one of them, Kiribeievich, is silent and gloomy, he asks the reason,
and the young Oprichnik confesses that he is in
love, and sings his song " When I go into the
garden," a Russian melody treated by Rubinstein in a purely cosmopolitan style. The
finale of the first act consists of dances by the
Skomorokhi and a chorus for the Oprichniki,
the music being rather pretentious and theatrical
in style. The opening scene of Act II. takes
place in the streets of Moscow, and begins with
a chorus of the people, who disperse on hearing
that the Oprichniki are in the vicinity. Alena,
the wife of the merchant Kalashnikov, now
comes out of her house on her way to vespers,
accompanied by a servant. She sings a quiet
recitative in which she tells the maid to go home
and await the return of the master of the house,
and reveals herself as a happy mother and
devoted wife. She goes her way to the church
alone, pausing however to sing a pretty,

common-place Italianised aria, " I seek the Holy Temple." Kıribeievich appears on the scene, makes passionate love to her and carries her off. An old gossip who has watched this incident now emerges from her hiding place and sings a song which introduces a touch of humour. Enter Kalashnikov, who learns from her of his wife's departure with the young Oprichnik ; but she gives a false impression of the incident. His recitative is expressive and touching. The scene ends with the return of the populace who sing a chorus. In the second scene Kalashnikov plays an important part and his doubts and fears after the return of Alena are depicted with power. This is generally admitted to be one of Rubinstein's few successful psychological moments, the realistic expression of emotion being one of his weak points. Kalashnikov's scene, in which he confers with his brothers, completes Act II. The curtain rises in Act III. upon a Square in Moscow where the people are assembling to meet the Tsar. Their chorus of welcome, " Praise to God in Heaven," is not to be compared for impressiveness with similar massive choruses in the operas of Moussorgsky and Rimsky-Korsakov. There are some episodes of popular life, such as the scene between a Tatar and the jester Nikitka, that are not lacking in humour ; and the latter has another tale about King David which is in the style of the so-called "spiritual songs" of the sixteenth century. The accusations brought by Kiribeievich are spirited. In a dramatic scene the Tsar listens to Alena's prayer for mercy, and pardons the bold Kalashnikov who has dared to defy his Pretorian guards, the Oprichniki. The opera winds up with a final chorus of the people who escort the Merchant from prison.

The Merchant Kalashnikov, although somewhat of a hybrid as regards style, with its Russian airs handled *à la Tedesca*, and its occasional lapses into vulgarity, has at the same time more vitality and human interest than most of Rubinstein's operas, so that it is to be regretted that it has remained so long unknown alike to the public of Russia and of Western Europe.

Rubinstein's Biblical operas have now practically fallen into oblivion. Seeing their length, the cost involved in mounting them, and their lack of strong, clear-cut characterisation, this is not surprising. The *Acts of Artaxerxes* and the *Chaste Joseph*, presented to the Court of Alexis Mikhaïlovich, could hardly have been more wearisome than *The Tower of Babel* and *The Shulamite*. These stage oratorios are like a series of vast, pale, pseudo-classical frescoes, and scarcely more moving than the officia odes and eclogues of eighteenth-century Russian literature. Each work, it is true, contains some saving moments, such as the Song of Victory, with chorus, "Beat the drums," sung by Leah, the heroic mother of the Maccabees, in the opera bearing that title, in which the Hebrew colouring is admirably carried out ; the chorus "Baal has worked wonders," from *The Tower of Babel ;* and a few pages from the closing scene of *Paradise Lost ;* but these rare flashes of inspiration do not suffice to atone for the long, flaccid Handelian recitatives, the tame Mendelssohnian orchestration, the frequent lapses into a pomposity which only the most naïve can mistake for sublimity of utterance, and the fluent dulness of the operas as a whole.

Far more agreeable, because less pretentious, is the early secular opera, a German adaptation of Thomas Moore's "Lalla Rookh," entitled *Feramors.* The ballets from this opera, the Dance of Bayadères, with chorus, in Act I., and The Lamplight Dance of the Bride of Kashmere (Act II.) are still heard in the concert room ; and more rarely, Feramor's aria, "Das Mondlicht träumt auf Persiens See." From the dramatic side the subject is weak, but, as Hanslick observes in his "Contemporary Opera"— in which he draws the inevitable parallel between Félicien David and the Russian composer– it was the oriental element in the poem that proved the attraction to Rubinstein. Yet how different is the conventional treatment of Eastern melody in *Feramors* from Borodin's natural and characteristic use of it in *Prince Igor* ! But although it is impossible to ignore Rubinstein's operas written to foreign texts for a foreign public, they have no legitimate place in the evolution of Russian national opera. It is with a sense of relief that we turn from him with his reactionary views and bigoted adherence to pre-Wagnerian conventions, to that group of enthusiastic and inspired workers who were less concerned with riveting the fetters of old traditions upon Russian music than with the glorious task of endowing their country with a series of national operas alive and throbbing with the very spirit of the people. We leave Rubinstein gazing westwards upon the setting sun of German classicism, and turn our eyes eastwards where the dawn is rising upon the patient expectations of a nation which has long been feeling its way towards a full and conscious self-realisation in music.

CHAPTER VIII

BALAKIREV AND HIS DISCIPLES

SOMETIMES in art, as in literature, there comes upon the scene an exceptional, initiative personality, whose influence seems out of all proportion to the success of his work. Such was Keats, who engendered a whole school of English romanticism ; and such, too, was Liszt, whose compositions, long neglected, afterwards came to be recognised as containing the germs of a new symphonic form. Such also was Mily Alexevich Balakirev, to whom Russian national music owes its second renaissance. Born at Nijny-Novgorod, December 31st, 1836 (O.S.), Balakirev was about eighteen when he came to St. Petersburg in 1855, with an introduction to Glinka in his pocket. He had previously spent a short time at the University of Kazan, but had actually been brought up in the household of Oulibishev, author of the famous treatise on Mozart. It is remarkable, and testifies to his sturdy independence of character—that the young man had not been influenced by his benefactor's limited and ultra-conservative views. Oulibishev, as we know, thought there could be no advance upon the achievements of his adored Mozart. Balakirev as a youth studied and loved Beethoven's symphonies and quartets, Weber's " Der Freischütz," Mendelssohn's Overtures and Chopin's works as a whole. He was by no means the incapable amateur that his academic detractors afterwards strove to prove him. His musical culture was solid. He had profited by Oulibishev's excellent library, and by the private orchestra which he maintained and permitted his young *protégé* to conduct. Although partially self-taught, Balakirev had already mastered the general principles of musical form, composition and orchestration. He was not versed in counterpoint and fugue ; and certainly his art was not rooted in Bach ; but that could hardly be made a matter of reproach, seeing that in Balakirev's youth the great poet-musician of Leipzig was neglected even in his own land, and it is doubtful whether the budding schools of Petersburg and Moscow, or even the long established conservatoires of Germany, would then have added much to his education in that respect. In his provincial home in the far east of Europe Balakirev stood aloof from the Wagnerian controversies. But his mind, sensitive as a seismograph, had already registered some vibrations of this distant movement which announced a musical revolution. From the beginning he was preoccupied with the question of transfusing fresh blood into the impoverished veins of old and decadent forms. Happily the idea of solving the problem by the aid of the Wagnerian theories never occurred to him. He had already grasped the fact that for the Russians there existed an inexhaustible source of fresh inspiration in their abundant and varied folk-music.

The great enthusiasm of his youth had been Glinka's music, and while living at Nijny-Novgorod he had studied his operas to good purpose. Filled with zeal for the new cause, Balakirev appeared in the capital like a St. John the Baptist from the wilderness to preach the new gospel of nationality in art to the adorers of Bellini and Meyerbeer. Glinka was on the point of leaving Russia for what proved to be his last earthly voyage. But during the weeks which preceded his departure he saw enough of Balakirev to be impressed by his enthusiasm and intelligence, and to point to him as the continuator of his work.

The environment of the capital proved beneficial to the young provincial. For the first time he was able to mix with other musicians and to hear much that was new to him, both at the opera and in the concert room. But his convictions remained unshaken amid all these novel experiences. From first to last he owed most to

himself, and if he soon became head and centre
of a new musical school, it was because, as
Stassov has pointed out, " he had every gift for
such a position : astonishing initiative, love and
knowledge of his art, and to crown all, untiring
energy."

Balakirev left no legacy of opera, but his influence on Russian music as a whole was so
predominant that it crops up in every direction,
and henceforth his name must constantly appear
in these pages. Indeed the history of Russian
opera now becomes for a time the history of a
small brotherhood of enthusiasts, united by a
common idea and fighting shoulder to shoulder
for a cause which ought to have been popular,
but which was long opposed by the press and the
academic powers in the artistic world of Russia,
and treated with contempt by the "genteel" amateur to whom a subscription to Italian opera stood
as the external sign of social and intellectual superiority. It was known as " Balakirev's set," or
by the ironical sobriquet of " the mighty band."

At the close of the 'fifties César Cui and
Modeste Moussorgsky had joined Balakirev's
crusade on behalf of the national ideal. A year
or two later Borodin and Rimsky-Korsakov
were admitted to the circle ; and subsequently a
gifted young amateur, Nicholas Lodyjensky,
attached himself for a time to the nationalists.
To these names must be added that of the writer,

Vladimir Stassov, whose active brain and pen
were always at the service of the new school.
Although Glinka had no further personal intercourse with Balakirev and his friends, Dargomijsky, as we have already seen, gladly opened
his house as a meeting place for this group of
young enthusiasts, who eagerly discussed questions of art with the older and more experienced
musician, and watched with keen interest the
growth of his last opera, *The Stone Guest.*

Rimsky-Korsakov, in his " Chronicle of my
Musical Life," gives some interesting glimpses of
the pleasant relations existing between the
members of the nationalist circle during the
early years of its existence. Rimsky-Korsakov,
who was studying at the Naval School, St.
Petersburg, made the acquaintance of Balakirev
in 1861. " My first meeting with Balakirev
made an immense impression upon me," he
writes. " He was an admirable pianist, playing
everything from memory. The audacity of
his opinions and their novelty, above all, his
gifts as a composer, stirred me to a kind of ven-
eration. The first time I saw him I showed him
my Scherzo in C minor, which he approved, after
passing a few remarks upon it, and some
materials for a symphony. He ordained that
I should go on with the symphony.[1] Of course

[1] Rimsky-Korsakov was the first of the Russian composers to write a symphony.

I was delighted. At his house I met Cui and Moussorgsky. Balakirev was then orchestrating the overture to Cui's early opera *The Prisoner in the Caucasus*. With what enthusiasm I took a a share in these actual discussions about instrumentation, the distribution of parts, etc! Through November and December I went to Balakirev's every Saturday evening and frequently found Cui and Moussorgsky there. I also made the acquaintance of Stassov. I remember an evening on which Stassov read aloud extracts from " The Odyssey," more especially for my enlightenment. On another occasion Moussorgsky read " Prince Kholmsky," the painter Myassedov read Gogol's " Viya," and Balakirev and Moussorgsky played Schumann's symphonies arranged for four hands, and Beethoven's quartets."

On these occasions the young brotherhood, all of whom were under thirty, with the exception of Stassov, aired their opinions and criticised the giants of the past with a frankness and freedom that was probably very naïve, and certainly scandalised their academic elders. They adored Glinka ; regarded Haydn and Mozart as old-fashioned ; admired Beethoven's latest quartets ; thought Bach—of whom they could have known little beyond the Well-Tempered Clavier—a mathematician rather than a musician ; they were enthusiastic over Berlioz, while, as yet, Liszt had not begun to influence them very greatly. " I drank in all these ideas," says Rimsky-Korsakov, "although I really had no grounds for accepting them, for I had only heard fragments of many of the foreign works under discussion, and afterwards I retailed them to my comrades (at the Naval School) who were interested in music, as being my own convictions." From the standpoint of a highly educated musician, a Professor at the St. Petersburg Conservatoire, Rimsky-Korsakov adopts a frankly mocking tone in his retrospective account of these youthful discussions; but it must be admitted that it was far better for the future development of Russian music that these young composers should have thought their own thoughts about their art, instead of taking their opinions ready-made from German text-books and the æsthetic dogmas laid down in the class rooms of the conservatoires.

For Rimsky-Korsakov these happy days were short-lived, for in 1862 he was gazetted to the cruiser " Almaz " and the next three years were spent on foreign service which took him as far afield as New York and Rio Janeiro.

Balakirev was distressed at this interruption to Rimsky's musical career. If the disciple idealised the master in those days, the latter in his turn treated the young sailor with fraternal affection, declaring that he had been providentially sent to take the place of a favourite pupil who had just gone abroad. A. Goussakovsky was a brilliant youth who had recently finished his course at the university and was specialising in chemistry. He appears to have been a strange, wild, morbid nature. His compositions for piano were full of promise, but he was unstable of purpose, flitted from one work to another and finished none. He did not trouble to write down his ideas, and many of his compositions existed only in Balakirev's memory. He flashes across this page of Russian musical history and is lost to view, like a small but bright falling star. Rimsky-Korsakov was endowed with far greater tenacity of purpose, and in spite of all difficulties he continued to work at his symphony on board ship and to post it piece by piece to Balakirev from the most out-of-the-way ports in order to have his advice and assistance.

Rimsky-Korsakov came back to St. Petersburg in the autumn of 1865 to find that some important changes had taken place in Balakirev's circle during his absence. In the first place, to the brotherhood was added a new member of whom great things were expected. This was Alexander Borodin, then assistant lecturer in chemistry at the Academy of Medicine. Secondly, Balakirev, in conjunction with Lomakin, one of Russia's most famous choir trainers, had founded the Free[1] School of Music, a most interesting experiment. It has been said that this institution was established in rivalry with the Conservatoire. The concerts given in connection with it, and conducted by its two initiators, were certainly much less conservative than those of the official organisation of the I. R. M. S. At the same time it must be borne in mind that during the 'sixties there was a great movement " towards the people," and that an enthusiastic temperament such as Balakirev's could hardly have escaped the passionate altruistic impulse which was stirring society. Individual effort, long restricted by official despotism, was becoming active in every direction. Between 1860-1870 a number of philanthropic schools were established in Russia, and the Free School, with its avowed aim of defending individual tendencies and upholding the cause of national music, was really only one manifestation of a widespread sentiment.

Other important events which Rimsky-Korsakov missed during his three years' cruise were the first production of Serov's opera *Judith*, and Wagner's visit to the Russian capital when he conducted the orchestra of the Philharmonic Society.

At this time, with the sole exception of Balakirev, every member of the nationalist circle

[1] Free in the sense of offering gratuitous instruction.

was earning his living by other means than music. Cui was an officer of Engineers, and added to his modest income by coaching. Moussorgsky was a lieutenant in the Preobrajensky Guards. Rimsky-Korsakov was in the Imperial navy, and Borodin was a professor of chemistry.

Rimsky-Korsakov and Borodin soon became intimate, notwithstanding the ten years difference in their ages. The former gives an interesting picture of the composer of *Prince Igor*, whose life was divided between chemistry and music, to both of which he was sincerely attached. " I often found him at work in his laboratory," writes Rimsky-Korsakov, " which communicated directly with his dwelling. When he was seated before his retorts, which were filled with colourless gases of some kind, forcing them by means of tubes from one vessel to another, I used to tell him he was spending his time in pouring water into a sieve. As soon as he was free he would take me to his living-rooms and there we occupied ourselves with music and conversation, in the midst of which Borodin would rush off to the laboratory to make sure that nothing was burning or boiling over, making the corridor ring as he went with some extraordinary passage of ninths or seconds. Then back again for more music and talk." Borodin's life, between his scientific work, his constant attendance at all kinds of boards and committee meetings,[1] and his musical interests, was strenuous beyond description. Rimsky-Korsakov, who grudged his great gifts to anything but music, says : " My heart is torn when I look at his life, exhausted by his continual self-sacrifice." He was endowed with great physical endurance and was utterly careless of his health. Sometimes he would dine twice in one day, if he chanced to call upon friends at mealtimes. On other occasions he would only remember at 9 p.m. that he had forgotten to take any food at all during the day. The hospitable board of the Borodins was generally besieged and stormed by cats, who sat on the table and helped themselves as they pleased, while their complacent owners related to their human guests the chief events in the biography of their feline *convives*. Borodin's wife was a woman of culture, and an accomplished pianist, who had profound faith in her husband's genius. Their married life was spoiled only by her failing health, for she suffered terribly from asthma and was obliged to spend most of the winter months in the drier air of Moscow, which meant long periods of involuntary separation from her husband.

Another meeting place of Balakirev's circle

[1] He was a warm advocate of the higher education of women, and one of the founders of the School of Medicine for Women at St. Petersburg.

was at the house of Lioudmilla Ivanovna Shestakov, Glinka's married sister. Here, besides the composers, came several excellent singers, mostly amateurs, including the sisters Karmalina and Mme. S. I. Zotov, for whom Rimsky-Korsakov wrote several of his early songs. Among those who sympathised with the aims of the nationalists were the Pourgold family, consisting of a mother and three daughters, two of whom were highly accomplished musicians. Alexandra Nicholaevna had a fine mezzo-soprano voice with high notes. She sang the songs of Cui, Balakirev and Rimsky-Korsakov with wonderful sympathy and insight, and "created" most of the female parts in the operas of "the mighty band" in the days when they had to be satisfied with drawing-room performances of their works. But her strong point was the interpretation of Moussorgsky's songs, which was a revelation of the composer's depth of feeling and close observation of real life and natural declamation. I had the privilege of visiting this gifted woman in later years when she was Mme. Molas,[1] and I can never forget the impression made upon me by her rendering of Moussorgsky's songs, "The Orphan," "Mush-

[1] She married a naval officer, the Admiral Molas who went down in the flagship *Petropavlovsk* at the entrance of the harbour of Port Arthur during the Russo-Japanese war. With him perished the great war painter, Vassily Verestchagin.

rooming," " Yeremoushka's Cradle Song," and more especially of the realistic pictures of child-life entitled "The Nursery." Her sister Nadejda Nicholaevna, who became Mme. Rimsky-Korsakov, was a pupil of Herke and Zaremba, Tchaikovsky's first master for theory. An excellent pianist and sight-reader, a musician to her finger-tips, she was always available as an accompanist when any new work by a member of the brotherhood needed a trial performance. She was also a skilful arranger of orchestral and operatic works for pianoforte.[1] The Pourgolds were devoted friends of Dargomijsky, and during the autumn of 1868 the entire circle met almost daily at his house, to which he was more or less confined by his rapidly failing health.

I have spoken of so many friends of "the mighty band" that it might be supposed that their movement was a popular one. This was not the case. With the exception of Stassov and Cui, who in their different styles did useful literary work for their circle, all the critics of the day, and the academical powers *en bloc*, were opposed to these musical Ishmaelites. Serov and Laroche carried weight, and were opponents worth fighting. Theophil Tolstoy

[1] Mme. Rimsky-Korsakov still takes an active interest in musical questions. Articles over her initials often appear in the Russian musical papers, and recently she has taken up her pen in defence of her husband's editorial work for Moussorgsky's operas.

(" Rostislav ") and Professor Famitzin, although they wrote for important papers, represented musical criticism in Russia at its lowest ebb, and would be wholly forgotten but for the spurious immortality conferred upon them in Moussorgsky's musical satire " The Peepshow." Nor was Anton Rubinstein's attitude to the new school either just or generous. Tchaikovsky, who, during the first years of their struggle for existence, was occupying the position of professor of harmony at the Moscow Conservatoire, started with more friendly feelings towards the brotherhood. His symphonic poem "Romeo and Juliet " (1870) was written under the influence of Balakirev, and his symphonic poem " The Tempest " (1873) was suggested by Vladimir Stassov. But as time went on, Tchaikovsky stood more and more aloof from the circle, and in his correspondence and criticisms he shows himself contemptuous and inimical to their ideals and achievements, especially to Moussorgsky, the force of whose innate genius he never understood. Throughout the 'sixties, the solidarity between the members of Balakirev's set was so complete that they could afford to live and work happily although surrounded by a hostile atmosphere. Rimsky-Korsakov's " Chronicle" of these early days oftens reminds us of the history of our own pre-Raphaelite Brotherhood, and we are moved to admire the devotion with which the members worked for one another and for the advancement of their common cause. A more ideal movement it would be difficult to find in the whole history of art, and all the works produced at this time were the outcome of single-minded and clear convictions, uninfluenced by the hope of pecuniary gain, and with little prospect of popular appreciation.

CHAPTER IX

GRADUAL DISSOLUTION OF THE CIRCLE OF FRIENDS

IT is difficult to fix the exact moment at which the little " rift within the lute " became audible in the harmony of Balakirev's circle. In 1872 Balakirev himself was in full opposition on many points with the policy of the I. R. M. S. and was maintaining his series of concerts in connection with the Free School in avowed rivalry with the senior institution. His programmes were highly interesting and their tendency progressive, but the public was indifferent, and his pecuniary losses heavy. In the autumn of that year he organised a concert at Nijny-Novgorod in which he appeared as a pianist, hoping that for once a prophet might not only find honour but substantial support in his own country. He was doomed to disappointment ; the room was empty and Balakirev used to allude to this unfortunate event as " my Sedan." He returned to St. Petersburg in low spirits and began to hold aloof from his former friends and pupils.

Eventually—so it is said—he took a clerkship in the railway service. At this period of his life he began to be preoccupied with those mystical ideas which absorbed him more or less until the end of his days.

After a time he returned to the musical life, and in the letters of Borodin and in Rimsky-Korsakov's " Chronicle " we get glimpses of the old ardent propagandist " Mily Alexe'ich." From 1867 to 1869 he was Director of the Imperial Chapel. But a few years later he again separated from his circle and this time he shut himself off definitely from society, emerging only on rare occasions to play at some charity concert, or visit the house of one of the few friends with whom he was still in sympathy. It was during these years that I first met him at the Stassovs' house. So few strangers ever came in contact with Mily Balakirev that I may be excused for giving my own personal impressions of this remarkable man.

From the moment when I first began to study Russian music, Balakirev's personality and genius exercised a great fascination for me. He was the spark from whence proceeded not only a musical conflagration but the warmth of my own poor enthusiasm. Naturally I was anxious to meet this attractive, yet self-isolated personality. It was an early summer's evening in St. Petersburg in 1901, and the excuses for the gathering were a birthday in the Stassov family, and the presence of an English enthusiast for Russian music. Balakirev was expected about 9 p.m. Stassov left the grand piano open like a trap set for a shy bird. He seemed to think that it would ensnare Mily Alexe'ich as the limed twig ensnares the bullfinch. The ruse was successful. After greeting us all round, Balakirev gravitated almost immediately to the piano. "I'm going to play three sonatas," he announced without further ceremony, "Beethoven's Appassionata, Chopin's B minor, and Schumann No. 3, in G minor." Then he began to play.

Balakirev was rather short. I do not know his pedigree, but he did not belong to the tall, fair type of Great Russia. There was to my mind a touch of the oriental about him : Tatar, perhaps, not Jewish. His figure was thickset, but his face was worn and thin, and his complexion brownish ; his air somewhat weary and nervous. He looked like a man who strained his mental energies almost to breaking point ; but his eyes—I do not remember their colour— were extraordinarily magnetic, full of fire and sympathy, the eyes of the seer and the bard. As he sat at the piano he recalled for a moment my last remembrance of Hans von Bülow. Something, too, in his style of playing confirmed this impression. He was not a master of sensational technique like Paderewski or Rosenthal. His execution was irreproachable, but one did not think of his virtuosity in hearing him play for the first time ; nor did he, as I expected, carry me away on a whirlwind of fiery emotion. A nature so ardent could not be a cold executant, but he had neither the emotional force nor the poetry of expression which were the leading characteristics of Rubinstein's art. What struck me most in Balakirev, and reminded me of Bülow, was the intelligence, the sympathy, and the authority of his interpretations. He observed, analysed, and set the work in a lucid atmosphere. He might have adopted Stendhal's formula : " *Voir clair dans ce qui est.*" It would be wrong, however, to think of Balakirev as a dry pedagogue. If he was a professor, he was an enlightened one—a sympathetic and inspired interpreter who knew how to reconstruct in imagination the period and personality of a composer instead of substituting his own.

Having finished his rather arduous but self-imposed programme, we were all afraid that he might disappear as quietly as he came. An inspiration on my part to address him some remarks, in extremely ungrammatical Russian, on the subject of his songs and their wonderful, independent accompaniments, sent him back to the piano, where he continued to converse with me, illustrating his words with examples of unusual rhythms employed in his songs, and gliding half unconsciously into some of his own and other people's compositions.   He could not be persuaded to play me " Islamey," the Oriental Fantasia beloved of Liszt, but I remember one delicate and graceful valse which he had recently written.   By this time the *samovar* was bubbling on the table and the room was filled with the perfume of tea and lemon.   Happily Balakirev showed no signs of departure.   He took his place at the table and talked with all his old passion of music in general, but chiefly of the master who had dominated the renaissance of Russian music—Michael Ivanovich Glinka.

Russians love to prolong their hospitality until far into the night.   But in May the nights in St. Petersburg are white and spectral.   At midnight the world is steeped in a strange light, neither twilight nor dawn, but something like the ghost of the departed day haunting the night that has slain it.   Instead of dreams one's mind is filled with fantastic ideas.   As I drove home through the streets, as light as in the daytime, I imagined that Balakirev was a wizard who had carried me back to the past— to the stirring period of the 'sixties so full of faith and generous hopes—so strong was the conviction that I had been actually taking part in the struggles and triumphs of the new Russian school.[1]

After this I never entirely lost sight of Balakirev. We corresponded from time to time and he was always anxious to hear the fate of his music in this country. Unfortunately I could seldom reassure him on this point, for his works have never roused much enthusiasm in the British public. He died on Sunday, May 29th, 1910. I had not long arrived in Petersburg when I heard that he was suffering from a severe chill with serious complications. Every day I hoped to hear that he was on the road to recovery and able to see me. But on the 16th I received from him a few pencilled lines— probably the last he ever wrote—in which he spoke of his great weakness and said the doctor still forbade him to see his friends. From that time until his death, he saw no one but Dimitri Vassileivich, Stassov's surviving brother, and his devoted friend and pupil Liapounov. He died, as he had lived for many years, alone, except for his faithful old housekeeper. He departed a true and faithful son of the Orthodox Church. In spite of his having spent nearly twenty years of his life in pietistic retirement, the news of his death reawakened the interest

[1] These impressions are taken from an article of mine (in French) published in the Sammelbände der Internationalen Musik Gesellschaft (Jahrgang IV. Heft I.), October-Dezember 1902. Leipzig, Breitkopf and Härtel.

of his compatriots. From the time of his passing away until his funeral his modest bachelor apartments could hardly contain the stream of people of all ages and classes who wished to take part in the short services held twice a day in the death chamber of the master. He was buried in the Alexander Nevsky Cemetery, not far from the graves of Dargomijsky, Glinka and Stassov.

The true reason for the loosening of the bonds between Balakirev and his former pupils cannot be ascribed to differences in their religious opinions. It was rather the inevitable result of the growth of artistic individuality. Balakirev could not realise this, and was disenchanted by the gradual neglect of his co-operative ideal. Borodin took a broad and sensible view of the matter in writing to one of the sisters Karmalina in 1876 :—" It is clear that there are no rivalries or personal differences between us ; this would be impossible on account of the respect we have for each other. It is thus in every branch of human activity ; in proportion to its development, individuality triumphs over the schools, over the heritage that men have gathered from their masters. A hen's eggs are all alike ; the chickens differ somewhat, and in time cease to resemble each other at all. One hatches out a dark-plumed truculent cock, another a white and peaceful hen. It is the same with us. We have all derived from the circle in which we lived the common characteristics of genus and species ; but each of us, like an adult cock or hen, bears his own character and individuality. If, on this account, we are thought to have separated from Balakirev, fortunately it is not the case. We are as fond of him as ever, and spare no pains to keep up the same relations as before. As to us, we continue to interest ourselves in each other's musical works. If we are not always pleased it is quite natural, for tastes differ, and even in the same person vary with age. It could not be otherwise."

The situation was no doubt rendered more difficult by Balakirev's unaccommodating attitude. " With his despotic character," says Rimsky-Korsakov, " he demanded that every work should be modelled precisely according to his instructions, with the result that a large part of a composition often belonged to him rather than to its author. We obeyed him without question, for his personality was irresistible." It was inevitable that, as time went on and the members of " the mighty band " found themselves less in need of guidance in their works than of practical assistance in bringing them before the public, Balakirev's circle should have become Belaiev's circle, and that the Mæcenas publisher and concert-giver should by degrees have acquired a preponderating influence in the nationalist school. This change took place during the 'eighties.

Mitrofane Petrovich Belaiev, born February 10th, 1836, was a wealthy timber merchant, with a sincere love of music. He was an exception to the type of the Russian commercial man of his day, having studied the violin and piano in his youth and found time amid the demands of a large business to occupy his leisure with chamber music. My recollections of Belaiev recall a brusque, energetic and somewhat choleric personality of the " rough diamond " type ; a passionate, but rather indiscriminate, enthusiast, and an autocrat. Wishing to give some practical support to the cause of national music, he founded a publishing house in Leipzig in 1885 where he brought out a great number of works by the members of the then new school, including a fine edition of Borodin's *Prince Igor*. He also founded the Russian Symphony Concerts, the programmes of which were drawn exclusively from the works of native composers. In 1889 he organised the Russian Concerts given with success at the Paris Exhibition ; and started the " Quartet Evenings " in St. Petersburg in 1891. Borodin, Rimsky-Korsakov, Glazounov and Liadov wrote a string quartet in his honour, on the notes B-la-f. Belaiev died in 1904, but the Leipzig house still continues its work under its original manager, Herr Scheffer.

Undoubtedly Belaiev exercised a powerful influence on the destinies of Russian music. Whether he was better fitted to be the central point of its activities at a certain stage of its development than Balakirev is a question which happily I am not called upon to decide. Money and business capacity are useful, perhaps indispensable, adjuncts to artistic progress in the present day, but they can never wholly take the place of enthusiasm and unstinted devotion. *" Les choses de l'âme n'ont pas de prix,"* says Renan ; nevertheless there is a good deal of bidding done for them in this commercial age. It is easy to understand the bitterness of heart with which the other-worldly and unconformable Balakirev saw the members of his school passing one by one into " the circle of Belaiev." He had steered the ship of their fortunes through the storms and shoals that beset its early ventures ; but another was to guide it into the haven of prosperity and renown. Rimsky-Korsakov, in his "Chronicle of my Musical Life," makes his recantation of old ideals and enthusiasms in the following terms : " Balakirev's circle was revolutionary ; Belaiev's progressive. Balakirev's disciples numbered five ; Belaiev's circle was more numerous, and continued to grow in numbers. All the five musicians who constituted the older school were eventually acknowledged as leading representatives of Russian music ; the later circle was made up of more varied elements ; some of its representatives were men of great creative gifts, others were less talented, and a few were not even composers, but conductors, like Dütsh, or executants like Lavrov. Balakirev's circle consisted of musicians who were weak—almost amateurish—on the technical side, who forced their way to the front by the sheer force of their creative gifts ; a force which sometimes replaced technical knowledge, and sometimes—as was frequently the case with Moussorgsky—did not suffice to cover their deficiences in this respect. Belaiev's circle, on the contrary, was made up of musicians who were well equipped and thoroughly educated. Balakirev's pupils did not interest themselves in any music prior to Beethoven's time ; Belaiev's followers not only honoured their musical fathers, but their remoter ancestors, reaching back to Palestrina. . . . The relations of the earlier circle to its chief were those of pupils to their teacher ; Belaiev was rather our centre than our head. . . . He was a Mæcenas, but not an aristocrat Mæcenas, who throws away money on art to please his own caprices and in reality does nothing to serve its interests. In what he did he stood on firm and honourable ground. He organised his concerts and publishing business without the smallest consideration for his personal profit. On the contrary, he sacrificed large sums of money, while concealing himself as far as possible from the public eye. . . . We were drawn to Belaiev by his personality, his devotion to art, and his wealth; not for its own sake but as the means to an end, applied to lofty and irreproachable aims, which made him the central attraction of a new musical circle which had only a few hereditary ties with the original ' invincible band.' "

This is no doubt a sincere statement of the relations between Belaiev and the modern Russian school, and it is only fair to quote this tribute to his memory. At the same time, when the history of Russian music comes to be written later in the century, both sides of the question will have to be taken into consideration. My own views on some of the disadvantages of the patronage system I have already expressed in the " Edinburgh Review " for July 1912, and I venture to repeat them here :

" He who pays the piper will, directly or indirectly, call the tune. If he be a Mæcenas of wide culture and liberal tastes he will perhaps call a variety of tunes ; if, on the other hand, he be a home-keeping millionaire with a narrowly patriotic outlook he will call only for tunes that awaken a familiar echo in his heart. So an edict—maybe an unspoken one—goes forth that a composer who expects his patronage must always write in the ' native idiom ' ; which is equivalent to laying down the law that a painter's pictures will be disqualified for exhibition if he uses more colours on his palette than those which appear in his country's flag. Something of this kind occurred in the ultra-national school of music in Russia, and was realised by some of its most fervent supporters as time went on. It is not difficult to trace signs of fatigue and perfunctoriness in the later works of its representatives. At times the burden of nationality seems to hang heavy on their shoulders ; the perpetual burning of incense to one ideal dulled the alertness of their artistic sensibilities. Less grew out of that splendid outburst of patriotic feeling in the 'sixties than those who hailed its first manifestations had reason to anticipate. Its bases were probably too narrowly exclusive to support an edifice of truly imposing dimensions. Gradually the inevitable has happened. The younger men threw off the restrictions of the folk-song school, and sought new ideas from the French symbolists, or the realism of Richard Strauss. There is very little native idiom, although there are still distinctive features of the national style, in the work of such latter day composers as Scriabin, Tcherepnin and Medtner. The physiognomy of Russian music is changing day by day, and although it is full of interest, one would welcome a development on larger and more independent lines."

In 1867 Nicholas Lodyjensky joined the circle. He was a young amateur gifted with a purely lyrical tendency, who played the piano remarkably well and improvised fluently. He composed a number of detached pieces and put together some fragments of a symphony and an opera, on the subject of " The False Dimitrius." Rimsky-Korsakov says his music showed a grace and beauty of expression which attracted the attention of the nationalist group, especially the music for the Wedding Scene of Dimitrius and Marina, and a setting for solo and chorus of Lermontov's " Roussalka" (The Water Sprite). But Lodyjensky, like Goussakovsky, was a typical dilettante ; almost inspired, but unable to concentrate on the completion of any important work. After a time he dropped out of the circle, probably because he had to earn his living in some other way, and the strain of a dual vocation discouraged all but the very strongest musical spirits.[1]

A musician of greater reputation who was partly attached to the nationalists was Anatol Liadov, whose work does not include any operatic composition.

[1] In 1908 he was Russian consul at New York.

Whatever the changes in the constitution of the nationalist party, Vladimir Stassov remained its faithful adherent through all vicissitudes. Some account of this interesting personality will not be out of place in a history of Russian opera. Vladimir Vassilievich Stassov, who may be called the godfather of Russian music—he stood sponsor for so many compositions of all kinds—was born in St. Petersburg, January 14th, 1825. He originally intended to follow his father's profession and become an architect. But eventually he was educated at the School of Jurisprudence and afterwards went abroad for a time. He studied art in many centres, but chiefly in Italy, and wrote a few articles during his travels. He returned to St. Petersburg, having acquired a command of many languages and laid the foundation of his wide critical knowledge. For a time he frequented the Imperial Public Library, St. Petersburg, where his industry and enthusiasm attracted the notice of the Director, Baron Korf, who invited him to become his temporary assistant. Subsequently Stassov entered the service of the Library and became head of the department of Fine Arts. This, at least, was his title, although at the time when I knew him his jurisdiction seemed to have no defined limits. A man of wide culture, of strong convictions and fearless utterance, he was a power

VLADIMIR STASSOV

in his day. Physically he had a fine appearance, being a typical Russian of the old school. The students at the Library used to call him the *Bogatyr*,[1] or with more irreverence the " Father," for he might have sat as an ideal model for the conventional representations of the First Person of the Trinity. Stassov's views on art were always on the large side ; but they were sometimes extreme and paradoxical. In polemics his methods were fierce, but not ungenerous. He was a kind of Slavonic Dr. Samuel Johnson, and there were times when one might as well have tried to argue calmly with the Car of Juggernaut. Those who were timid, inarticulate, or physically incapable of sustaining a long discussion, would creep away from his too-vigorous presence feeling baffled and hurt, and nursing a secret resentment. This was unfortunate, for Stassov loved and respected a relentless opponent, and only those who held their own to the bitter end enjoyed the fine experience of a reconciliation with him. And how helpful, considerate and generous he was in dispensing from his rich stores of knowledge, or his modest stores of worldly possessions, there must be many to testify ; for his private room at the Public Library was the highway of those in search of counsel or assistance of any kind.

[1] The *Bogatyri* were the heroes of ancient and legendary days.

He had a remarkable faculty for imparting to others a passion for work, a most beneficial power in the days when dilettantism was one of the worst banes of Russian society. In his home, too, he clung to the old national ideal of hospitality for all who needed it, and no questions asked. With all his rugged strength of character he had moments of childlike vanity when he loved to appear before his admiring guests attired in the embroidered scarlet shirt, wide velveteen knickers and high boots which make up the holiday costume of the Russian peasant ; or dressed like a boyard of old. With all this, he was absolutely free from the snobbishness which is sometimes an unpleasant feature of the Russian *chinovnik*, or official. Naturally many stories were related of Vladimir Stassov, but I have only space for two short anecdotes here. The first illustrates the Russian weakness for hot, and often futile, discussion ; the second, Stassov's enthusiasm for art and indifference to social conventions.

Once he had been arguing with Tourgeniev, whose cosmopolitan and rather supercilious attitude towards the art of young Russia infuriated the champion of nationalism. At last Tourgeniev, wearied perhaps with what he called " this chewing of dried grass," and suffering acutely from rheumatic gout, showed signs of yielding to Stassov's onslaughts. " There," cried the latter triumphantly, " now I see you agree with me ! " This acted like the dart planted in the hide of the weary or reluctant bull. Tourgeniev sprang from his chair and shuffled on his bandaged feet to the window, exclaiming : " Agree with you indeed ! If I felt I was beginning to think like you, I should fling open the window (here he suited the action to the word) and scream to the passers-by, ' Take me to a lunatic asylum ! I agree with Stassov ! ! ' "

On another occasion " Vladimir Vassilich " returned late one evening from his country cottage at Pargolovo, without troubling to change the national dress which he usually wore there. This costume was looked upon with disfavour in the capital, as savouring of a too-advanced liberalism and sympathy with the people. On arriving home, his family reminded him that Rubinstein was playing that night at a concert of the I. R. M. S. and that by the time he had changed he would be almost too late to hear him. " I cannot miss Rubinstein," said Vladimir Vassilich, " I must go as I am." In vain his family expostulated, assuring him that " an exalted personage " and the whole Court would be there, and consequently he must put on more correct attire. " *I will not* miss Rubinstein," was all the answer they got for their pains. And Stassov duly appeared in the Salle de la

Noblesse in a red shirt with an embroidery of cocks and hens down the front. He was forgiven such breaches of etiquette for the sake of his true nobility and loyalty of heart.

Such was the doughty champion of the nationalists through good and evil fortune. His writings on musical questions form only a small part of his literary output, the result of over sixty years of indefatigable industry ; for he was an authority on painting, architecture and design. Like Nestor, the faithful chronicler of mediæval Russia, he worked early and late. He did great service to native art by carefully collecting at the Imperial Public Library all the original manuscript scores of the Russian composers, their correspondence, and every document that might afterwards serve historians of the movement. He was the first to write an important monograph on Glinka, and this, together with his book on Borodin, his exhaustive articles on Dargomijsky and Moussorgsky, and his general surveys of musical progress in Russia, are indispensable sources of first-hand information for those who would study the question of Russian music *à fonds*.[1] As a critic, time has proved that, in spite of his ardent crusade on

[1] Collected Works (Sobranye Sochinenie, 4 volumes). "Twenty-five years of Russian Art " (musical section), Vol. I. " In the Tracks of Russian Art " (musical section),

behalf of modernism and nationality, his judgments were usually sound ; as an historian he was painstaking and accurate ; as regards his appreciation of contemporary art, he showed a remarkable *flair* for latent talent, and sensed originality even when deeply overlaid by crudity of thought and imperfect workmanship. He was apparently the first to perceive the true genius and power concealed under the foppishness and dilettantism of Moussorgsky's early manhood. He considered that neither Balakirev, Cui, nor Rimsky-Korsakov appreciated the composer of *Boris Godounov* at his full value. He upheld him against all contemptuous and adverse criticism, and the ultimate triumph of Moussorgsky's works was one of the articles in his artistic creed.

Vol. I. "A. S. Dargomijsky." "A. N. Serov." "Gabriel Lomakin." "Perov and Moussorgsky" (Vol. II.), are among his chief contributions to musical literature. But there are a number of critical articles on first performances, etc., which cannot be enumerated here.

CHAPTER X

MOUSSORGSKY

WE have seen that Glinka and Dargomijsky represented two distinct tendencies in Russian operatic music.
The one was lyrical and idealistic ; the other
declamatory and realistic. It would seem that
Glinka's qualities were those more commonly
typical of the Russian musical temperament,
since, in the second generation of composers, his
disciples outnumbered those of Dargomijsky, who
had actually but one close adherent : Modeste
Moussorgsky. Cui, Borodin and Rimsky-Korsakov were all—as we shall see when we come
to a more detailed analysis of their works—
attracted in varying degrees to melodic and
lyric opera. Although in the first flush of
enthusiasm for Dargomijsky's music-drama *The
Stone Guest*—which Lenz once described as " a
recitative in three acts "—the younger nationalists were disposed to adopt it as " the
Gospel of the New School," Moussorgsky alone
made a decisive attempt to bring into practice
the theories embodied in this work. Taking

Dargomijsky's now famous dictum : *I want the note to be the direct representation of the word—I want truth and realism,* as his starting-point, Moussorgsky proceeded to carry it to a logical conclusion. Rimsky-Korsakov speaks of his having passed through an early phase of idealism when he composed his Fantasia for piano " St. John's Eve " (afterwards remodelled for orchestra and now known as " Night on the Bare Mountain"), " The Destruction of Sennacherib," and the song " Night," to a poem by Poushkin. But although at first he may not have been so consciously occupied in the creation of what Rimsky-Korsakov calls " grey music," it is evident that no sooner had he found his feet, technically speaking, than he gripped fast hold of one dominant idea—the closer relationship of music with actual life. Henceforward musical psychology became the absorbing problem of his art, to which he devoted himself with all the ardour of a self-confident and headstrong nature. In a letter to Vladimir Stassov, dated October 1872, he reveals his artistic intentions in the following words : " Assiduously to seek the more delicate and subtle features of human nature—of the human crowd—to follow them into unknown regions, and make them our own : this seems to me the true vocation of the artist. Through the storm, past shoal and sunken rock, make for new shores without fear, against all hindrance ! . . . In the mass of humanity, as in the individual, there are always some subtle impalpable features which have been passed by, unobserved, untouched by anyone. To mark these and study them, by reading, by actual observation, by intuition—in other words, to feed upon humanity as a healthy diet which has been neglected—there lies the whole problem of art." However greatly we may disagree with Moussorgsky's æsthetic point of view, we must confess that he carried out his theories with logical sequence, and with the unflinching courage of a clear conviction. His operas and his songs are human documents which bear witness to the spirit of their time as clearly as any of the great works of fiction which were then agitating the public conscience. In this connection I may repeat what I have said elsewhere : that " had the realistic schools of painting and fiction never come into being through the efforts of Perov, Repin, Dostoievsky and Chernichevsky, we might still reconstruct from Moussorgsky's works the whole psychology of Russian life." [1]

In order to understand his work and his attitude towards art, it is necessary to realise something of the period in which Moussorgsky lived. He was a true son of his time, that

[1] My article on Moussorgsky in Grove's " Dictionary of Music."

MOUSSORGSKY
From a portrait by Repin painted shortly before his death

stirring time of the 'sixties which followed the emancipation of the serfs, and saw all Russian society agitated by the new, powerful stimulants of individual freedom and fraternal sympathy. Of the little group of musicians then striving to give utterance to their freshly awakened patriotism, none was so passionately stirred by the literary and political movements of the time as this born folk-composer. Every man, save the hide-bound official, or the frivolous imitator of Byron and Lermontov, was asking himself in the title of the most popular novel of the day : " What shall we do ? " And the answer given to them was as follows : " Throw aside artistic and social conventions. Bring down Art from the Olympian heights and make her the handmaid of humanity. Seek not beauty but truth. Go to the people. Hold out the hand of fellowship to the liberated masses and learn from them the true purpose of life." The ultra romanticism of Joukovsky and Karamzin, the affectation of Byronism, and the all too aristocratic demeanour of the admirers of Poushkin, invited this reaction. Men turned with disgust to sincere and simple things. The poets led the way : Koltsov and Nikitin with their songs of peasant life ; Nekrassov with his revolt against creeds and social conventions. The prose writers and painters followed, and the new spirit invaded music when it found a congenial soil in Moussorgsky's sincere and unsophisticated nature. Of the young nationalist school, he was the one eminently fitted by temperament and early education to give expression in music to this democratic and utilitarian tendency ; this contempt for the dandyism and dilettantism of the past generation ; and, above all, to this deep compassion for " the humiliated and offended."

Modeste Moussorgsky was born March 16/28, 1839, at Karevo, in the government of Pskov. He was of good family, but comparatively poor. His childhood was spent amid rural surroundings, and not only the music of the people, but their characteristics, good and bad, were impressed upon his mind from his earliest years. He was equally conversant with the folk literature, and often lay awake at night, his youthful imagination over-excited by his nurse's tales of witches, water-sprites and wood-demons. This was the seedtime of that wonderful harvest of national music which he gave to his race as soon as he had shaken off the superficial influences of the fashionable society into which he drifted for a time. His father, who died in 1853, was not opposed to Modeste's musical education, which was carried on at first by his mother, an excellent pianist. The young man entered the Preobrajensky Guards, one of the smartest regiments in the service, before he was eighteen. Borodin met him for the first time at this period of his existence and described him in a letter to Stassov as a typical military dandy, playing selections from Verdi's operas to an audience of appreciative ladies. He met him again two or three years later, when all traces of foppishness had disappeared, and Moussorgsky astonished him by announcing his intention of devoting his whole life to music ; an announcement which Borodin did not take seriously at the time. During the interval Moussorgsky had been frequenting Dargomijsky's musical evenings, where he met Balakirev, under whose inspiring influence he had undergone something like a process of conversion, casting the slough of dandyism, and becoming the most assiduous of workers.

While intercourse with Dargomijsky contributed to the forced maturing of Moussorgsky's ideas about music, the circumstances of his life still hindered his technical development. But he was progressing. His early letters to Cui and Stassov show how deeply and independently he had already thought out certain problems of his art. Meanwhile Balakirev carried on his musical education in a far more effective fashion than has ever been admitted by those who claim that Moussorgsky was wholly self-taught, or, in other words, completely ignorant of his craft. The " Symphonic Inter-

mezzo," composed in 1861, shows how insistent
and thorough was Balakirev's determination
that his pupils should grasp the principles of
tradition before setting up as innovators. Here
we have a sound piece of workmanship, showing
clear traces of Bach's influence ; the middle
movement, founded on a national air, being
very original in its development, but kept
strictly within classical form. His earliest operatic attempt, dating from his schooldays, and
based upon Victor Hugo's " Han d'Island,"
was quite abortive as regards the music. Of
the incidental music to " Œdipus," suggested
by Balakirev, we have Stassov's testimony that
a few numbers were actually written down, and
performed at some of the friendly gatherings of
the nationalist circle ; only one, however, has
been preserved, a chorus sung by the people
outside the Temple of the Eumenides, which does
not in any way presage Moussorgsky's future
style.

Faced with the prospect of service in a
provincial garrison, Moussorgsky resolved to
leave the army in 1859. His friends, and more
particularly Stassov, begged him to reconsider
his determination ; but in vain. He had now
reached that phase of his development when
he was impatient of any duties which inter-
fered with his artistic progress. Unfortunately
poverty compelled him to accept a small post

under the government which soon proved as irksome as regimental life. In 1856 he fell ill, and rusticated for a couple of years on an out-of-the-way country property belonging to his brother. During this period of rest he seems to have found himself as a creative artist. After working for a time upon an opera founded upon Flaubert's novel " Salammbô," he turned his attention to song, and during these years produced a number of his wonderful vocal pictures of Russian life, in its pathetic and humorous aspects. The music which he composed for *Salammbô* was far in advance of the *Œdipus*. Already in this work we find Moussorgsky treating the people, " the human crowd," as one of the most important elements of opera. " In conformity with the libretto," says Stassov, " certain scenes were full of dramatic movement in the style of Meyerbeer, evoking great masses of the populace at moments of intense pathos or exaltation." Much of the music of this opera was utilised in later works. Stassov informs us that Salammbô's invocation to Tanit is now the recitative of the dying Boris ; the opening of the scene in the Temple of Moloch has become the *Arioso* in the third act of *Boris Godounov ;* while the Triumphal Hymn to Moloch is utilised as the people's chorus of acclamation to the False Demetrius in the same opera.

Moussorgsky's next operatic essay took the form which he described as "opera dialogué." The subject—Gogol's prose comedy "The Match-Maker"—was admirably suited to him, and he started upon the work full of enthusiasm for the task. His methods are shown in a letter written to César Cui in the summer of 1868, in which he says : " I am endeavouring as far as possible to observe very clearly the changes of intonation made by the different characters in the course of conversation ; and made, so it appears, for trifling reasons, and on the most insignificant words. Here, in my opinion, lies the secret of Gogol's powerful humour. . . . How true is the saying : ' the farther we penetrate into the forest the more trees we find ! ' How subtle Gogol is ! He has observed old women and peasants and discovered the most fascinating types. . . . All this is very useful to me ; the types of old women are really precious." Moussorgsky abandoned *The Match-Maker* after completing the first act. This was published by Bessel, in 1911, under the editorship of Rimsky-Korsakov, and contains the following note : " I leave the rights in this work of my pupilage unconditionally and eternally to my dear Vladimir Vassilievich Stassov on this his birthday, January 2nd, 1873. (Signed) Modeste Moussoryanin, alias Moussorgsky. Written with a quill pen in

Stassov's flat, Mokhovaya, House Melnikov, amid a considerable concourse of people."

" The said MOUSSORGSKY."

Moussorgsky originally designated this work as " an attempt at dramatic music set to prose." The fragment, with its sincere and forcible declamation, is interesting as showing a phase in the evolution of his genius immediately preceding the composition of *Boris Godounov*. The four scenes which it comprises consist of conversations on the subject of marriage carried on between four sharply defined and contrasted characters : Podkolessin, a court councillor and petty official in the Civil Service ; Kocharev, his friend ; Tekla Ivanovna, a professional match-maker, and Stepan, Podkolessin's servant. Rimsky-Korsakov, who often heard the music sung and played by its author, says in his preface to the work that it should be executed *à piacere ;* that is to say, that for each individual a particular and characteristic *tempo* must be observed : for Podkolessin—a good-natured, vain and vacillating creature—a slow and lazy time throughout ; a more rapid movement for his energetic friend Kocharev, who literally pushes him into matrimony ; for the Match-maker a moderate *tempo*, somewhat restrained, but alert ; and for Stepan rather a slow time. Stassov thought highly of this work, and believed that as traditional prejudices vanished, and opera became a more natural form of art, this prose comedy, the music of which fits closely as a glove to every passing feeling and gesture suggested by the text, would come to be highly appreciated.

One more unfinished opera engages our attention before we pass on to consider Moussorgsky's two masterpieces. Fragments, consisting of an introduction and several " Comic Scenes," based upon Gogol's " The Fair at Sorochinsi," have been recently published by Bessel, with Russian text only. The subject is peculiarly racy and the humour not very comprehensible to those ignorant of Malo-Russian life ; but the music, though primitive, is highly characteristic, and may be commended to the notice of all who wish to study Moussorgsky in as full a light as possible.

The idea of basing a music-drama on Poushkin's tragedy " Boris Godounov " was suggested by Prof. Nikolsky. From September 1868, to June 1870, Moussorgsky was engaged upon this work. Each act as it was finished was tried in a small circle of musical friends, the composer singing all the male rôles in turn, while Alexandra Pourgold (afterwards Mme. Molas) created the women's parts. Dargomijsky, who heard a portion of it before his death in 1869, declared that Moussorgsky had entirely surpassed him in his own sphere.

Boris Godounov was rejected by the Direction of the Imperial Opera on the ground that it gave too little opportunity to the soloists. The unusual form of the opera, the bold treatment of a dramatic, but unpopular, episode in national history, and the democratic sentiment displayed in making the People the protagonist in several scenes of the work, were probably still stronger reasons for the attitude of disapproval always shown by the " powers that be " towards *Boris Godounov*. Very unwillingly, yielding only to the entreaties of his friends, the composer consented to make some important changes in his work. The original plan of the opera consisted of the following scenes : The crowd awaiting the election of Boris, and his Coronation ; Pimen in his cell ; the scene in the Inn, on the Lithuanian frontier ; Boris and his children, and the interview with Shouisky ; the scene in the Duma, and the death of Boris ; the peasant revolt, and the entry of the Pretender. It will be seen that the feminine element was curiously neglected. The additional scenes, composed on the advice of Stassov and the distinguished Russian architect V. Hartmann, were partially designed to rectify this omission. They include the scenes in the house of the Polish grandee Mnishek ; the song of the Hostess of the Inn ; portions of the first scene of Act I. ; the episodes of the Chiming Clock and the Parrakeet ; also some fine passages in the scene between Pimen and Gregory (Scene 1, Act II.). Portions of *Boris* were given at Kondratiev's benefit, at the Maryinski Theatre, in February, 1873, but the production of the opera in its entirety was delayed until January 24th, 1874. How often has Stassov described to me the excitement of the days that followed ! The old-fashioned subscribers to the Opera sulked at this interruption to its routine ; the pedants of the Conservatoire raged ; the critics —Moussorgsky had already satirised them in " The Peepshow "—baffled, and consequently infuriated, " foamed at the mouth." So stupid were the intrigues organised against *Boris* that some wreaths offered by groups of young people and bearing messages of enthusiastic homage to the composer, were intercepted at the doors of the opera house and sent to Moussorgsky's private residence, in order to suppress a public recognition of his obnoxious genius. For it was the young generation that took *Boris* straight to their hearts, and in spite of all organised opposition, the work had twenty performances, the house being always crowded ; while students sang the choruses from the opera as they went home through the streets at midnight.

While this controversy was raging, Moussorgsky was already occupied with a new music-drama upon an historical subject, suggested to

SHALIAPIN AS BORIS GODOUNOV

him by Stassov, dealing with the tragic story of the Princes Khovansky and the rising of the old Archers-of-the-Guard—the Streltsy. He was full of confidence in his project, and just before the first performance of *Boris* in 1873, wrote to Stassov in the following characteristic strain : " Now for judgment ! It is jolly to feel that we are actually thinking of and living for *Khovanstchina* while we are being tried for *Boris*. Joyfully and daringly we look to the distant musical horizon that lures us onward, and are not afraid of the verdict. They will say : ' You are violating all laws, human and divine ' ; and we shall reply, ' Yes ' ; thinking to ourselves, ' so we shall again.' They will warn us, ' You will soon be forgotten for ever and a day ' ; and we shall answer, ' Non, non, et non, madame.' " This triumphant moment in Moussorgsky's life was fleeting. *Boris Godounov* was not suffered to become a repertory opera, but was thrust aside for long periods. Its subsequent revivals were usually due to some star artist who liked the title-rôle and insisted on performing the work on his benefit night ; and also to private enterprise.

In 1871 Moussorgsky shared rooms with Rimsky-Korsakov until the marriage of the latter in 1873. Then he took up his abode with the gifted poet Count Golenishtiev-Koutouzov, whose idealistic and mystical tendencies were

not without influence on the champion of realism,
as may be seen from the two song-cycles,
" Without sunshine " and " Songs and dances
of death," composed to his verses. " The
Nursery," a series of children's songs, the " Pictures from an exhibition," inspired by Hartmann's drawings, and the orchestral piece,
" Night on the Bare Mountain," date from this
period. Meanwhile the stress of poverty and
the growing distaste for his means of livelihood
—a singularly unsuitable official appointment—
were telling on his health. Feeling, perhaps,
that his time on earth was short, he worked with
feverish energy. Finally, some friction with
the authorities ended in his resigning his post
in 1879, and undertaking a tour in South Russia
with the singer, Madame Leonova. The appreciation shown to him during this journey afforded
him some moments of happiness ; but his constitution was hopelessly shattered, and in 1880
he was obliged to rest completely. A series of
terrible nervous attacks compelled him at last
to take refuge in the Nicholas Military Hospital,
where he died on his forty-second birthday,
March 16/28, of paralysis of the heart and the
spinal marrow.

The historical drama " Boris Godounov " was
one of the fruits of the poet Poushkin's exile at
Mikhaïlovsky in 1824. Virtually imprisoned
on his father's estate to repent at leisure some

youthful delinquencies, moral and political, Poushkin occupied his time with the study of Karamzin's History of Russia and Shakespeare's plays. " Boris Godounov " marks a transition from the extreme influence of Byron to that of the creator of " Macbeth." Ambition coupled with remorse is the moving passion of the tragedy. The insane cruelty of Ivan the Terrible deprived Russia of almost every strong and independent spirit with the exception of the sagacious and cautious Boyard, Boris Godounov, the descendant of a Tatar family. Brother-in-law and Regent of Ivan's weak-witted heir, Feodor, Boris was already, to all intents and purposes, ruler of Russia before ambition whispered that he might actually wear the crown. Only the Tsarevich Dmitri, a child of six, stood between him and the fulfilment of his secret desire. In 1581 Dmitri was murdered, and suspicion fell upon Boris, who cleverly exculpated himself, and in due course was chosen to succeed Feodor. He reigned wisely and with authority ; but his Nemesis finally appeared in the person of the monk Gregory, the False Demetrius, whose pretentions were eagerly supported by the Poles. Boris, unhinged by the secret workings of conscience, was brought to the verge of madness just at the moment when the people—who had never quite resigned themselves to a ruler of Tatar origin—wavered in their allegiance. Urged by Rome, the Poles took advantage of the situation to advance upon Moscow. At this critical juncture Boris was seized with a fatal illness. The Tsars, as we know, may appoint their own successors ; Boris with his last breath nominated his son (also a Feodor), and died in his fifty-sixth year, in April 1605.

The intellectual power and fine workmanship which Poushkin displayed in " Boris Godounov " entitle this drama to rank as a classic in Russian literature. It contains moments of forcible eloquence, and those portions of the play which deal with the populace are undoubtedly the strongest. Here Poushkin disencumbers himself of all theatrical conventions, and shows not only accurate knowledge of the national temperament, but profound observation of human nature as a whole. Such a subject accorded well with Moussorgsky's genius, which, as we have seen, was eminently democratic.

Moussorgsky arranged his own text for *Boris Godounov*, retaining Poushkin's words intact wherever that was practicable, and simplifying, remodelling, or adding to the original material when necessary. The result is a series of living-pictures from Russian history, somewhat disconnected if taken apart from the music, which is the coagulating element of the work. The welding of these widely contrasting scenes is effected partially by the use of recurrent leading motives, but chiefly by a remarkable homogeneity of musical style. Moussorgsky, as may be proved from his correspondence, was consciously concerned to find appropriate musical phrases with which to accompany certain ideas in the course of opera ; but he does not use leading motives with the persistency of Wagner. No person or thing is labelled in *Boris Godounov*, and we need no thematic guide to thread our way through the psychological maze of the work. There is one motive that plays several parts in the music-drama. Where it occurs on page 49 of the pianoforte score of 1908 (just after Pimen's words to Gregory : " He would now be your age, and should be Tsar to-day "), it evokes the memory of the murdered Tsarevich Dmitri ; but it also enters very subtly into the soul-states of the impostor who impersonates him, and those of the remorseful Boris. There are other characteristic phrases for Boris, suggesting his tenderness for his children and his ruthless ambition.

The opera opens with a prologue in which the people are gathered in the courtyard of the many-towered monastery of Novo-Dievichy at Moscow, whither Boris had withdrawn after the assassination of the Tsarevich. The crowd moves to and fro in a listless fashion ; it hardly knows why it is there, but hopes vaguely that

the election of a new ruler may bring some
amelioration of its sad lot.   Meanwhile the
astute Boris shows no unseemly haste to snatch
at the fruit of his crime.   The simplicity and
economy of means with which Moussorgsky
produces precisely the right musical atmosphere
is very striking.   The constable enters, and
with threats and blows galvanises the weary
and indifferent throng into supplications addressed to Boris.   The secretary of the Duma
appears, and announces that Boris refuses the
crown ; the crowd renews its entreaties.   When
the pilgrims enter, the people wake to real
life, pressing around them, and showing that
their enthusiasm is for spiritual rather than for
temporal things.   In the second scene, which
shows the coronation procession across the Red
Square in the Kremlin, the Song of Praise
(*Slavsia*) is sung with infinitely greater hearti-
ness ; for now the Tsar comes into personal
contact with his people.   The scenes of the
Prologue and the Coronation move steadily
on, just as they would do in real life ; there is
scarcely a superfluous bar of musical accompaniment, and the ordinary operatic conventions
being practically non-existent, we are completely
convinced by the realism of the spectacle and
the strangely new, undisciplined character of
the music.   The truth is forcibly brought home
to us of M. Camille Bellaigue's assertion that

every collective thought, or passion, needs not only words, but music, if we are to become completely sensible to it.

The text of the òpening scene of Act I. is taken almost intact from Poushkin's drama. Played as it now usually is between the strenuous animation of the Prologue and the brilliant Coronation Scene, its pervading atmosphere of dignity and monastic calm affords a welcome interlude of repose. Moussorgsky handles his ecclesiastical themes with sure knowledge. In early days Stassov tells us that he learnt from the chaplain of the Military Academy " the very essence of the old Church music, Greek and Catholic." The scene in the Inn, where Gregory and the vagabond monks, Varlaam and Missail, halt on their flight into Lithuania, is often cut out of the acting version. It contains, however, two characteristic and popular solos : a lively folk-song for the Hostess, and a rollicking drinking-song for Varlaam (bass) ; besides frequent touches of the rough-hewn, sardonic humour which is a distinguishing quality of Moussorgsky's genius. The unabashed " naturalism " of this scene displeased a fashionable Russian audience ; although it was found possible to present it to a London audience which must have travelled much farther from the homely ribaldry of Elizabethan days than had the simple-minded " big public " of Russia to whom Moussorgsky's work was designed to appeal a generation ago.

With the opening of Act II. we feel at once that Moussorgsky is treading on alien ground. This portion of the opera—for which he was his own librettist—was added in order that some conventional love interest might be given to the work. The glamour of romance is a borrowed quality in Moussorgsky's art ; and, in spite of the charm of the scenic surroundings, and some moments of sincere passion, the weakness of the music proclaims the fact. He, who penetrates so deeply into the psychology of his own people, finds no better characterisation of the Polish temperament than the use of the polacca or mazurka rhythms. True, he may intend by these dance measures to emphasise the boastful vanity of the Polish nobles and the light, cold nature of Marina Mnishek ; but the method becomes monotonous. Marina's solo takes this form, and again in the duet by the fountain we are pursued by the eternal mazurka rhythm.

The second scene of Act II. is packed full of varied interest, and in every episode Moussorgsky is himself again. The lively dancing-songs for the young Tsarevich and the Nurse are interrupted by the sudden entry of Boris. In the scene which follows, where the Tsar forgets for a moment the cares of State and the

sting of conscience, and gives himself whole-
heartedly to his children, there is some exquisitely tender music, and we begin for the first
time to feel profound pity for the usurper.   The
Tsarevich's recital of the incident of the para-
keet, reproducing with the utmost accuracy
and transparent simplicity the varied inflec-
tions of the child's voice, as he relates his tale
without a trace of self-consciousness, is equal
to anything of the kind which Moussorgsky
has achieved in " The Nursery " song cycle.
This delightful interlude of comedy gives place
on the entrance of Shouisky to the first shadows
of approaching tragedy.   Darker and darker
grows the mind of the Tsar, until the scene ends
in an almost intolerable crisis of madness and
despair.   From the moment of Boris's terrible
monologue the whole atmosphere of the work
becomes vibrant with terror and pity.   But
realistic as the treatment may be, it is a realism
—like that of Shakespeare or Webster—that
is exalted and vivified by a fervent and forceful
imagination.

In the opening scene of Act III., enacted
amid a winter landscape in the desolate forest
of Kromy, Moussorgsky has concentrated all
his powers for the creation of a host of national
types who move before our eyes in a dazzling
kaleidoscopic display.   They are not attractive
these revolted and revolting peasants, revenging

themselves upon the wretched aristocrat who
has fallen into their hands ; for Moussorgsky,
though he raises the Folk to the dignity of a
protagonist, never idealises it, or sets it on a
pedestal.   But our pulses beat with the emotions
of this crowd, and its profound groan of anguish
finds an echo in our hearts.   It is a living and
terrible force, and beside it all other stage
crowds seem mechanical puppets.   In the fore-
ground of this shifting mass is seen the village
idiot, ' God's fool,' teased by the thoughtless
children, half-reverenced, half-pitied, by the
men and women.   After the False Demetrius
has passed through the forest, drawing the
crowd in his wake, the idiot is left sitting alone
in the falling snow.   He sings his heart-breaking
ditty :   " Night and darkness are at hand.
Woe to Russia ! "   and the curtain falls to the
sound of his bitter, paroxysmal weeping.

The last scene is pregnant with the " horror
that awaits on princes."   The climax is built
up step by step.   After the lurking insanity
of Boris, barely curbed by the presence of the
Council ; after his interview with Pimen, who
destroys his last furtive hope that the young
Tsarevich may not have been murdered after
all ; after his access of mental and physical
agony, and his parting with his beloved son—
it is with a feeling of relief that we see death
put an end to his unbearable sufferings.

Although *Khovanstchina* may in some ways approach more nearly to the conventional ideal of opera, yet foreigners, I think, will find it more difficult to understand than *Boris Godounov*. To begin with it lacks the tragic dominant figure, swayed by such universal passions as ambition, remorse, and paternal tenderness, which gives a psychological unity to the earlier work. Here the dramatic interest is more widely dispersed ; it is as though Moussorgsky sought to crowd into this series of historical pictures as many different types of seventeenth-century Russia as possible ; and these types are peculiarly national. Except that it breaks through the rigid traditions of Byzantine art, the figures being full of vitality, *Khovanstchina* reminds us of those early *ikons* belonging to the period when the transport of pictures through the forests, bogs, and wildernesses of Russia so restricted their distribution, that the religious painter resorted to the expedient of representing on one canvas as many saints as could be packed into it.

Stassov originated the idea of utilising the dramatic conflict between old and new Russia at the close of the seventeenth century as the subject of a music-drama. It was his intention to bring into relief a group of representative figures of the period : Dositheus, head of the sect known as the Rasskolniki, or Old

Believers,[1] a man of lofty character and prophetic insight; Ivan Khovansky, typical of fanatical, half-oriental and conservative Russia; Galitsin, the westernised aristocrat, who dreams of a new Russia, reformed on European lines; two contrasting types of womanhood, both belonging to the Old Believers—the passionate, mystical Martha, falling and redeeming herself through the power of love, and Susan, in whom fanaticism has dried up the well-springs of tenderness and sympathy; the dissolute young Andrew Khovansky, ardently attracted by the pure, sweet young German girl, Emma; the egotistical Scrivener, who has his humorous side; the fierce Streltsy, and the oppressed and suffering populace—" all these elements," says Stassov, " seemed to suggest characters and situations which promised to be intensely stirring." It was also part of his original design to bring upon the scene the young Tsar, Peter the Great, and the Regent, the Tsarevna Sophia. But much of Stassov's original scenarium had perforce to be dropped; partly because it would have resulted in the building up of a work on an unpractically colossal scale, but also because

---

[1] In the reign of Alexis the revision of the Bible carried out by the Patriarch Nicon (1655) resulted in a great schism in the Orthodox Church, a number of people clinging to the old version of the Scriptures in spite of the errors it contained. Thus was formed the sect of the Old Believers which still exists in Russia.

Moussorgsky's failing health spurred him on to complete the drama at all costs. Had he lived a few years longer, he would probably have made of *Khovanstchina* a far better balanced and a more polished work.

From the musical point of view there is undoubtedly more symmetry and restraint in *Khovanstchina* than in *Boris*. We are often impressed by the almost classic simplicity of the music. A great deal of the thematic material is drawn from ecclesiastical sources.

Khovanstchina opens with an orchestral Prelude, descriptive of daybreak over Moscow, than which nothing in Russian music is more intensely or touchingly national in feeling. The curtain rises upon the Red Square in the Kremlin, just as the rising sun catches the domes of the churches, and the bells ring for early matins. A group of Streltsy relate the havoc they have worked during the preceding night. The Scrivener, a quaint type of the period, appears on the scene and is roughly chaffed. When the Streltsy depart, the Boyard Shaklovity enters and bribes the Scrivener to write down his denunciation of the Khovanskys. No sooner is this done, than the elder Khovansky and his suite arrive, attended by the Streltsy and the populace. In virtue of his office as Captain of the Old Guard, the arrogant nobleman assumes the airs of a sovereign, and issues autocratic commands, while the people, impressed by his grandeur, sing him a song of flattery. When the crowd has departed the Lutheran girl, Emma, runs in, hotly pursued by the younger Khovansky. She tries in vain to rid herself of his hateful attentions. At the climax of this scene, Martha, the young Rasskolnik whom Prince Andrew has already loved and betrayed, comes silently upon the stage and saves Emma from his embraces. Martha approaches Andrew, who tries to stab her ; but she parries the blow, and in one of her ecstatic moods prophesies his ultimate fate. The elder Khovansky and his followers now return, and the Prince inquires into the cause of the disturbance.   Prince Ivan admires Emma and orders the Streltsy to arrest her ; but Andrew, mad with jealousy, declares she shall not be taken alive.   At this juncture Dositheus enters, rebukes the young man's violence, and restores peace.

Act II. shows us Prince Galitsin reading a letter from the Tsarevna Sophia, with whom he has formerly had a love-intrigue. In spite of his western education Galitsin is superstitious. The scene which follows, in which Martha, gazing into a bowl of water, as into a crystal, foretells his downfall and banishment, is one of the most impressive moments in the work. Galitsin, infuriated by her predictions, orders his servants to drown Martha on her homeward way. A long scene, devoted to a dispute between Galitsin and Khovansky, is rather dry. Dositheus again acts as peacemaker.

Act III. takes place in the quarter of Moscow inhabited by the Streltsy. Martha, seated near the house of Andrew Khovansky, recalls her passion for him in a plaintive folk-song. The song closes with one of her prophetic allusions to the burning of the Old Believers. Susan, the old fanatic, overhears Martha and reproves her for singing " shameless songs of love." She threatens to have her brought before the Brethren and tried as a witch ; but Dositheus intervenes and sends Susan away, terrified at the idea that she is the prey of evil spirits. Night falls, and the stage is empty. Enter Shaklovity, who sings of the sorrows of his country in an aria that is one of the most beautiful things in the music-drama. The next scene is concerned with the Streltsy, who march in to a drinking song. They encounter their womenfolk, who, unlike the terrified populace of Moscow, have no hesitation in falling upon them and giving them a piece of their mind. Undoubtedly the Streltsy were not ideal in their domestic relations. While they are quarrelling, the Scrivener comes in breathless, and announces the arrival of foreign troopers and Peter the Great's bodyguard, " the Petrovtsy."

The cause of Old Russia is lost. Sobered and fear-
ful, the Streltsy put up a prayer to Heaven,
for the religious instinct lurks in every type of
the Russian people, and even these savage
creatures turn devout at a moment's notice.

In Act IV. the curtain rises upon a hall in
Prince Ivan Khovansky's country house, where
he is taking his ease, diverted by the songs of
his serving-maids and the dances of his Persian
slaves.   Shaklovity appears, and summons him
to attend the Tsarevna's Council.   As Khovansky in his robes of ceremony is crossing the
threshold, he is stabbed, and falls with a great
cry.   The servants disperse in terror, but
Shaklovity lingers a moment to mock the corpse
of his enemy.   The scene now changes to the
open space in front of the fantastic church of
Vassily Blajeny, and Galitsin is seen on his way
to exile, escorted by a troop of cavalry.   When
he has gone by, Dositheus soliloquises on the
state of Russia.   Martha comes in and tells
him that the foreign mercenaries have orders
to surround the Old Believers in their place
of assemblage and put them all to death.
Dositheus declares that they will sooner perish
in self-ignited flames, willing martyrs for their
faith.   He enjoins Martha to bring Prince
Andrew among them.   During the meeting
between Martha and Andrew, the young Prince
implores her to bring back Emma, and learning

SHALIAPIN AS DOSITHEUS IN "KHOVANSTCHINA"

that the girl is safely married to her lover, he curses Martha for a witch, and summons his Streltsy to put her to death. In vain the Prince blows his horn, his only reply is the hollow knelling of the bell called " Ivan Veliky." Presently the Streltsy enter, carrying axes and blocks for their own execution. At the last moment a herald proclaims that Peter has pardoned them, and they may return to their homes.

In the fifth and last Act the Old Believers are assembled by moonlight at their hermitage in the woods near Moscow. Dositheus encourages his followers to remain true to their vows. Martha prays that she may save Andrew's soul by the power of her love for him. Presently she hears him singing an old love song which echoes strangely amid all this spiritual tension. By sheer force of devotion she induces him to mount the pyre which the Brethren, clothed in their white festal robes, have built up close at hand. The trumpets of the troopers are heard drawing nearer, and Martha sets a light to the pyre. The Old Believers sing a solemn chant until they are overpowered by the flames. When the soldiers appear upon the scene, they fall back in horror before this spectacle of self-immolation ; while the trumpets ring out arrogantly, as though proclaiming the passing of the old faith and ideals and the dawning of a new day for Russia.

" My first introduction to the works of Moussorgsky came through Vladimir Stassov. Together we went through the earlier edition of *Boris Godounov* (1875), and *Khovanstchina*, already issued with Rimsky-Korsakov's revisions. ' There is more vitality in Moussorgsky than in any of our contemporary composers,' Stassov would declare to me in my first moments of doubtful enthusiasm. ' These operas will go further afield than the rest, and you will see their day, when I shall no longer be here to follow their fortunes in Western Europe.' How surely his predictions regarding this, and other questions, were destined to be fulfilled is a fact borne in upon me every year that I live and work in the world of music. Later on he gave me the new edition of *Boris* (1896), edited by the composer's life-long friend, who was in some degree his teacher—Rimsky-Korsakov. Theoretically, Stassov was fully opposed to these editorial proceedings ; for, while admitting Moussorgsky's technical limitations, and his tendency to be slovenly in workmanship, he thought it might be better for the world to see this original and inspired composer with all his faults ruthlessly exposed to view, than clothed and in his right mind with the assistance of Rimsky-Korsakov. Stassov's attitude to Moussorgsky reminds me of the Russian vagabond who said to Mr. Stephen Graham : ' Love us while we are dirty, for when we are clean all the world will love us.' We who loved Moussorgsky's music in spite of all its apparent dishevelment may not unnaturally resent Rimsky-Korsakov's conscientious grooming of it. But when it actually came to the question of producing the operas, even Stassov, I am sure, realised the need for practical revisions, without which Moussorgsky's original scores, with all their potential greatness, ran considerable risk of becoming mere archæological curiosities. In 1908 Bessel published a later edition of *Boris*, restoring the scenes cut out of the version of 1896. This is the edition now generally used ; the first one, on which I was educated, having become somewhat of a rarity." [1]

At the present moment it is impossible to write of Moussorgsky's operas without touching on this vexed question of Rimsky-Korsakov's right to improve upon the original drafts of his friend's works, since it is daily agitating the musical press of Russia and Paris.

Throughout his whole life, it was Rimsky-Korsakov's lot to occupy at frequent intervals the most delicate, difficult and thankless position which can well be thrust upon a man, when, time after time, he was asked to complete works left unfinished in consequence of the illness,

[1] Quoted from an article by me, "Moussorgsky's Operas," in the "Musical Times," July 1st, 1913.

untimely death, or incompetence of their authors. That he attacked this altruistic work in a self-sacrificing and perfectly honest spirit cannot for a moment be doubted by anyone who knew him personally. But his temperament was not pliable, and as time went on and his æsthetic theories became more set, it grew increasingly difficult for him to see a work in any light but that of his own clearly illumined orderly vision. The following conversation between himself and V. Yastrebtsiev—if it contains no note of exaggeration—shows the uncompromising view which he took of his editorial duties. In 1895 he had expressed his intention of writing a purely critical article on " the merits and demerits of *Boris Godounov*." But a year later he changed his mind, because he said : " a new revised pianoforte score and a new orchestral score will be a more eloquent testimony to future generations of my views on this work, not only as a whole, but as regards the details of every bar ; the more so, because in this transcription of the opera for orchestra, personality is not concerned, and I am only doing that which Moussorgsky himself ought to have done, but which he did not understand how to carry out, simply because of his lack of technique as a composer. I maintain that in my intention to reharmonise and re-orchestrate this great opera of Moussorgsky there is certainly nothing for which I can be blamed ; in any case I impute no sin to myself. And now," he concluded, " when I have finished my revisions of *Boris* and *Sadko* it will be necessary to go through the entire score of Dargomijsky's *The Stone Guest* (which was orchestrated by me), and should I find anything in the instrumentation which seems to me not good (and I think I shall find much) I will correct it, in order that in the future none will be able to reproach me with carelessness as regards the works of others. Only when I have revised the whole of Moussorgsky's works shall I begin to be at peace and feel that my conscience is clear ; for then I shall have done all that can and ought to be done for his compositions and his memory."[1]

Rimsky-Korsakov was a noble and devoted friend, but he was before all things a craftsman of the highest excellence. When it came to a question of what he believed to be an offence against art, he saved his friend's musical soul at the expense of his individuality. We have therefore to weigh his close personal knowledge of Moussorgsky's aims and technical incapacity against the uncompromising musical rectitude which guided his editorial pen. When the question arises whether we are to hear Moussorgsky according to Rimsky-Korsakov,

[1] Published by V. Yastrebtsiev in the Moscow weekly, "Musika." No. 135, June 22 (O.S.), 1913.

or according to Diaghilev-Ravel-Stravinsky, for my own part, having grown accustomed to the versions of Rimsky-Korsakov—which still leave in the operas so much of Moussorgsky's essential genius that they have not hitherto failed in their profound psychological impression—I feel considerable doubt as to the wisdom of flying from them to evils that we know not of. For, after all, Rimsky-Korsakov was no purblind pedant, but a gifted musician with an immense experience of what was feasible on the operatic stage and of all that could militate against the success of a work.

CHAPTER XI

WITH Borodin we return to a position midway between the original type of national lyric opera which Glinka inaugurated in *A Life for the Tsar* and the dramatic realism of Moussorgsky.

Alexander Porphyrievich Borodin, born at St. Petersburg in 1834, was the illegitimate son of a Prince of Imeretia, one of the fairest of the Georgian provinces which the Russian General Todleben rescued from Turkish occupation in 1770. The reigning princes of Imeretia boasted that they were direct descendants of King David the Psalmist, and quartered the harp and sling in their arms. Borodin's education was chiefly confided to his mother. As a boy, his capacities were evenly balanced between music and science, but, having to make his living, he decided in favour of the latter and became a distinguished professor of chemistry at the College of Medicine in St. Petersburg. As regards music, he remained until his twenty-eighth year merely an intelligent amateur. He played the piano, the violoncello and the flute, all with some facility ; he wrote a few songs and enjoyed taking part in Mendelssohn's chamber music. It is clear that until he met Balakirev in 1862 there was never any serious conflict between duty and inclination. Borodin was a man of sane and optimistic temperament which disposed him to be satisfied with the career he had chosen, in which he seemed destined for unusual success. Unlike Tchaikovsky, who felt himself an alien among the bureaucrats and minor officials with whom he was associated in the Ministry of Justice, Borodin was genuinely interested in his work. But no one with a spark of artistic enthusiasm could pass under Balakirev's influence and be the same man as before. Within a short time of their first meeting, the story of Cui and Moussorgsky was repeated in Borodin. All his leisure was henceforth consecrated to the serious study of music. Harmony and musical analysis he worked up under Balakirev ; and all his contemporaries agree in asserting that counterpoint came to him by intuition. His early marriage to a woman of considerable talent as a musician was an important factor in his artistic development.

Borodin's youth had been spent chiefly in cities ; consequently he did not start life with that intimate knowledge of the folk-music which Balakirev and Moussorgsky had acquired. But his perception was so quick and subtle, that no sooner had his attention been called to the national element in music than he began to use it with mastery. This is already noticeable in his first Symphony, in E flat major. This work is not free from the faults of inexperience, but it displays all the potential qualities of Borodin's talent—poetical impulse, a fine taste, an originality which is not forced, and a degree of technical facility that is astonishing, when we realise that music was merely the occupation of his rare leisure hours.

Stassov saw in Borodin the making of a true national poet, and encouraged his secret ambition to compose an epic opera. He first took up the subject of Mey's drama " The Tsar's Bride ; " but his progress was so frequently interrupted that his interest flagged. It needed a subject of unusual attraction to keep him faithful amid many professional preoccupations to such a long and difficult task. But in 1869 Stassov believed he had found an ideal source from which to draw the libretto of a great national opera, and sketched out a rough plot which he persuaded Borodin to consider. It is not easy to convey to those who have not studied the early Slavonic literature any just and clear idea of the national significance of " The Epic of the Army of Igor." The original manuscript of this Rhapsody or Saga was bought from a monk by Count Moussin-Poushkin as late as 1795, and published by him in 1800. Unfortunately the original document was among the many treasures which perished in the burning of Moscow in 1812. Its authenticity has since been the cause of innumerable disputes. Many scholars, including the late Professor of Slavonic languages at Oxford, Mr. W. R. Morfill, have been disposed to regard it as one of those many ingenious frauds—like the Poems of Ossian—which were almost a feature of literary history in the eighteenth century. Others affirm that all the Russian poets of the eighteenth century put together had not sufficient imagination to have produced a single line of " The Epic of Igor." In any case, it so far surpasses in interest most of the mediæval Slavonic chronicles that it has taken a strong hold on the popular imagination, and the majority prefer to believe in its genuine origin in spite of differences of opinion among the learned. In order to give some idea of its significance and interest, perhaps I may compare it—in certain respects—with the Arthurian Legends. The period is of course much later—the close of the twelfth century.

The book of *Prince Igor*, planned by Stassov and written by Borodin, runs as follows :

The Prologue takes place in the market-place of Poultivle, the residence of Igor, Prince of

Seversk. The Prince and his army are about
to start in pursuit of the Polovtsy, an Oriental
tribe of Tatar origin. Igor wishes to meet his
enemies in the plains of the Don, whither they
have been driven by a rival Russian prince,
Sviatoslav of Kiev. An eclipse of the sun
darkens the heavens, and at this fatal passage
the people implore Igor to postpone his expedi-
tion. But the Prince is resolute. He departs
with his youthful son Vladimir Igorievich,
commending his wife Yaroslavna to the care
of his brother-in-law, Prince Galitsky, who
remains to govern Poultivle, in the absence of
its lord. The first scene depicts the treachery
and misrule of this dissolute nobleman, who tries
to win over the populace with the assistance of
two deserters from Igor's army. Eroshka and
Skoula are players on the *goudok*, or rebeck,
types of the gleemen, or minnesingers, of that
period. They are the comic villains of the
opera. In the second scene of Act I. some
young girls complain to the Princess Yaroslavna of the abduction of one of their companions, and implore her protection from Prince
Galitsky. Yaroslavna discovers the perfidy
of her brother, and after a violent scene drives
him from her presence, at the very moment
when a messenger arrives with the news that
Igor's army has been defeated on the banks of
the Kayala. "At the third dawn," says the

rhapsody, " the Russian standards fell before the foe, for no blood was left to shed.", Igor and Vladimir are taken prisoners and the Polovsty are marching on Poultivle. The news of this heroic disaster causes a reaction of loyal sentiment, and, as the curtain falls, the Boyards draw their swords and swear to defend Yaroslavna to the death.

The second and third acts take place in the enemy's camp, and are full of Oriental colour. Khan Konchak, as depicted in the opera, is a noble type of Eastern warrior. He has one beautiful daughter, Konchakovna, with whom the young Prince Vladimir falls passionately in love. The serenade which he sings before her tent is perhaps the most fascinating number in the whole work. There is also a fine bass solo for Prince Igor, in which he gives vent to the grief and shame he suffers in captivity. Ovlour, one of the Polovetz soldiers, who is a Christian convert, offers to facilitate Igor's escape. But the Prince feels bound by the chivalrous conduct of Khan Konchak to refuse his offer. In the second act the Khan gives a banquet in honour of his noble captive, which serves as a pretext for the introduction of Oriental dances, choruses, and gorgeous scenic effects.

In the third act the conquering army of the Polovsty return to camp, bringing the prisoners and spoils taken from Poultivle. At this sight,

Igor, filled with pity for the sorrows of his wife and people, consents to flee. While the soldiers are dividing the spoil from Poultivle, Ovlour plies them liberally with koumiss and, after a wild orgy, the whole camp falls into a drunken sleep. Borodin has been severely censured by certain critics for the robust realism with which he has treated this scene. When the Khan's daughter discovers their secret preparations for flight, she entreats Vladimir not to forsake her. He is on the point of yielding, when his father sternly recalls him to a sense of duty. But Konchakovna's glowing Oriental passion is not to be baulked. At the last moment, when Ovlour gives the signal for escape, she flings herself upon her lover, and holds him back until Igor has mounted and galloped out of the camp, unconscious that his son is left behind. Detained against his will, Vladimir finds no great difficulty in accommodating himself to circumstances. The soldiers would like to kill him in revenge for his father's escape. But the Khan philosophically remarks : " Since the old falcon has taken flight, we must chain the young falcon by giving him a mate. He must be my daughter's husband." In the fourth Act Yaroslavna sings her touching lament, as she stands on the terrace of her ruined palace and gazes over the fertile plains, now ravaged by the hostile army. Even while she bemoans the cruelty of fate, two horsemen come in sight. They prove to be Igor and the faithful Ovlour, returned in safety from their perilous ride. The joy of reunion between husband and wife may be perhaps a trifle over-emphasised. It is the man who speaks here, rather than the artist ; for Borodin, who lived in perfect domestic happiness with his wife, knew, however, many long and enforced separations from her. The picture of conjugal felicity which he gives us in *Igor* is undoubtedly reflected from his own life.

The opera closes with a touch of humour. Igor and Yaroslavna enter the Kremlin at Poultivle at the same moment as the two deserters Eroshka and Skoula. The precious pair are shaking in their shoes, for if Igor catches sight of them they are lost. To get out of their difficulty they set the bells a-ringing and pretend to be the first bearers of the glad tidings of Igor's escape. Probably because they are merry ruffians and skilful with their *goudoks*, no one reveals their treachery and they get off scot-free.

When we consider that *Prince Igor* was written piecemeal, in intervals snatched between medical commissions, boards of examination, lectures, and laboratory work, we marvel to find it so astonishingly cohesive, so delightfully fresh. Borodin describes the difficulties he had to contend with in a letter to an intimate friend.

" In winter," he says, " I can only compose
when I am too unwell to give my lectures. So
my friends, reversing the usual custom, never
say to me, ' I hope you are well ' but ' I do hope
you are ill.' At Christmas I had influenza,
so I stayed at home and wrote the Thanksgiving
Chorus in the last act of *Igor*."

Borodin took his work very seriously, as we
might expect from a scientist. He had access
to every document bearing on the period of his
opera, and he received from Hunfalvi, the
celebrated traveller, a number of melodies
collected among the tribes of Central Asia
which he employed in the music allotted to the
Polovtsy. But there is nothing of meticulous
pedantry apparent in Borodin's work. He has
drawn a vivid picture of the past, a worthy
pendant to the historical paintings of his contemporary Vasnietsov, who has reconstructed
mediæval Russia with such astonishing force
and realism. Borodin modelled his opera upon
Glinka's *Russlan and Liudmilla* rather than
on Dargomijsky's *The Stone Guest*. He had his
own personal creed as regards operatic form.
" Recitative does not conform to my temperament," he says, " although according to some
critics I do not handle it badly. I am far more
attracted to melody and cantilena. I am more
and more drawn to definite and concrete forms.
In opera, as in decorative art, minutiæ are

out of place. Bold outlines only are necessary.
All should be clear and fit for practical performance from the vocal and instrumental stand-
points.   The voices should take the first place ;
the orchestra the second."

Prince Igor, in its finished form, is a compromise between the new and the old methods ;
for the declamation, although not of such
primary importance as with Dargomijsky, is
more developed than with Glinka. Borodin
keeps to the accepted divisions of Italian opera,
and gives to Igor a long aria quite in the
traditional style. The music of *Prince Igor* has
some features in common with Glinka's *Russlan*,
in which the Oriental element is also made to
contrast with the national Russian colouring.
But the Eastern music in Borodin's opera is
more daring and characteristic. Comparing
the two operas, Cheshikin says : " The epic
beauty of *Prince Igor* reminds us of the serene
poetry of Goncharov, of the so-called ' poetry
of daily life ' ; while Glinka may be more
suitably compared to Poushkin. Borodin's
calm, cheerful, objective attitude towards the
national life is manifested in the general style
of the opera ; in the wonderfully serene
character of its melody ; in the orchestral
colour, in the transparency of the harmony,
and the lightness and agility of the counterpoint. In spite of his reputation as an innovator,

Borodin has introduced nothing startlingly new into this opera ; his orchestral style is still that of Glinka. . . . The poetry of common things exercised such a fascination for Borodin that he completely forgot the heroic tendencies of Glinka. His folk, as represented by him amid an epidemic of alcoholism, and the hard-worked, ubiquitous *goudok* players, Eroshka and Skoula, throw into the shade the leading characters whose musical outlines are somewhat sketchy and impermanent. Borodin's Igor recalls Glinka's Russlan ; Yaroslavna is not a very distinguished personality ; Galitsky is not far removed from Eroshka and Skoula ; and Konchakovna and Vladimir are ordinary operatic lovers. The chief beauty of Glinka's *Russlan* lies in the solo parts and in a few concerted numbers. On the other hand, the principal hero of Borodin's opera is ' the folk ' ; while its chief beauty is to be found in the choruses based on Russian and Tatar folk-song themes. What affects us chiefly in the music may be traced to that normal optimism with which the whole work is impregnated." Borodin, it should be added, had far more humour than Glinka, who could never have created two such broadly and robustly comic types as Skoula and Eroshka. There is a distinctly Shakespearian flavour in the quality of Borodin's humour. In this respect he approaches Moussorgsky.

In the atmosphere of healthy, popular optimism which pervades it throughout ; in the prevalence of major over minor keys ; in the straightforwardness of its emotional appeal—*Prince Igor* stands almost alone among Russian operas. The spirit of pessimism which darkens Russian literature inevitably crept into the national opera ; because music and literature are more closely associated in Russia than in any other country. Glinka's *A Life for the Tsar* is a tragedy of loyal self-sacrifice ; Tchaikovsky took his brooding melancholy into his operatic works, which are nearly all built on some sad or tragic libretto ; Cui deals in romantic melodrama ; Moussorgsky depicts the darkest phases in Russian history. *Prince Igor* comes as a serene and restful interlude after the stress and horror which characterise many Russian national operas. Nor is it actually less national because of its optimistic character. There are two sides to the Russian temperament ; the one overshadowed by melancholy and mysticism ; prone to merciless analysis ; seeing only the contradictions and vanities of life, the mortality and emptiness of all that is. I doubt if this is the true Russian temperament ; if it is not rather a morbid condition, the result of sudden and copious doses of culture, administered too hastily to a people just emerging from a semi-barbaric state—the kind of result

ALEXIS BORODIN

that follows alcohol taken on an empty stomach ;
a quick elation, an equally speedy reaction to
extreme depression. The other side of the
Russian character is really more normal. It
shows itself in the popular literature. The
folk-songs and *bylini* are not all given up to
resentful bitterness and despair. We find this
healthier spirit in the masses, where it takes the
form of a desire for practical knowledge, a
shrewdness in making a bargain and a co-
operative spirit that properly guided would
accomplish wonders. It shows itself, too, in a
great capacity for work which belongs to the
vigorous youth of the nation and in a cheerful
resignation to inevitable hardships. Borodin
was attracted by temperament to this saner
aspect of national character.

The most distinctive feature of Russian art
and literature is the power to reflect clearly, as
in a glass, various phases of popular life. This
has also been the aim of the Russian composers,
with few exceptions. They cheerfully accepted
the limitations imposed by the national vision,
and have won appreciation abroad by the
sheer force of genius manifested in their works.
They resolutely sought the kingdom of the
Ideal, and would have been greatly surprised to
find such things as universal fame added to
them. Borodin, for example, cherished no
illusions as to winning the approval of Berlin

or Paris for his work. *Prince Igor*, he said, with admirable philosophy, " is essentially an opera for the Russians. It would never bear transplantation." For many years, however, it could not even be said to be " a work for the Russians " in the fullest sense, because it was not offered to the right public. Works like *Prince Igor* and *Boris Godounov*, which should have been mounted at a People's Palace in St. Petersburg, for the enjoyment of a large and really popular audience, were laid aside for many years awaiting the patriotic enterprise of rich men like Mamantov, who occasionally gave a series of Russian operas at their own expense, or the generous impulse of artists such as Melnikov and Shaliapin, who were willing to risk the production of a national masterpiece on their benefit nights.

César Cui offers in most respects a complete contrast to the composer of *Prince Igor*. It is true that he shares with Borodin the lyrical, rather than the declamatory, tendency in operatic music, but whereas the latter is a follower of Glinka in his close adherence to the national style, we find in the music of César Cui a strong blend of foreign influences. As in Tchaikovsky's dramatic works we discern from first to last some traces of his earliest love in music—the Italian opera—so in Cui's compositions we never entirely lose sight of his

French descent. Cui's position as a composer must strike us as paradoxical. The first disciple to join Balakirev, and always a staunch supporter of the new Russian school, we might naturally expect to find some strong, progressive, and national tendency in his music. We might suppose that he would assume the virtue of nationality even if he had it not. But this is not the case. The French element, combined, curiously enough, with Schumann's influence, is everywhere predominant. Nevertheless, Cui has been a distinct force in the evolution of modern Russian music, for to him is generally attributed the origin of that " second generation " of composers with whom inspiration ranks after the cult of form, and " the idea " becomes subordinate to elaborate treatment. This tendency is also represented by Glazounov in his early work, and still more strongly by Liadov and one or two composers for the pianoforte.

Cui was born at Vilna, in Poland, in 1835. His father had served in Napoleon's army, and was left behind during the retreat from Moscow in 1812. He afterwards married a Lithuanian lady and settled down as teacher of French in the Vilna High School. Here Cui received his early education. He showed a precocious musical talent and, besides learning the pianoforte, picked up some theoretical knowledge from

Moniuszko ; but he never—as is sometimes stated—received regular instruction from the Polish composer. Except for what he owed in later life to Balakirev's guidance, Cui is actually that *rara avis*, a self-taught composer.

From the time he entered the School of Military Engineering in 1850, until he passed out with honours in 1857, Cui had no time to devote to his favourite pursuit. On obtaining officer's rank he was appointed sub-Professor of Fortification, and lecturer on the same subject at the Staff College and School of Artillery. Among his pupils he reckoned the present Emperor, Nicholas II. Cui has now risen to be a Lieut.-General of Engineers and President of the I. R. M. S. At first his military appointments barely sufficed to keep him, and when he married —early in life—he and his wife were obliged to add to their income by keeping a preparatory school for boys intended eventually for the School of Engineering. Here Cui taught all day, when not lecturing in the military schools ; while his nights were largely devoted to the study of harmony, and afterwards to composition and musical criticism. Very few of the Russian composers, with their dual occupations to fulfil, have known the luxury of an eight hours' day.

Cui first met Balakirev in 1856, and was introduced by him to Dargomijsky. His earliest

operatic attempt, a work in one act entitled
The Mandarin's Son, was a very slight composition in the style of Auber. An opera composed
about the same time (1858-1859) on Poushkin's
dramatic poem *The Captive in the Caucasus* was
a much more ambitious effort. Many years
later—in 1881—Cui considered this work worth
remodelling, and he also interpolated a second
act. The patch is rather obvious, but *The Captive in the Caucasus* is an interesting work to
study, because it reveals very clearly the difference between Cui's earlier and later styles.
Cui's reputation as an operatic composer
actually began, however, with the performance
of *William Ratcliff*, produced at the Maryinsky
Theatre, St. Petersburg, in February 1869, under
the direction of Napravnik, on the occasion of
Mme. Leonova's benefit. A composer who is
also a critic is certainly at a disadvantage in
many respects. Cui, who contributed during
the 'sixties a whole series of brilliant—and
often mercilessly satirical—articles to the
Russian press,[1] gave his adversaries an excellent opportunity to attack him for inconsistency when *Ratcliff* made its appearance.
Cui's literary precepts do undoubtedly move
somewhat in advance of his practice as a
composer, and *Ratcliff* conforms in very few

[1] He was appointed musical critic of the St. Petersburg
" Viedomosty " in 1864.

respects to the creed of the new Russian
school as formulated by him in his well-known
articles "La Musique en Russie." That is
to say, instead of following the example
of Dargomijsky in *The Stone Guest*, Cui to a
great extent replaces free-recitative by arioso ;
while at the same time the absence of such
broad and flowing melody as we find in the
operas of Glinka, Borodin, and Tchaikovsky
places *William Ratcliff* in a position midway
between declamatory and lyric opera. Some
of the hostile criticisms showered upon this
work are not altogether unjust. The subject
of Heine's early tragedy, the outcome of his
" Sturm und Drang " period, is undoubtedly
crude and sensational ; even in Plestcheiev's
fine translation it was hardly likely to be accept-
able to a nation who was beginning to base its
dramatic traditions on the realistic plays of
Gogol and Ostrovsky, rather than upon the
romanticism of Schiller's " Robbers," and kindred dramas. The music is lacking in realistic
power and certainly makes no pretensions to
fulfil Dargomijsky's dictum that " the note
must represent the word." Although the action
of *William Ratcliff* takes place across the border,
neither the sentiment nor the colour of the
music would satisfy a Scottish composer. But
Cui's critics show a lack of perception when they
neglect to praise the grace and tenderness which

characterise his heroine Mary, and the sincerity and warmth of emotion which occasionally kindles and glows into passion as in the love-duet between William and Mary in the last act.

The public verdict which began by echoing that of the critics, with the inimical Serov at their head, afterwards became more favourable, and *William Ratcliff*, when produced in 1900 by the Private Opera Company in Moscow, was received with considerable enthusiasm.

Tchaikovsky, writing of this opera in 1879, says : " It contains charming things, but unfortunately it suffers from a certain insipidity, and from over-elaboration in the development of the parts. It is obvious that the composer has spent a long time over each individual bar, and lovingly completed it in every detail, with the result that his musical outline has lost its freedom and every touch is too deliberate. By nature Cui is more drawn towards light and piquantly rhythmic French music ; but the demands of ' the invincible band,' which he has joined, compel him to do violence to his natural gifts and to follow those paths of would-be original harmony which do not suit him. Cui is now forty-four years of age and has only composed two operas and two or three dozen songs. He was engaged for ten years upon his opera *Ratcliff*. It is evident that the work was composed piecemeal, hence the lack of any unity of style." This criticism contains a germ of carefully observed truth. The score of *William Ratcliff*, which looks deceptively simple and seems to be packed with dance rhythms in the style of Auber (Leslie's song in Act II. for instance might be a chansonette from " Fra Diavolo "), shows on closer examination rather a tiresome succession of harmonic surprise tricks, intended perhaps to draw attention from themes which have not in themselves an impressive dramatic quality. At the same time, only prejudice could ignore the true poetry and passion expressed in the love scenes between William and Mary.

William Ratcliff was followed by a series of admirable songs which indicated that Cui's talent as a vocal composer was rapidly maturing. A new opera, in four acts, entitled *Angelo*,[1] was completed and performed in St. Petersburg in February 1876, under the direction of Napravnik, the occasion being the benefit of the great baritone Melnikov. The book of *Angelo* is based upon a play of Victor Hugo—a tale of passionate love ; of rivalry between two beautiful and contrasting types of womanhood ; of plotted revenge, and final atonement, when

[1] Ponchielli has used the same subject for his opera " Gioconda " ; while Mascagni, influenced possibly by the Russian realists, made a literal setting of Heine's poem " William Ratcliff " in the style of *The Stone Guest* (" Guglielmo Ratcliff," Milan 1895.)

Tisbe saves the life of her rival at the expense
of her own.   The scene is laid in Padua during
the middle of the sixteenth century.   This
work is generally regarded as the fruit of Cui's
maturity.   The subject is more suited to his
temperament than Heine's " Ratcliff," and lends
itself to the frequent employment of a chorus.
Here Cui has been very successful, especially
in the lighter choruses written in Italian dance
rhythms, such as the tarantella " The moon
rides in the clear bright sky," in the third act,
and the graceful valse-like chorus " Far o'er
the sea."   The love duet between Catarina
and Rodolfo is preferred by many to the great
love duet in *Ratcliff*.   Cui, whose heroines are
more convincing than his male types, has
found congenial material in Catarina and
Tisbe, who have been described as " Woman in
Society and Woman outside it " ; thus com-
bining in two typical personalities " all women
and all womanhood."   There is power, too, in
the purely dramatic moments, as when Ascanio
addresses the populace.   The opera concludes
with a fine elegiac chorus, in which the character of the period and locality—mediæval
Italy, tragic and intense—is not unsuccessfully
reflected.

In *Angelo* Cui made a supreme effort to achieve
breadth of style and to break through the limitations he had imposed upon himself by adopting

the methods and peculiarities of such composers as Schumann and Chopin. But this effort seems to have been followed by a speedy reaction. After the appearance of *Angelo* his manner becomes more distinctly finical and artificial. His military duties and his literary work made increasing demands on his time, and the flow of inspiration dropped below its highest level. Songs and miniatures for pianoforte were now his chief preoccupation, and, greater undertakings being perhaps out of the question, he became absorbed in the cult of small and finished forms, and fell increasingly under the influence of Schumann. It was at this time that he wrote the additional act for *The Captive in the Caucasus*, to which reference has already been made. Here the contrast between the simplicity and sincerity of his first style, and the formal polish and " preciousness " of his middle period, is very pronounced. The use of local colour in *The Captive in the Caucasus* is not very convincing. Cui is no adept in the employment of Oriental themes, and the Caucasus has never been to him the source of romantic inspiration it has proved to so many other Russian poets and composers.

Another four-act opera *The Saracen*, the subject taken from a play by the elder Dumas entitled "Charles VII. chez ses grands Vasseaux," was first performed at the Maryinsky Theatre in St. Petersburg in 1899, and revived by the Private Opera Company at Moscow in 1902. The subject is gloomy and highly dramatic, with sensational elements almost as lurid as anything in *William Ratcliff*. The interest of the opera fluctuates between the love of the King for Agnes Sorel—two figures which stand out in relief from the dark historical background of that period, when Jeanne d'Arc was fighting the battles of her weak and indolent sovereign—and the domestic affairs of the saturnine Count Saverny and his wife Bérangère ; complicated by the inner drama which is carried on in the soul of the Saracen slave Jakoub, who is in love with the Countess, and finally murders her husband at her instigation. As usual, Cui is most successful in the purely lyrical numbers—the love scenes between the King and Agnes Sorel. Here the music, almost effeminately tender, has that touching and sensuous quality which caused a celebrated French critic to write of Cui as " the Bellini of the North." The " berceuse," sung, strangely enough, by the harsh Count de Saverny as he keeps watch over the King's son on the threshold of his bed-chamber, is a strikingly original number which should be better known in the concert-room.

Le Flibustier, composed between 1888-1889, was dedicated to that distinguished amateur the Countess Mercy-Argenteau, whose influence counted for so much in Cui's later musical development. This work, written to a French libretto from a play by Jean Richepin, was originally produced at the Opéra Comique, Paris, in 1894. It is described as a " Comédie lyrique en trois actes." It is frankly French in style and contains some graceful and effective music, but lacks the natural emotion and ardour which in Ratcliff and Angelo atone for some limitations of expression and for the lack of unity of style.

An opera in one act, Mam'selle Fifi, based upon Guy de Maupassant's well-known tale of the Franco-Prussian war, was produced by the Private Opera Company at the Hermitage Theatre in the autumn of 1903. The work was well received by the public. The scene is laid in a chateau near Rouen which is occupied by a detachment of Prussians and their commanding officers. Bored by their life of inaction, the officers induce some young women from Rouen to come and amuse them. They entertain them at dinner, and sub-lieutenant von Eirich (nicknamed Mam'selle Fifi) pays attention to the patriotic Rachel ; but while at table he irritates her to such a degree by his insulting remarks and vulgar jokes that she seizes a knife and stabs him mortally in the throat. Afterwards she makes her escape. Kashkin says : " The music

of this opera flows on smoothly in concise declamatory scenes, only interrupted from time
to time by the chorus of officers, and the light-
hearted songs of Amanda. Rachel's aria introduces a more tragic note. The music is so
closely welded to the libretto that it appears
to be an essential part of it, clothing with
vitality and realism scenes which would otherwise be merely the dry bones of opera."

While I was in Russia in the spring of 1901,
Cui played to me a " dramatic scene," or one-
act opera, entitled *A Feast in Time of Plague.*
It proved to be a setting of a curious poem by
Poushkin which he pretended to have translated
from Wilson's " City of the Plague." Walsingham, a young English nobleman, dares to indulge
in " impious orgies " during the visitation of
the Great Plague. The songs of the revellers
are interrupted at intervals by a funeral march,
as the dead-cart goes its round to collect its
victims. Cui has set Poushkin's poem word for
word, consequently this little work is more
closely modelled upon Dargomijsky's *The Stone
Guest* than any other of his operas. When I
heard the work, I was under the impression that
it was intended only as a dramatic cantata,
but it was afterwards produced as an opera
at the New Theatre, Moscow, in the autumn of
1901. The song sung by Walsingham's mistress, Mary (" Time was "), which is Scotch in

character, has considerable pathetic charm, and struck me as the most spontaneous number in the work, which, on the whole, seems an effort to fit music not essentially tragic in character to a subject of the gloomiest nature.

In summing up Cui's position as a composer, I must return to my assertion that it is paradoxical. First, we may conclude from the preponderance of operatic music and songs that Cui is more gifted as a vocal than as an instrumental composer ; that, in fact, he needs a text to bring out his powers of psychological analysis. But when we come to examine his music, the methods—and even the mannerisms— of such instrumental composers as Chopin and Schumann are reflected in all directions. A style obviously founded on Schumann will necessarily lack the qualities which we are accustomed to regard as essential to a great operatic style. Cui has not the luminous breadth and powerful flow of simple and effective melody which we find in the older type of opera; nor the pre-eminent skill in declamation which is indispensable to the newer forms of music-drama. His continuous use of arioso becomes monotonous and ineffective, because, with him, the clear edges of melody and recitative seem perpetually blurred. This arises partly from the fact that Cui's melody, though delicate and refined, is not strongly individual. He is not a plagiarist in the worst sense of the word, but the influences which a stronger composer would have cast off at maturity seem to obtain a stronger hold on him as time goes on. His talent reminds me of those complex recipes for pot-pourri which we find in the day-books of our great-grandmothers. It is compounded of many more or less delightful ingredients : French predilections, Schumannesque mannerisms, some essence distilled from the grace and passion of Chopin, a dash of Russian sincerity—a number of fragrant and insidious aromas, in which the original element of individuality is smothered in the rose leaves and lavender winnowed from other people's gardens. Then there is a second perplexing consideration which follows the study of Cui's music. Possessed of this fragrant, but not robust, talent, Cui elects to apply it to themes of the ultra-romantic type with all their grisly accompaniments of moonlit heaths, blood-stained daggers, vows of vengeance, poison-cups, and the rest. It is as though a Herrick were posing as a John Webster. Surely in these curious discrepancies between the artist's temperament and his choice of subject and methods of treatment we find the reason why of all Cui's operas not one has taken a permanent hold on the public taste in Russia or abroad. And this in spite of their lyrical charm and graceful workmanship.

Cui is now the sole remaining member of

" the invincible band " who originally gathered
round Balakirev for the purpose of founding a
national school of music. He is now in his
eightieth year, but still composes and keeps up
his interest in the Russian musical world.
Within the last three years he has published
a four-act opera on the subject of Poushkin's
tale, " The Captain's Daughter."[1]

---

[1] The opera was produced in St. Petersburg in February,
1911, the Emperor and Empress being present.   It will be
given shortly by the Zimin Opera Company, in Moscow.
Published by Jurgenson, Moscow.

CHAPTER XII

RIMSKY-KORSAKOV

A contemporary critic has pointed to Rimsky-Korsakov and Tchaikovsky as having, between them, built up Russian music to its present proud condition, " constructing their majestic edifice upon the everlasting foundation laid by Glinka." Making some allowance for grandiloquence of language, this observation is particularly true as applied to Rimsky-Korsakov, for not only was he consistently true to the national ideal in all his works, but during his long activity as a teacher he trained a whole group of distinguished musicians—Liadov, Arensky, Ippolitov-Ivanov Grechyaninov, Tcherepnin, Stravinsky—who have all added their stones to the building up of this temple of Russian art. At the same time, we must regard Rimsky-Korsakov as the last of those national composers who chose to build with exclusively local materials and in purely Russian style. The younger generation are shaping their materials under more varied influences. Rimsky-Korsakov, therefore, stands out in the history of Russian opera as one of the most distinguished and distinctively racial composers of that circle to whom we owe the inauguration of the national school of music in Russia.

The subject of this chapter was born in the little village of Tikvin, in the government of Novgorod, on March 6th, 1844, and, until he was twelve years old, he continued to live on his father's estate, among the lakes and forests of northern Russia, where music was interwoven with every action of rustic life. His gifts were precocious ; between six and seven he began to play the pianoforte, and made some attempts at composition before he was nine. It was almost a matter of tradition that the men of the Korsakov family should enter the navy ; consequently in 1856, Nicholas Andreivich was sent to the Naval College at St. Petersburg, where he remained for six years. Not without difficulty he managed to continue his pianoforte lessons on Sundays and holidays with the excellent teacher Kanillé. The actual starting point of his musical career, however, was his introduction to Balakirev and his circle. From this congenial companionship Rimsky-Korsakov was abruptly severed in 1863, when he was ordered to sea in the cruiser " Almaz." The ship was absent on foreign service for three years, during which she practically made the round of the world. While on this voyage Rimsky-Korsakov wrote and revised a Symphony, Op. 1 in E Minor, and surely never was an orchestral work composed under stranger or less propitious conditions. Balakirev performed this work at one of the concerts of the Free School of Music in the winter of 1866. It was the first symphony ever composed by a Russian, and the music, though not strong, is agreeable ; but like many other early *opus* numbers it bears evidence of strong external influences.

In the chapters dealing with Balakirev and his circle I have given a picture of the social and artistic conditions in St. Petersburg to which the young sailor returned in the autumn of 1865. In common with other members of this school, Rimsky-Korsakov's musical development at this time was carried on as it were *à rebours*, Schumann, Berlioz, Liszt and Glinka being his early ideals and models. During the years of his pupilage with Balakirev, he composed, besides his first symphony, the Symphonic Picture " Sadko," a Fantasia on Servian Themes, the Symphony with an Oriental programme entitled " Antar," and the opera *The Maid of Pskov*, now usually given abroad under the title of *Ivan the Terrible*. In his " Chronicle of my Musical Life " Rimsky-Korsakov shows clearly that after passing through a phase of

blind idolatry for Balakirev and his methods, he
began, largely by reason of his orderly, industrious, and scrupulously conscientious
nature, to feel the need of a more academic
course of training. He realised the defects in
his theoretical education most keenly when,
in 1871, Asanchievsky, who had just succeeded Zaremba as Director of the St. Petersburg Conservatoire, offered him a post as
professor of practical composition and also
the direction of the orchestral class. Urged
by his friends, and prompted by a certain
self-assurance which he asserts was born of
his ignorance, Rimsky-Korsakov accepted the
post, being permitted at the same time to
remain in the naval service. Although he
had composed " Sadko," " Antar," and other
attractive and well-sounding compositions, he
had worked, so far, more or less intuitively
and had not been grounded in the particular
subjects which form the curriculum of a musical
academy. Probably it mattered much less
than his scrupulous rectitude prompted him
to suppose, that he felt unfit to lecture upon
rondo-form, and had his work as a conductor
yet to learn. The main thing was that he
brought a fresh, breezy, and wholly Russian
current of thought into the stuffy atmosphere of pedantic classicism which must have
been engendered under Zaremba's direc-

torate.[1] Indeed, according to his own modest account, things seem to have gone well with the orchestral and instrumentation classes. From this time, however, began that strong reaction in favour of classicism and " the schools," upon which his progressive friends looked with dismay ; to them his studies appeared merely the cult of musical archæology—a retrogressive step to be deeply deplored. On the other hand Tchaikovsky hailed it as a sign of grace and repentance. " Rimsky-Korsakov," writes the composer of the " Pathetic " symphony to N. von Meck, in 1877, " is the one exception (in the matter of conceit and stiff-necked pride) to the rest of the new Russian school. He was overcome by despair when he realised how many profitable years he had lost and that he was following a road which led nowhere. He began to study with such zeal that during one summer he achieved innumerable exercises in counterpoint and sixty-four fugues, ten of which he sent me for inspection." Rimsky-Korsakov may have felt himself braced and strengthened by

[1] It will be remembered that Zaremba was satirized in Moussorgsky's humorous Scena " The Musician's Peep show " as that " denizen of cloudland " who used to deliver to his bewildered classes inspired dictums something in this style :

> " Mark my words : the minor key
> Is the source of man's first downfall ;
> But the major still can give
> Salvation to your erring souls."

this severe course of musical theory ; it may have been a relief to his extremely sensitive artistic conscience to feel that henceforward he he could rely as much on experience as on intuition ; but his remorse for the past—supposing him ever to have felt the sting of such keen regret—never translated itself into the apostasy of his earlier principles. After the sixty-four fugues and the exhaustive study of Bach's works, he continued to walk with Berlioz and Liszt in what Zaremba would have regarded as the way of sinners, because in his opinion it coincided with the highway of musical progress, as well as with his natural inclinations. He knew the forms demanded by his peculiar temperament. Genius, and even superior talent, almost invariably possess this intuition. No one should have known better than Tchaikovsky that in spite of well-intentioned efforts to push a composer a little to the right or the left, the question of form remains—and will always remain—self-selective. Rimsky-Korsakov, after, as before, his initiation into classicism, chose the one path open to the honest artist—musician, painter, or poet—the way of individuality.

In 1873 Rimsky-Korsakov, at the suggestion of the Grand Duke Constantine, was appointed Inspector of Naval Bands, in which capacity he had great opportunities for practical experiments in instrumentation. At this time, he tells us, he went deeply into the study of acoustics and the construction and special qualities of the instruments of the orchestra. This appointment practically ended his career as an officer on the active list, at which he must have felt considerable relief, for with all his " ideal conscientiousness " it is doubtful whether he would ever have made a great seaman. The following letter, written to Cui during his first cruise on the " Almaz," reveals nothing of the cheery optimism of a true " sea-dog "; but it does reveal the germ of " Sadko " and of much finely descriptive work in his later music. " What a thing to be thankful for is the naval profession," he writes ; " how glorious, how agreeable, how elevating ! Picture yourself sailing across the North Sea. The sky is grey, murky, and colourless ; the wind screeches through the rigging ; the ship pitches so that you can hardly keep your legs ; you are constantly besprinkled with spray, and sometimes washed from head to foot by a wave ; you feel chilly, and rather sick. Oh, a sailor's life is really jolly ! "

But if his profession did not benefit greatly by his services, his art certainly gained something from his profession. It is this actual contact with nature, choral in moments of stress and violence, as well as in her milder rhythmic moods, that we hear in " Sadko " the orchestral fantasia, and in *Sadko* the opera. We feel the weight of the wind against our bodies and the sting of the brine on our faces. We are left buffeted and breathless by the elemental fury of the storm when the Sea King dances with almost savage vigour to the sound of Sadko's *gusslee*, or by the vehement realism of the shipwreck in " Scheherezade."

Of his early orchestral works, " Sadko " displays the national Russian element, while the second symphony, " Antar," shows his leaning towards Oriental colour. These compositions prove the tendency of his musical temperament, but they do not show the more delicate phases of his work. They are large and effective canvases and display extraordinary vigour and much poetical sentiment. But the colour, although laid on with science, is certainly applied with a palette knife. We must go to his operas and songs to discover what this artist can do in the way of discriminating and exquisite brush-work. In speaking of Korsakov's work, it seems natural to drop into the language of the studio, for, to me, he always appears as a descriptive poet, or still more as a landscape painter who has elected music for his medium. Gifted with a brilliant imagination, yet seeing with a realist's vision, he is far more attracted to what is capable of definite expression than towards abstract thought. Lyrical he is ; but more in the sense of Wordsworth than of Shelley. With a nature to which the objective world makes so strong an appeal, impassioned self-revelation is not a primary and urgent necessity. In this respect he is the antithesis of Tchaikovsky. The characteristic vein of realism which we have found in all our Russian composers, and most strongly marked in Moussorgsky, exists also in Korsakov ; but in his case it is controlled by an almost fastidious taste, and a love of beautiful details which sometimes stifle the fundamental idea of his work. From these preliminary remarks you will have formed for yourselves some idea as to the spirit in which this composer would approach the sphere of dramatic music.

He came to it first by way of Russian history. The *Maid of Pskov* (" Pskovityanka " [1]) was completed in 1872, and performed in St. Petersburg in January, 1873. The caste was a remarkably good one : Ivan the Terrible—Petrov ; Michael Toucha—Orlov ; Prince Tokmakov—Melnikov ; Olga—Platonova ; Vlassievna—Leonova. Napravnik was the conductor. Opinions as to its success vary greatly, but the early fate of the work does not seem to have been happy, partly because, as Stassov

[1] This opera is now given abroad under the title of *Ivan the Terrible*, which brings home to foreigners some realisation of its period and of its gloomy central figure.

says, the public, accustomed only to Italian opera, were incapable of appreciating this attempt at serious historical music-drama, and partly because the opera suffered severely at the hands of the critics and the Censor.

In *The Maid of Pskov* (" Ivan the Terrible ") Rimsky-Korsakov started under the influence of Dargomijsky's *The Stone Guest*, to the theory of which all the new Russian school at first subscribed. Afterwards Rimsky-Korsakov, like Tchaikovsky, alternated between lyrical and declamatory opera and occasionally effected a union of the two styles. In *The Maid of Pskov* the solo parts consisted at first chiefly of mezzo-recitative of a somewhat dry quality, relieved by great variety of orchestral colour in the accompaniments. The choruses, on the other hand, were very national in style and full of melody and movement. The work underwent many revisions before it appeared in its present form. In 1877 the composer added the Overture to the Prologue and the Entr'actes. At this time he was assisting to edit the " monumental " edition of Glinka's operas which the master's sister Liudmilla Shestakov was bringing out at her own expense. " This occupation," says Rimsky-Korsakov, " proved to be an unexpected schooling, and enabled me to penetrate into every detail of Glinka's structural style." The first revision of *The Maid of Pskov* and the editing of *A Life for the Tsar* and *Russlan* were carried on simultaneously. Therefore it is not surprising that Rimsky-Korsakov set himself to polish and tone down many youthful crudities which appeared in the original score of his own opera. Cui, Moussorgsky and Stassov, although at first they approved his resolution to revise the work, showed some disappointment at the results ; while the composer's wife deeply regretted its first form. It was evident to all that what the work had gained in structure and technical treatment it had lost in freshness and lightness of touch. In 1878 the composer offered it once more, in this revised edition, to Baron Kistner, Director of the Imperial Opera, but without success. The work was laid aside until 1894, when it was again re-modelled and revived by the initiative of an amateur society at the Panaevsky Theatre, St. Petersburg, in April 1895. In this version it was mounted at the Imperial Opera House, Moscow, when Shaliapin appeared in the part of Ivan the Terrible. On this occasion the opera was preceded by the Prologue *Boyarinya Vera Sheloga*, composed in 1899. Its reception was extremely enthusiastic, and in the autumn of 1903—thirty years after its first performance—it was restored to the repertory of the St. Petersburg Opera.

The subject of *The Maid of Pskov* is taken from one of Mey's dramas, dealing with an episode

from the history of the sixteenth century when
Ivan the Terrible, jealous of the enterprise and
independence of the twin cities of Pskov and
Novgorod, resolved to humble their pride and
curtail their power. Novgorod fell ; but the
awful doom of Pskov was mitigated by the
Tsar's discovery that Olga, who passes for the
daughter of Prince Tokmakov, the chief magis-
trate of the city, was in reality his own natural
child, the daughter of Vera Sheloga whom he
had loved in youth, and for whose memory the
tyrant could still feel some spark of affection and
some pangs of remorse. One of the finest
moments in the opera is the summoning of the
Vêche, or popular assembly, in the second act.
The great city of mediæval Russia, with all it
contained of characteristic energy, of almost
Elizabethan vigour and enterprise, is set before
us in this musical picture. The stress and anger
of the populace ; the fine declamatory monologue for Prince Tokmakov ; the song sung by
Michael Toucha, Olga's lover, who leads the
rebellious spirits of Pskov ; the impressive
knell of the tocsin calling the citizens to attend
the *Vêche*—all unite to form a dramatic scene
worthy to compare with the finale of Glinka's
Russlan and Liudmilla, or with the *Slavsia*
(the chorus of acclamation) which makes the
Kremlin ring in *A Life for the Tsar*. Russians,
as everyone knows who has lived in their

country, have a passion for bells, and often
reproduce their effects in their music : witness the orchestral prelude " Dawn Breaking
over Moscow " in Moussorgsky's *Khovanstchina*
and the familiar Overture "1812 " by Tchaikovsky. The bell effects in *The Maid of Pskov* are
extraordinarily moving. Recalling, as it does,
traditions of political liberty and free speech,
this bell—so I have been told—appeared in the
eyes of the Censor the most objectionable and
revolutionary character in the whole opera.
The scenes in which the old nurse Vlassievna
takes part—a *Nianka* is so much a part of
domestic life in Russia that no play or opera
seems complete without one—are full of quiet
humour and tenderness. The love-music for
Michael and Olga is graceful rather than
passionate, more warmth and tenderness being
shown in the relations between the young girl
and the Tsar, for whom she has an instinctive
filial feeling. Psychologically the later scenes
in the opera, in which we see the relentless and
superstitious heart of Ivan gradually softening
under the influence of paternal love, interest and
touch us most deeply. In 1899 Rimsky-Korsakov added, at Shaliapin's request, the aria now
sung by the Tsar in his tent, in the last act.
This number reveals much of Ivan's strange and
complex nature ; in it he is alternately the
despot, the remorseful lover, and the weary old

man aching for a daughter's tenderness. Cheshi-kin points out the remarkable effect which the composer produces at the end of this solo, where the key fluctuates between B flat major and G minor, with the final cadence in D major, giving a sense of weakness and irresolution appropriate to Ivan's weariness of body and soul. The final scene in the opera, in which the death of Olga snatches from the wretched Tsar his last hope of redemption through human love, has but one fault : that of almost unendurable poignancy.

With the accession of Alexander III. in 1881 began a more encouraging period for Russian composers. The Emperor showed a distinct predilection for native opera, and particularly for the works of Tchaikovsky. A series of musical events, such as the raising of the Glinka monument at Smolensk by national subscription (1885), Rubinstein's jubilee (1889), the publication of Serov's critical works, and the public funeral accorded to Tchaikovsky (1893), all had his approval and support, and in some instances were carried out entirely at his own expense. Henceforth the repertory of Russian music-dramas was not permitted to languish, and after the death of Tchaikovsky, the Direc-torate of the Opera Houses seems to have turned to Rimsky-Korsakov in the expectation of at least one novelty in each season. Consequently his achievement in this sphere of music far exceeds that of his immediate predecessors and contemporaries, amounting in all to thirteen operatic works. Of this number, none can be said to have been really a failure, and only one has dropped completely out of the repertory of the two capitals and the provinces, although some are undoubtedly more popular than others. To speak in detail of all these works would require a volume devoted to the subject. I propose, therefore, to give a brief account of the greater number, devoting a little more space to those which seem most likely ever to be given in this country.

The two operas which follow in 1879 and 1880, while possessing many features in common with each other, differ wholly in character from *The Maid of Pskov*. In *A Night in May* and *The Snow Maiden* (" Sniegourochka ") the dramatic realism of historical opera gives place to lyrical inspiration and the free flight of fancy. *A Night in May* is taken from one of Gogol's Malo-Russian tales. *The Snow Maiden : a Legend of Springtide* is founded upon a national epic by the dramatist Ostrovsky. Both operas offer that combination of legendary, picturesque and humorous elements which always exercised an attraction for Rimsky-Korsakov's musical temperament. In both works he shows that he has attained to a supreme mastery of orchestration, and the

accompaniments in every instance go far to
atone for his chief weakness—a certain dryness
of melodic invention, except where the style
of the melody coincides with that of the folk
tune. *A Night in May* reveals the composer
as a humorist of delicate and fantastic quality.
Rimsky-Korsakov's humour is entirely native
and individual, having nothing akin to the
broad, saturnine, biting wit of Moussorgsky,
nor to the vigorous humour of Borodin's comic
villains Eroshka and Skoula, in *Prince Igor*.
Rimsky-Korsakov can be sprightly, fanciful,
and arch ; his humour is more often expressed
by witty orchestral comments upon the text
than by the melodies themselves.

The first performance of *A Night in May*
took place at the Maryinsky Theatre, St.
Petersburg, in January 1880, but it was soon
withdrawn from the repertory and only revived
in 1894, at the Imperial Mikhaïlovsky Theatre.
In 1896 it was given at the Folk Theatre, in
Prague ; and produced for the first time in
Moscow in 1898. Besides being more lyrical
and melodious in character than *The Maid of
Pskov*, this opera shows evidences of Rimsky-
Korsakov's intervening studies in the contrapuntal treatment of the choruses and concerted
numbers. The scene of *A Night in May*,
as in several of Gogol's tales, is laid near
the village of Dikanka in Little Russia. Levko

(tenor), the son of the Golova or Headman of the hamlet, is in love with Hanna (mezzo-soprano), but his father will not give consent to the marriage, because he admires the girl himself. In the first act Levko is discovered serenading Hanna in the twilight. Presently she emerges from her cottage and they sing a love duet. Then Hanna asks Levko to tell her the legend of the old deserted manor house that stands beside the mere. He appears reluctant, but finally relates how once a Pan (a Polish gentleman) dwelt there with the Pannochka, his fair daughter. He was a widower, and married again, but his second wife proved to be a witch who caused him to turn his daughter out of the house. The girl in despair drowned herself in the mere and became a Roussalka. She haunted the lake at night, and at last, catching her stepmother perilously near the edge of the water, she lured her down into its depths. Levko tells his sweetheart that the present owner wants to erect a distillery on the site of the mansion and has already sent a distiller there. The lovers then say good-bye and Hanna re-enters her cottage. Next follows an episode in which the village drunkard Kalenik (baritone) tries to dance the *Gopak* while the village girls sing a chorus of mockery. When the stage is empty the Headman (bass) appears and sings a song to Hanna in which,

while he implores her to listen to his love, he
tells her that she ought to be very proud to have
him for a suitor. Hanna, however, will have
nothing to say to him. Levko, who has overheard this scene and wishes to teach his father
the lesson " of leaving other people's sweet-
hearts alone," points him out to some woodcutters on their way home from work and
encourages them to seize him and hold him up
to ridicule. The Headman, however, pushes
them aside and makes his escape. The act
ends with a song for Levko and the chorus of
woodcutters.

In the second act the curtain rises on the
interior of the Headman's hut, where, with his
sister-in-law and the Distiller, he is discussing
the fate of the old manor house. Levko and
the woodcutters are heard singing their im-
pertinent song outside the house. The Headman, beside himself with rage, rushes out and
catches one of the singers, who is dressed in a
sheepskin coat turned inside out. Now follows
a farcical scene of tumult ; the singer escapes,
and the Headman, by mistake, shuts up his
sister-in-law in a closet. There is a general hue
and cry after the culprit and the wrong people
are continually being arrested, including the
village drunkard Kalenik. In the last act
Levko is discovered singing a serenade to the
accompaniment of the Little-Russian *bandoura*

before the haunted manor house by the mere. Apparently the wraith of the Pannochka appears at one of the windows. Then the Roussalki are seen on the edge of the lake, where they sit weaving chaplets of water-plants. At the request of the Pannochka-Roussalka, Levko leads the choral dances with his *bandoura*. Afterwards the Pannochka rewards him by giving him a letter in which she orders the Headman not to oppose Levko's marriage with Hanna. When the dawn breaks, the Headman, accompanied by the Scrivener, the Desyatsky (a kind of village superintendent) and others, arrive upon the scene, still in search of the culprit, who proves to be his own son. Levko gives the letter to his father, who feels obliged to consent to the young people's marriage. Hanna with her girl friends now come upon the scene and the opera ends with a chorus of congratulations to the bride and bridegroom.

Perhaps the most graceful of all Rimsky-Korsakov's early operas is *The Snow Maiden*, in the music of which he has reflected the indelible impressions of a childhood spent amid sylvan surroundings. There is something of the same vernal impulse in pages of *The Snow Maiden* of which we are conscious in Wagner's Forest Murmurs. What a profound loss to the poetry of a nation is the disappearance of its forests ! It is not only the rivers which grow drier and poorer for the ruthless wielding of the axe. None of Korsakov's operas show a greater profusion of little lyrical gems than this one, which embodies the Slavonic legend of the spring. The Snow Maiden is the daughter of jolly King Frost and the Fairy Spring. She is brought up by her parents in the solitary wintry woods, because envious Summer has foretold her death when the first ray of sunlight and love shall touch her icy beauty. But the child is attracted by the songs of the shepherd Lel, whom she has seen sporting with the village girls in the meadows. She longs to lead a mortal's life, and her parents unwillingly consent, and confide her to a worthy peasant couple who promise to treat her as a daughter. The Fairy Spring bids her child to seek her should she be in trouble—" you will find me by the lakeside in the valley and I will grant your request whatever it may be " are the parting words of her mother. Then the Snow Maiden begins her sad mortal existence. She admires the gay shepherd, who does not respond to her fancy. Mizgyr, a young Tatar merchant, falls madly in love with her, and for her sake deserts his promised bride Kupava. The passionate Kupava appears at the Court of the king of Berendei and demands justice. The fickle lover makes but one defence : " O, Tsar," he says, " if you could but see the Snow Maiden." At

this juncture she appears, and the King, behold-
ing her beauty, cannot believe that she is
heartless. He promises her hand and rich
rewards to any one of his young courtiers who
can woo and win her before the next sunrise.
In a wonderful forest scene we are shown the
arcadian revels of the people of Berendei. Lel
makes love to the deserted Kupava; while
Mizgyr pursues the Snow Maiden with his
passionate addresses. The wood-spirits interfere on her behalf and Mizgyr gets lost in the
forest. The Snow Maiden sees Lel and Kupava wandering together under the trees and
endeavours to separate them, but in vain. In
her trouble she remembers her mother and seeks
her by the lake-side. The Fairy Spring appears,
and moved by her daughter's entreaties, she
accords her the power to love like a mortal.
When the Snow Maiden sees Mizgyr again she
loses her heart to him, and speaks of the new,
sweet power of love which she feels stirring
within her. But even as she speaks, a ray of
sunlight pierces the clouds, and, falling on the
young girl, melts her body and soul into the
rising spring waters. Mizgyr, in despair, kills
himself, and the opera closes with a song of
thanksgiving to the Midsummer Sun.

The poetical death-scene of the Snow Maiden;
Kupava's passionate love song and her incantation to the bees; the pastoral songs of the

shepherd Lel ; the folk-song choruses ; sometimes with accompaniments for the *gusslee* ; the
fairy scene in the forest and the return of the
birds with the flight of winter—these things
cannot fail to charm those who have not
altogether outgrown the glamour of the world's
youth with its belief in the personification of
natural forces.   This opera is truly national,
although it deals with legendary rather than
historical events.   This, however, as M. Camille
Bellaigue points out, does not mean that its
nationality is superficial or limited.   Speaking of
the wonderful scene in the palace of the King of
Berendei, where he is seen sitting on his throne
surrounded by a company of blind bards singing
solemn airs to the accompaniment of their
primitive harps, the French critic says : " Such
a chorus as this has nothing in common with
the official chorus of the courtiers in old-
fashioned opera.   In the amplitude and originality of the melody, in the vigour of the
arpeggio accompaniment, in the exotic savour
of the cadence and the tonality, we divine
something which belongs not merely to the
unknown but to infinitude. . . . But there is
something which the music of Rimsky-Korsakov
expresses with still greater force and charm,
with an originality which is at once both
stronger and sweeter, and that is the natural
landscape, the forms and colours, the very face

of Russia itself. In this respect the music is something more than national, it is to a certain extent native, like the soil and sky of the country."[1]

In 1889 Rimsky-Korsakov began a fourth opera, the history of which is connected with the co-operative tendency that distinguished the national school of musicians. The composition of collective works was, I believe, one of Balakirev's early ideals ; the Paraphrases, a set of clever variations on a childish theme, dedicated to Liszt by Borodin, Cui, Liadov and Rimsky-Korsakov, and the Quartet in honour of Balaiev are examples of this spirit of combination. In 1872 Gedeonov, then Director of the Opera, proposed that Borodin, Moussorgsky, Cui and Rimsky-Korsakov should each undertake one act of a ballet-opera for a plot of his own providing, entitled *Mlada*. The music was written, but lack of funds prevented the enterprise from being carried out, and each composer utilised the material left on his hands in his own way. Rimsky-Korsakov incorporated his share with the fantastic scenes of *A Night in May*. In 1889, however, he took up the subject once more and *Mlada* was completed by the autumn of the same year. Produced at the Maryinsky Theatre in October 1892, it failed to win the

[1] *Impressions Musicales et Littéraires*, par Camille Bellaigue.

success it undoubtedly deserved. In the opera
the part of Prince Mstivoy was taken by
Stravinsky, and that of the Czech minstrel,
Liumir, by Dolina. In the ballet, the Shade
of Mlada was represented by the famous
ballerina Petipa, and the Shade of Cleopatra
by Skorsiouka. The subject is taken from the
history of the Baltic Slavs in the ninth century ;
but although in this work he returns to an
historical episode, the composer does not go back
to the declamatory style of *The Maid of Pskov.*
Cheshikin considers that *Mlada* is highly effective from the theatrical point of view. Moreover, the old Slavonic character of the music
is cleverly maintained throughout, the ordinary
minor scale being replaced by the " natural
minor " (the Æolian Mode). The scenes representing the ancient Pagan customs of the Slavs
are highly picturesque and, except on the
grounds of its expensive setting, it is difficult
to understand why this work should have
passed out of the repertory of the Russian opera.

The most distinctly humorous of all Rimsky-
Korsakov's operas is the *Christmas Eve Revels,*
a subject also treated by Tchaikovsky under
the title of *Cherevichek* and re-published as *Le
Caprice d'Oxane).* The composer, as we have
seen, rarely went outside his own land for
literary material. But even within this circle
of national subjects there exist many shades

of thought and sentiment. Gogol's characters differ widely from those portrayed in such a legend as " Sadko." The Malo-Russian and Cossack population are more vivacious, and also more dreamy and sentimental, than the Great Russians. In fact the difference between the inhabitants of the Ukraine and those of the government of Novgorod is as great as that between a southern Irishman and a Yorkshire-man, and lies much in the same directions.

The *Christmas Eve Revels* opens with an orchestral introduction, " The Holy Night," descriptive of the serene beauty of the night upon which the Christ Child came into the world to put all the powers of darkness under his feet. It is based upon two calm and solemn themes, the first rather mystical in character, the second of child-like transparency. But with the rising of the curtain comes an entire change of sentiment, and we are immediately brought into an atmosphere of peculiarly national humour. This sudden change from the mystical to the grotesque recalls the Russian miracle plays of the Middle Ages. The moon and stars are shining on a Little-Russian village ; the hut of Choub the Cossack occupies the central position. Out of the chimney of one of the huts emerges the witch-woman Solokha, riding upon a broom-stick. She sings a very old " Kolyadka," or Christmas song. Now the Devil appears upon the scene to enjoy the beauty of the night. These shady characters confide their grievances to each other. Solokha has a weakness for the Cossack Choub, but her son Vakoula the Smith is making love to Choub's beautiful daughter Oxana, and this is a great hindrance to her own plans, so she wishes to put an end to the courtship if possible. To-night Choub is going to supper with the Sacristan and Vakoula is sure to take that opportunity of visiting his sweetheart, who is, however, deaf to all his entreaties. The Devil has his own grudge against Vakoula, because he has drawn a caricature of his satanic majesty upon the wall of the village church. The Devil and the Witch decide to help each other. They steal the moon and stars and fly off, leaving the village plunged in darkness. Ridiculous complications occur. Choub and the Sacristan go out, but wander round in a circle, and after a time find themselves back at the Cossack's hut, where Vakoula is making love to Oxana. In the darkness Vakoula mistakes Choub for a rival lover and drives him out of his own courtyard. Matters are set right by the return of the moon and stars, who have managed to escape from the Devil and his companion.

In the end Oxana declares she will only accept Vakoula on condition that he presents her with a pair of the Empress's shoes. The

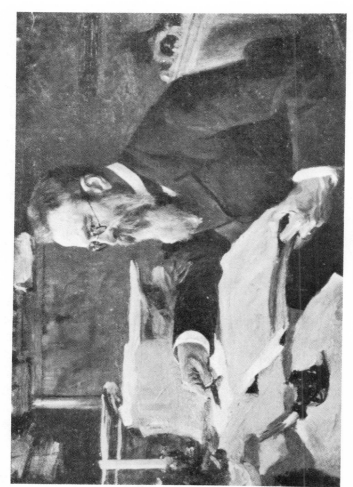

RIMSKY-KORSAKOV
From a portrait by Repin

Smith departs upon this unpromising errand.
Thanks to his Cossack friends he finds his way
into the palace. During the festivities of the
evening, the Cossacks are called upon to
perform their national dances in order to amuse
the Court. The Empress, in high good humour,
is informed of Vakoula's quest, and good-
naturedly gives him her shoes. He returns in
triumph to his native village and marries his
capricious beauty.

Although Rimsky-Korsakov had apparently
abandoned the original operatic theories of the
new school, Dargomijsky's methods must still
have exercised some attraction for him, for in
1897 he set Poushkin's dramatic duologue
Mozart and Salieri without making the least
change in the text, and dedicated it to the
memory of the composer of *The Stone Guest.*
Its production by the Private Opera Company
at Moscow, in 1898, was memorable for a
wonderful interpretation by Shaliapin of the
part of Salieri. Mozart (tenor) was sung by
Shkafer, the conductor being Esposito. The
same artists sang in the work when it was given
in St. Petersburg in the following year. In
Mozart and Salieri, which is not called an opera
but merely a dramatic scene, we have melodic
recitative without any relapse into cantilena.
The declamation of the two musical heroes is
relieved and embellished by apt comments

heard in the accompaniments. For instance, when Salieri speaks of a " simple scale," a scale is heard in the orchestra ; when he mentions an organ, a pedal point is introduced into the accompaniment. This sounds extremely naïve, but in reality this miniature music-drama is remarkably clever as regards craftsmanship and musical repartee. The style of the work is completely in keeping with the period—the eighteenth century—and excellent imitations of Mozart's style occur when the master sits down to the piano and plays two tiny movements, *allegretto semplice* and *grave.*

Rimsky-Korsakov wrote one more work in a similar style to *Mozart and Salieri,* the Dramatic Prologue in one act *Boyarinya Vera Sheloga,* which was really intended to precede *The Maid of Pskov* and elucidate the history of Olga, the heroine of that opera. The little work was first performed in this way by the Private Opera Company at Moscow in 1898. It tells in fuller detail the story of the two sisters Vera and Nadejda Nassonov, to which Prince Tokmakov refers in his conversation with Matouta in the first act of *The Maid of Pskov,* and introduces the Boyard Ivan Sheloga and Vlassievna, the faithful nurse of the orphaned Olga. The work contains a charming lullaby sung by Vera to her little daughter. This number is published apart from the Prologue and has become extremely popular with amateur singers.

Sadko, A Legendary Opera (Opera-bylina), in seven tableaux, composed between 1895-1896, is a compromise between lyrical and declamatory opera so skilfully effected that this work has come to be regarded as the perfect fruit of Rimsky-Korsakov's maturity, and the most complete exposition of his artistic creed. The work was produced by the Private Opera Company at Moscow in December, 1897, and introduced to St. Petersburg by the same company in the following year.

Sekar-Rojansky, a young tenor possessed of a beautiful fresh voice, created the title rôle. The work was received with extraordinary enthusiasm, and shortly afterwards the Directorate of the Imperial Operas, who had at first refused to consider it, took up the opera and staged it with great magnificence. A. M. Vaznietsov, brother of the artist who painted the frescoes of the cathedral of Kiev, was sent to Old Novgorod and other parts of northern Russia to make sketches for the scenery. The archæological details and the landscapes on the margin of Lake Ilmen were faithfully reproduced. The first performance took place at the Maryinsky Theatre in January, 1901, under Napravnik's direction ; on this occasion Davidov impersonated the hero.

At the outset of his career, Rimsky-Korsakov was attracted by this legend of the eleventh century belonging to the Cycle of Novgorod. Sadko is a poor but adventurous minstrel, often referred to in the folk-songs as " the nightingale of Novgorod." He does not win his renown by chivalrous actions and prowess in the field, like Ilya Mouramets and the heroes of the Cycle of Kiev. The Novgorodians were an energetic but commercial race. Sadko, driven to desperation by poverty, lays a wager against the rich merchants of Novgorod that he will catch gold-fish in Lake Ilmen. The merchants stake their goods, the minstrel all he has—a far more valuable asset—" his dare-devil head," as the legends say. How Sadko charms the Sea King by his singing and playing upon the *gusslee*, how he secures the gold-fish and, with them, all the wealth of Novgorod, is told in the ballad of Nejata, the young minstrel. After a while Sadko grows restless in spite of his good fortune. He sets sail with his fleet of merchant vessels in search of fresh adventures. The ships are overtaken by a tempest, and it becomes necessary to propitiate the wrath of the Sea King. Lots are cast, and the unlucky one invariably falls to Sadko. It is characteristic of the astute merchant-hero that he cheats in every possible way in order to avert his doom! Finally, he is cast overboard and drifts away

upon a plank, clinging to his cherished *gusslee* :
a pagan Jonah; a Slavonic Arion. His adventures at the bottom of the seas ; the Sea King's
welcome to his virtuoso-guest ; his efforts to
marry Sadko to one of his daughters ; the
procession of these beautiful sea-maidens—
some three hundred in number—demanding of
Sadko a judgment far more difficult and delicate
than anything Paris was called upon to pro-
nounce ; the cleverness with which Sadko
extricates himself from the difficult situation,
by selecting the only plain lady of the party, so
that there is no risk of permanently falling in
love with her and forgetting his wife in Novgorod ; the wild glee of the Sea King at the
playing of the famous minstrel, and his dance,
which imperils the earth and can only be stopped
by the shattering of the precious *gusslee* ;
Sadko's return to his faithful and anxious wife
—all these incidents are set forth in the opera
with a Wagnerian luxury of stage accessories
and scenic effects.

As regards structure, *Sadko* combines—as I
have said—the lyrical and declamatory elements. It is pre-eminently a national opera
in which the composer has conveyed a truthful
picture of the customs and sentiments of an
archaic period. In *Sadko* we find many melodies
completely modal in character. The Sea Queen's
slumber song in the seventh scene is Dorian,

Sadko's aria in the fifth scene is Phrygian, and so on. The song of Nejata has an accompaniment for harps and pianino which gives the effect of the *gusslee*.

Besides the national element, Rimsky-Korsakov introduces characteristic songs of other countries. In the scene in which Sadko generously restores to the merchants the goods won from them in his wager, keeping only a fleet of merchant vessels for himself, he requests some of the foreign traders to sing the songs of their distant lands. The Varangian guest sings a song in a brisk, energetic rhythm, quite Scandinavian in character ; the Venetian complies with a graceful barcarolle, while the Indian merchant charms the audience with an Oriental melody of rare beauty. The musical interest of *Sadko* is in fact very great.

If there is any truth in the suggestion that Rimsky-Korsakov composed *Mozart and Salieri* and dedicated it to Dargomijsky as a kind of recantation of certain Wagnerian methods, such as a limited use of *leitmotifs* to which he had had recourse in *Sadko*, then his return to the purely lyrical style in his ninth opera, *The Tsar's Bride* (*Tsarsky Nievesta*), may equally have been a kind of apology to the memory of Glinka. But it seems far more probable that he worked independently of all such ideas and suited the musical style to the subject of the opera. *The Tsar's Bride,* in three acts, was produced by the Private Opera Company at Moscow in 1899, Ippolitov-Ivanov being the conductor. From Moscow it travelled first to the provinces, and reached St. Petersburg in the spring of 1900. As it is perhaps the most popular of all Rimsky-Korsakov's operas, and one that is likely to find its way abroad, it is advisable to give some account of the plot. It is based on one of Mey's dramas, the subject of which had temporarily attracted Borodin some twenty years earlier. The Oprichnik Gryaznoy falls madly in love with Martha, the beautiful daughter of a merchant of Novgorod named Sobakin; but she is betrothed to the Boyard Lykov. Gryaznoy vows she shall never marry another, and procures from Bomely, court-physician to Ivan the Terrible, a magic potion which is to help his cause. His former mistress Lioubasha overhears the conversation between the Oprichnik and Bomely. She makes a desperate effort to win Gryaznoy back to her, but in vain. In the second act the people are coming away from vespers and talking about the Tsar's choice of a bride. Martha, with two companions, comes out of the church. While she is standing alone, two men emerge from the shadow of the houses, one of whom is Ivan the Terrible in disguise. He gazes intently at Martha and then goes his way, leaving her vaguely terrified. Meanwhile Lioubasha has been watching Martha from a window. Then she in her turn goes to Bomely and asks him for some potion that will injure her rival. He replies that he will give her what she requires, but the price of it will be a kiss from her lips. Reluctantly she consents. In the third act, Lykov and Gryaznoy are seated at table with the merchant Sobakin, who has just informed them that the wedding of Lykov and Martha must be postponed. Lykov asks Gryaznoy what he would do in his place if by any chance the Tsar's choice should fall upon Martha. The Oprichnik gives an evasive answer. Meanwhile, in one of the cups of mead poured out by the host, he drops his magic potion, and when Martha joins them at table he offers it to her to drink. Suddenly the maidservant rushes in with the news that a deputation of boyards has arrived, and a moment later Maliouta enters to announce that the Tsar has chosen Martha to be his bride. In the final scene, which takes place in an apartment in the Tsar's palace, Sobakin is seen bewailing his daughter's illness. Gryaznoy enters with an order from Ivan to inquire after her health. The Oprichnik believes that her illness is caused by the potion he administered. Presently Maliouta with the rest of the Oprichniki come upon the scene. Gryaznoy informs Martha

that her former suitor Lykov, having confessed
to the fiendish design of poisoning her, has been
executed by order of the Tsar.   Martha gives a
cry and becomes unconscious.   When she
comes to herself her mind is affected, and she
mistakes Gryaznoy for her lover Lykov, calling
him "Ivan" and speaking caressingly to him.
Gryaznoy now sees that his plot for getting rid
of Lykov has been a failure.   Touched by
Martha's madness he is prepared to give himself
up to Maliouta for judgment; but the latter
gives him an opportunity of inquiring into the
deception played upon by him Bomely.   Lioubasha now comes forward and confesses that
she changed the potion.   Gryaznoy stabs her
and then imploring Martha's forgiveness,
quits the scene, while the poor mad girl, still
mistaking him for her lost lover, cries after him
"Come back to-morrow, my Ivan."

The music of *The Tsar's Bride* is melodious;
and the orchestration, though simpler than is
generally the case with Rimsky-Korsakov, is
not lacking in variety and colour.   Though by
no means the strongest of his operas, it seems to
exercise a great attraction for the public;
possibly because its nationalism is less strenu-
ously demonstrated than in some of its predecessors.

*The Legend of Tsar Saltan, of his Son the
famous and doughty Warrior, Prince Gvidon*

Saltanovich, and of the beautiful Tsarevna Liebed
(the Swan-queen), an opera in four acts with a
Prologue, the libretto drawn from Poushkin's
poem of the same title, was produced by the
Private Opera Company in Moscow in December
1906. Previously to the first performance of
the work, an orchestral suite consisting of three
of the entr'actes was played in St. Petersburg at one of the concerts of the I. R. M. S.
The work follows the model of *Sadko* rather
than that of purely lyrical operas. Here Rimsky-Korsakov makes a more extended and
systematic use of the *leitmotif*. The leading
characters, Saltan, Militrissa, Tsarevna Liebed
and the Sea Rovers, have their characteristic
themes, but a number of minor motives are
used in connection with particular sentiments
and even to represent various natural objects.
The story, which is too long to give in all its
details, deals with the adventures of Tsar
Saltan and the Three Sisters; the two elders—
recalling the story of Cinderella—are jealous of
the youngest Militrissa who marries the Tsar's
son, and during Saltan's absence from home
they revenge themselves upon her by sending
a false message announcing that she has borne
her husband a daughter instead of a son. The
tale offers a strange mixture of the fantastic
and the realistic. The opera is remarkable for
its fine orchestral numbers and the novelty and

brilliancy of its instrumentation, and for the free use of folk melodies.[1]

In his eleventh opera, *Servilia*, Rimsky-Korsakov makes one of his rare excursions in search of a subject outside Russian folk-lore or history. The libretto is based upon a drama by his favourite author Mey, but the scene of the plot is laid in Rome. In *Servilia* Rimsky-Korsakov returns once more to the declamatory style, as exemplified in *Mozart and Salieri*, without, however, entirely abandoning the use of the *leitmotif*. The first performance of the work took place at the Maryinsky Theatre in the autumn of 1902. Servilia's passionate love for the Tribune Valerius Rusticus, from which she suddenly turns on her conversion to Christianity in the last act of the opera, offers considerable opportunities for psychological delineation. But "the inward strife between her pagan passion and ascetic instincts," says Cheshikin, "is not enacted on the stage; it takes place chiefly behind the scenes and the

[1] There are no less than ten true folk-themes contained in the opera of *Tsar Saltan*. The theme of the Elder Sisters, in the Introduction, may be found in Rimsky-Korsakov's collection of National Songs, No. 24, communicated by Balakirev. The theme of the Tale of the Old Grandfather is a street cry ("Any fruit or greens"); a theme used by the Prince Gvidon is taken from a child's song, No. 66, in Korsakov's collection; others may be found in the same volume; also in the collections of Stakhovich and Prach.

spectator is shown only the result." It is not surprising that the success of the opera does not lie in the delineation of the heroine but in certain interesting details, and especially in the skilful use of local colour. The Hymn to Athena in the first act ; the Anacreontic song for Montanus in the second act (in the Mixolydian), with its characteristic figures of accompaniment for flute ; the Dance of the Mænads ; and a graceful Spinning-song for female voices in the third act, are the most successful numbers in the work. On the whole, *Servilia* is regarded by Russian critics as a retrograde step after *Sadko* and *Tsar Saltan.*

Kastchei the Immortal is described as " a legend of the autumn" in one act and three scenes, with uninterrupted music throughout. The sketch of the libretto was given to the composer by E. M. Petrovsky and is a free adaptation of a very old fairy tale. The opera was produced by the Private Opera Company in Moscow in 1902, and aroused a good deal of comment in consequence of several new procedures on the part of the composer, revealing a more decisive tendency to follow in the steps of Wagner. The charge of imitation is based upon the use of *leitmotifs* and also upon the content of the libretto, in which, as in many of Wagner's operas, the idea of redemption plays a prominent part. Kastcheievna, the daughter of the wicked

wizard Kastchei, is redeemed by intense suffering from her own jealous fury, when she lets
fall a tear, in the crystal sphere of which Kastchei
has enclosed his own fate. But Rimsky-Korsakov does not give us merely an internal drama
in the Wagnerian sense, for we see enacted upon
the stage the wholly external drama of the
rescue of the unhappy Tsarevna, spell-bound
by the evil Kastchei, at the hands of Ivan
Korolevich. The opera ends with the downfall
of the barriers which shut out the gloomy,
autumnal, sin-oppressed kingdom of Kastchei
from the happier world outside. " This symbolism," says Cheshikin, " may be taken in its
widest acceptation ; but in anything which is
freed from a despotic power, our public is
prepared to see a social tendency which is to their
taste and they applaud it with satisfaction."
Kastchei chanced to be the opera which was
represented in St. Petersburg (in March, 1905)
at the moment when Rimsky-Korsakov was
expelled from his professorship at the Conservatoire in consequence of his frank criticisms
of the existing bureaucracy, and each representation was made the occasion of an ovation
in his honour. The opera contains many fine
moments, such as the fierce chorus—a kind of
trepak—sung by the snow-spirits at the close
of the first act ; the two contrasting love-
duets, one which Ivan Korolevich sings with

Kastcheievna, and a later one in which the Tsarevna takes part, in the third act ; and the sinister slumber-song which the unhappy Tsarevna is forced to sing for Kastchei, while wishing that his sleep was the sleep of death, is distinguished for its marked originality. As regards harmony, Rimsky-Korsakov in *Kastchei* indulges in a good deal that is piquant and unusual ; there is much chromaticism in the fantastic scenes and a general tendency to what one critic describes as "studied cacophany," which is unusual in the work of this composer. *Kastchei* stands out as one of the most Wagnerian among Russian operas.

Pan Voyevode was completed in 1903, and produced by the Private Opera Company in St. Petersburg in October, 1904. The scene of the libretto is laid in Poland about the beginning of the seventeenth century, and the story concerns the love affairs of Chaplinsky, a young nobleman, and Maria, a poor orphan girl of good family. While out hunting, Pan Voyevode— governor of the district—sees Maria and loses his heart to her. At his command the lovers are separated by force, and the Voyevode declares his intention of marrying Maria. Yadviga, a rich widow, who has claims upon the Voyevode, determines to prevent the marriage at any cost. She takes counsel with a sorcerer, from whom she procures poison. The preparations for the wedding are all made, and the Voyevode is entertaining his friends at a banquet, when Yadviga appears, an uninvited guest, to warn him that Chaplinsky and his friends are coming to effect the rescue of Maria. At the banquet Maria sings the "Song of the Swan," but its yearning sadness oppresses the Voyevode and his guests. Suddenly the injured lover bursts into the hall with his followers and a wild scuffle ensues. In the last act, Chaplinsky having been taken prisoner and condemned to death, the interrupted festival recommences. In the meantime Yadviga has poured poison into Maria's goblet. Needless to say that in the end the cups get changed and it is the Voyevode who drinks the fatal potion. Maria, after a prayer by his dead body, orders the release of Chaplinsky and all ends happily.

Pan Voyevode gives occasion for a whole series of Polish dances, a Krakoviak, a Kazachok, or Cossack dance, a Polonaise, and a Mazurka. The incantation scene, when Yadviga seeks the sorcerer, and the Song of the Swan are favourite numbers in the work. *Pan Voyevode* was produced in Moscow in 1905 under the conductorship of Rachmaninov.

The idea of the Legendary Opera, *The Tale of the Invisible City of Kitezh and the Maiden Fevronia*, was in Rimsky-Korsakov's mind for nearly ten years before he actually composed the work between 1903-1905. The first performance in St. Petersburg took place at the Maryinsky Theatre early in the spring of 1907, and Moscow heard the opera in the following season. The opera starts with an orchestral introduction based upon a folk-melody. There is great charm in the opening scene laid in the forests surrounding Little Kitezh, where Fevronia is discovered sitting among the tall grasses and singing a song in praise of all living creatures. There she is joined by a bear, and a crane, and other birds, all of which she welcomes as friends ; and there the young Prince Vsievolod sees her and loses his heart to the beautiful child of nature. Their love scene is interrupted by the sound of horns, introducing a company of archers in search of the Prince. Fevronia then finds out her lover's identity. The next act shows the market-place in Little Kitezh crowded with all manner of archaic Russian types : a showman leading a bear, a minstrel singing and playing the *gusslee*, old men and women, young men and girls—one of those animated canvases which recall certain pages in Moussorgsky's operas and are the precursors of similar scenes in Stravinsky's *Petroushka*. Some " Superior People " are grumbling at the marriage of the Prince to the unknown and homeless girl Fevronia. Soon the bride appears accompanied by the wedding procession. She receives the congratulations of the populace, but the " Superior People " show some disdain. Suddenly a fresh group of people rush on in terror, followed by the Tatars who break up the crowd and seize Fevronia. Under threats of torture they compel the crazy drunkard Kouterma to guide them to Kitezh the Great. Fevronia puts up a prayer for the city as the Tatars carry her off on one of their rough carts.

The scene changes to Kitezh the Great, where the old Prince and his son, the bridegroom, are listening to the account given by the fugitives of the destruction of Little Kitezh by the Tatars. All are horrified to hear that Fevronia has fallen into their ruthless hands. The Prince assembles his soldiers and goes out to meet the enemy. While the women are singing a chorus of lamentation, the church bell begins to ring of its own accord. The old Prince declares it is a miraculous sign that the town will be saved. The curtain rises next on the Tatar encampment on the shores of the Shining Lake. Fevronia in despair is still sitting in the Tatars' cart. The half-crazy Kouterma has been bound hand and foot because the Tatars suspected him. Their two leaders have fought; one is left dead on the ground ; all the others have fallen asleep. Fevronia takes a knife from the dead Tatar chief and cuts Kouterma's bonds. He is about to escape when the sound of a bell arrests him. He rushes madly to the lake with the intention of drowning himself, but at that moment a ray of sunlight falls on the water in which he sees reflected the city of Kitezh the Invisible. Now he really makes his escape, taking Fevronia with him. The Tatars are awakened, and running to the edge of the lake, they, too, see the miraculous reflection and exclaim in terror : " Awful in truth is the God of the Russians."

Fevronia passes some terrible hours alone in the gloom of the enchanted forest with Kouterma ; but she prays, and presently he leaves her. Then little lamps appear in the trees, and gold and silver flowers spring up in the grass, while the Paradise Birds, Aklonost and Sirin, sing to comfort her. Aklonost tells her he is the messenger of death. She replies that she has no fear of death, and weaves herself a garland of immortal flowers. Presently the the spirit of the young Prince appears to her. He tells her that he has been killed, " but now," he says, " thank God, I am alive." He gives Fevronia some bread, bidding her eat before she starts on her long journey ; " who tastes our bread knows eternal happiness," he says. Fevronia eats and throws some of the crumbs to the birds ; then with a prayer, " Christ receive me into the habitations of the just," she disappears with the spirit of the Prince. After an orchestral interlude, the curtain rises upon the apotheosis of the City of Kitezh, and the Paradise Birds are heard proclaiming : " The Celestial gates are open to us ; time has ceased ; Eternity has begun." The people come out to welcome Fevronia and the Prince, and sing their epithalamium. Fevronia now learns that Kitezh did not fall, but only disappeared; that the northern lights bore the prayers of the just to heaven; and also the cause of the blessed and miraculous sound heard by Kouterma. Then the Prince leads his bride into the cathedral while the people sing : " Here shall there be no more tears or sorrow, but everlasting joy and peace."

Rimsky-Korsakov died of angina pectoris on June 8th, 1908 at Lioubensk, near St. Petersburg, where he was spending the summer with his family. In the previous year he had finished his last opera *The Golden Cock*, the production of which was not sanctioned by the Censor during the composer's lifetime. It is said that this vexation, following upon his difficulties with the authorities of the Conservatoire, helped to hasten his end.

The Golden Cock is composed to a libretto by V. Bielsky, based upon Poushkin's well-known poem. The author of the book says in his preface to the opera : " the purely human nature of Poushkin's *Golden Cock*—that instructive tragi-comedy of the unhappy consequences following upon mortal passions and weaknesses—permits us to place the plot in any region and in any period." In spite of the Eastern origin of the tale, and the Italian names, Duodo and Guidone, all which constitutes the historical character of the story and recalls the simple customs and the daily life of the Russian people, with its crude, strong colouring, its exuberance and liberty, so dear to the artist. The work opens with a Prologue, in which the Astrologer tells us that although the opera is

"A fairy-tale, not solid truth,
It holds a moral good for youth."

In the first scene we are introduced to a hall in the Palace of King Dodon, where he is holding a council with his Boyards. He tells them that he is weary of kingly responsibilities and especially of the perpetual warfare with his hostile neighbours, and that he longs to rest for a while. First he asks the advice of his heir, Prince Gvidon, who says that instead of fighting on the frontier he should withdraw his troops and let them surround the capital, which should first be well provisioned. Then, while the enemy was destroying the rest of the country, the King might repose and think of some new way of circumventing him. But the old Voyevode Polkan does not approve of the

project, for he thinks it will be worse to have the
hostile army surrounding the city, and perhaps
attacking the King himself. Nor does he agree
with the equally foolish advice of the King's
younger son Aphron. Very soon the whole
assembly is quarrelling as to the best way out
of the difficulty, when the Astrologer arrives
upon the scene. He offers King Dodon a
present of a Golden Cock which would always
give warning in case of danger. At first the
King does not believe him, but the cock is
brought in and cries at once : " Kikeriki,
kikerikou ! Be on your guard, mind what
you do ! " The King is enchanted and feels
that he can now take his ease. He offers to
give the Astrologer whatever reward he asks.
The latter replies that he does not want
treasures or honours, but a diploma drawn
up in legal form. " Legal," says the King,
" I don't know what you mean. My desires
and caprices are the only laws here ; but you
may rest assured of my gratitude." Dodon's
bed is brought in, and the chatelaine of the
Palace tucks him up and keeps watch by him
until he falls into a sound sleep. Suddenly
the shrill crowing of the Golden Cock awakens
the King and all his attendants. The first
time this happens he has to send his unwilling
sons to the war ; the second time he is obliged
to go himself. There is a good deal of comic

business about the departure of the King, who is obviously afraid of his warhorse.

In the second act Dodon and the Voyevode Polkan, with their army, come to a narrow pass among the rocks which has evidently been the scene of a battle. The corpses of the warriors lie pale in the moonlight, while birds of prey hover around the spot. Here Dodon comes suddenly upon the dead bodies of his two sons, who have apparently killed each other. The wretched, egotistical king is reduced to tears at the sight. His attention is soon distracted, for, as the distant mist clears away, he perceives under the shelter of the hillside a large tent lit up by the first rays of the sun. He thinks it is the tent of the hostile leader, and Polkan endeavours to lead on the timid troops in hopes of capturing him. But, to the great astonishment of the King and his Voyevode, a beautiful woman emerges from the tent followed by her slaves bearing musical instruments. She sings a song of greeting to the dawn. Dodon approaches and asks her name. She replies modestly, with downcast eyes, that she is the Queen of Shemakha. Then follows a long scene in which she lures on the old King until he is hopelessly infatuated with her beauty. Her recital of her own attractions is made without any reserve, and soon she has completely turned Dodon's head. She insists on his singing, and mocks at his unmusical voice ; she forces him to dance until he falls exhausted to the ground, and laughs at his uncouth movements. This scene really constitutes the ballet of the opera. Finally the Queen of Shemakha consents to return to his capital and become his bride. Amid much that is genuinely comic there are a few touches of unpleasant realism in this scene, in which the ineffectual, indolent, and sensual old King is fooled to the top of his bent by the capricious and heartless queen. Here we have travelled far from the beautiful idealism of *The City of Kitezh ;* the humour of the situation has a sharp tang to it which belies the spirit of Poushkin and Russian humour in general ; we begin to speculate as to whether Bielsky has not studied to some purpose the plays of George Bernard Shaw, so much read in Russia.

The curtain rises in the third act upon another of those scenes of bustle and vigorous movement characteristic of Russian opera. The people are awaiting the return of King Dodon. " Jump and dance, grin and bow, show your loyalty but don't expect anything in return," says the sardonic chatelaine, Amelfa. There enters a wonderful procession which reminds us of an Eastern fairy tale : the advance guard of the King; the Queen of Shemakha, in a bizarre costume, followed by a grotesque cortege of giants, dwarfs, and black slaves. The spectacle for the time being allays the evident anxiety of the people. As the King and Queen pass by in their golden chariot the former appears aged and care-worn ; but he gazes on his companion with uxorious tenderness. The Queen shows evident signs of boredom. At this juncture the Astrologer makes his appearance and a distant storm, long threatening, bursts over the city. The King gives a flattering welcome to the Astrologer and expresses his readiness to reward him for the gift of the Golden Cock. The Astrologer asks nothing less than the gift of the Queen of Shemakha herself. The King refuses with indignation, and orders the soldiers to remove the Astrologer. But the latter resists, and reminds Dodon once more of his promise. The King, beside himself with anger, hits the Astrologer on the head with his sceptre. General consternation in the crowd. The Queen laughs a cold, cruel laugh, but the King is terrified, for he perceives that he has killed the Astrologer. He tries to recover himself and takes comfort from the presence of the Queen, but now she openly throws off all pretence of affection and drives him away from her. Suddenly the Cock gives out a shrill, threatening cry ; he flies on to the King's head and with one blow of his beak pierces his skull. The King falls dead. A loud clap of thunder is followed by darkness, during which the silvery laugh of the Queen is heard. When it grows light again Queen and Cock have both disappeared. The unhappy and bewildered people sing a chorus of regret for the King : " Our Prince without a peer, was prudent, wise, and kind ; his rage was terrible, he was often implacable ; he treated us like dogs ; but when once his rage was over he was a Golden King. O terrible disaster ! Where shall we find another king ! " The opera concludes with a short Epilogue in which the Astrologer bids the spectators dry their tears, since the whole story is but fiction, and in the kingdom of Dodon there were but two real human beings, himself and the Queen.

The music of this opera is appropriately wild and barbaric. We feel that in spite of forty years development it is essentially the work of the same temperament that produced the Symphonic Poems " Sadko " and the Oriental symphony " Antar."

A close study of the works of Rimsky-Korsakov reveals a distinguished musical personality ; a thinker ; a fastidious and exquisite craftsman ; in a word—an artist of a refined and discriminating type who concerns himself very little with the demands and appreciation of the general public. Outside Russia, he has been censured for his subserviency to national influences, his exclusive devotion to a patriotic ideal.   On the other hand, some Russian critics have accused him of introducing Wagnerism into national opera.   This is only true in so far that he has grafted upon opera of the older, more melodic type the effective employment of some modern methods, more particularly the moderate use of the *leitmotif*.   As regards orchestration, I have already claimed for him the fullest recognition.   He has a remarkable faculty for the invention of new, brilliant, prismatic orchestral effects, and is a master in the skilful employment of onomatopœia.   Those who assert—not entirely without reason—that Rimsky-Korsakov is not a melodist of copious and vivid inspiration must concede the variety, colour, independence and flashing wit of his accompaniments.   This want of balance between the essential and accessory is certainly a characteristic of his music.   Some of his songs and their accompaniments remind me of those sixteenth-century portraits in which some slim, colourless, but distinguished Infanta is gowned in a robe of brocade rich enough to stand by itself, without the negative aid of the wearer.

Rimsky-Korsakov does not correspond to our stereotyped idea of the Russian temperament. He is not lacking in warmth of feeling, which kindles to passion in some of his songs ; but his moods of exaggerated emotion are very rare. His prevailing tones are bright and serene, and occasionally flushed with glowing colour. If he rarely shocks our hearts, as Moussorgsky does, into a poignant realisation of darkness and despair, neither has he any of the hysterical tendency which sometimes detracts from the impressiveness of Tchaikovsky's *cris de cœur*.

When a temperament, musically endowed, sees its subject with the direct and observant vision of the painter, instead of dreaming it through a mist of subjective exaltation, we get a type of mind that naturally tends to a programme, more or less clearly defined. Rimsky-Korsakov belongs to this class. Labelled or not, we feel in all his music the desire to depict.

This representative of a school, reputed to be revolutionary, who has arrayed himself in the full panoply of musical erudition and scholarly restraint ; this poet whose imagination revels in the folk-lore of Russia and the fantastic legends of the East ; this professor who has written fugues and counterpoints by the dozen ; this man who looked like an austere schoolmaster, and can on occasion startle us with an almost barbaric exuberance of colour and energy, offers, to my mind, one of the most fascinating analytical studies in all contemporary music.

CHAPTER XIII

TCHAIKOVSKY

TYPICALLY Russian by temperament and in his whole attitude to life; cosmopolitan in his academic training and in his ready acceptance of Western ideals; Tchaikovsky, although the period of his activity coincided with that of Balakirev, Cui, and Rimsky-Korsakov, cannot be included amongst the representatives of the national Russian school. His ideals were more diffused, and his ambitions reached out towards more universal appreciation. Nor had he any of the communal instincts which brought together and cemented in a long fellowship the circle of Balakirev. He belonged in many respects to an older generation, the " Byroniacs," the incurable pessimists of Lermontov's day, to whom life appeared as " a journey made in the night time." He was separated from the nationalists, too, by an influence which had been gradually becoming obliterated in Russian music since the time of Glinka—I allude to the influence of Italian opera.

The first æsthetic impressions of an artist's childhood are rarely quite obliterated in his subsequent career. We may often trace some peculiar quality of a man's genius back to the very traditions he imbibed in the nursery. Tchaikovsky's family boasted no skilled performers, and, being fond of music, had an orchestrion sent from the capital to their official residence among the Ural Mountains. Peter Ilich, then about six years old, was never tired of hearing its operatic selections ; and in after life declared that he owed to this mechanical contrivance his passion for Mozart and his unchanging affection for the music of the Italian school.

It is certain that while Glinka was influenced by Beethoven, Serov by Wagner and Meyerbeer, Cui by Chopin and Schumann, Balakirev and Rimsky-Korsakov by Liszt and Berlioz, Tchaikovsky never ceased to blend with the characteristic melody of his country an echo of the sensuous beauty of the South. This reflection of what was gracious and ideally beautiful in Italian music is undoubtedly one of the secrets of Tchaikovsky's great popularity with the public. It is a concession to human weakness of which we gladly avail ourselves ; although, as moderns, we have graduated in a less sensuous school, we are still willing to worship the old gods of melody under a new name.

Tchaikovsky began quite early in life to

frequent the Italian Opera in St. Petersburg ; consequently his musical tastes developed far earlier on the dramatic than on the symphonic side. He knew and loved the operatic master-pieces of the Italian and French schools long before he knew the Symphonies of Beethoven or any of Schumann's works. His first opera, *The Voyevode*, was composed about a year after he left the St. Petersburg Conservatoire, in 1866. He had just been appointed professor of harmony at Moscow, but was still completely unknown as a composer. At this time he was fortunate enough to make the acquaintance of the great dramatist Ostrovsky, who generously offered to supply his first libretto. In spite of the prestige of the author's name, it was not altogether satisfactory, for Ostrovsky had origin-ally written *The Voyevode* as a comedy in five acts, and in adapting it to suit the requirements of conventional opera many of its best features had to be sacrificed.

The music was pleasing and quite Italian in style. The work coincides with Tchaikovsky's orchestral fantasia " Fatum " or " Destiny," and also with the most romantic love-episode of his life—his fascination for Madame Désiré-Artôt, then the star of Italian Opera in Moscow. Thus all things seemed to combine at this juncture in his career to draw him to dramatic art, and especially towards Italianised opera.

The Voyevode, given at the Grand Opera, Moscow, in January, 1869, provoked the most opposite critical opinions. It does not seem to have satisfied Tchaikovsky himself for, having made use of some of the music in a later opera (*The Oprichnik*), he destroyed the greater part of the score.

The composer's second operatic attempt was made with *Undine*. This work, submitted to the Director of the Imperial Opera in St. Petersburg in 1869, was rejected, and the score mislaid by some careless official. When, after some years, it was discovered and returned to the composer, he put it in the fire without remorse. Neither of these immature efforts are worth serious consideration as affecting the development of Russian opera.

The Oprichnik was begun in January 1870, and completed in April 1872. Tchaikovsky attacked this work in a complete change of spirit. This time his choice fell upon a purely national and historical subject. Lajechnikov's tragedy "The Oprichnik" is based upon an episode of the period of Ivan the Terrible, and possesses qualities whch might well appeal to a composer of romantic proclivities. A picturesque setting; dramatic love and political intrigue; a series of effective—even sensational—situations, and finally several realistic pictures from national life; all these things might have been turned to excellent account in the hands of a skilled librettist. Unluckily the book was not well constructed, while, in order to comply with the demands of the Censor, the central figure of the tragedy—the tyrant himself—had to be reduced to a mere nonentity. The most serious error, however, was committed by Tchaikovsky himself, when he grafted upon *The Oprichnik*, with its crying need for national colour and special treatment, a portion of the pretty Italianised music of *The Voyevode*. The interpolation of half an act from a comedy subject into the libretto of an historical tragedy confused the action without doing much to relieve the lurid and sombre atmosphere of the piece.

The " Oprichniki," as we have already seen in Rubinstein's opera *The Bold Merchant Kalashnikov*, were the " Bloods " and dandies of the court of Ivan the Terrible—young noblemen of wild and dissolute habits who bound themselves together by sacrilegious vows to protect the tyrant and carry out his evil desires. Their unbridled insolence, the tales of their Black Masses and secret crimes, and their utter disrespect for age or sex, made them the terror of the populace. Sometimes they masqueraded in the dress of monks, but they were in reality robbers and murderers, hated and feared by the people whom they oppressed.

Here is the story of *The Oprichnik* briefly

stated : Andrew Morozov, the descendant of a noble but impoverished house, and the only son of the widowed Boyarinya Morozova, is in love with the beautiful Natalia, daughter of Prince Jemchoujny. His poverty disqualifies him as a suitor. While desperately in need of money, Andrew falls in with Basmanov, a young Oprichnik, who persuades him to join the community, telling him that an Oprichnik can always fill his own pockets. Andrew consents, and takes the customary oath of celibacy. Afterwards, circumstances cause him to break his vow and marry Natalia against her father's wish. Prince Viazminsky, the leader of the Oprichniki, cherishes an old grudge against the family of Morozov, and works for Andrew's downfall. On his wedding-day he breaks in upon the feast with a message from the Tsar. Ivan the Terrible has heard of the bride's beauty, and desires her attendance at the royal apartments. Andrew, with gloomy forebodings in his heart, prepares to escort his bride, when Viazminsky, with a meaning smile, explains that the invitation is for the bride alone. Andrew refuses to let his wife go into the tyrant's presence unprotected. Viazminsky proclaims him a rebel and a traitor to his vows. Natalia is carried away by force, and the Oprichniki lead Andrew into the market-place to suffer the death-penalty at their hands.

Meanwhile Boyarinya Morozova, who had cast off her son when he became an Oprichnik, has softened towards him, and comes to see him on his wedding-day. She enters the deserted hall where Viazminsky, alone, is gloating over the success of his intrigue. She inquires unsuspectingly for Andrew, and he leads her to the window. Horror-stricken, she witnesses the execution of her own son by his brother Oprichniki, and falls dead at the feet of her implacable enemy.

During its first season, this work was given fourteen times; so that its success—for a national opera—may be reckoned decidedly above the average. Those who represented the advanced school of musical opinion in Russia condemned its forms as obsolete. Cui, in particular, called it the work of a schoolboy who knew nothing of the requirements of the lyric drama, and pronounced it unworthy to rank with such masterpieces of the national school as Moussorgsky's *Boris Godounov* or Rimsky-Korsakov's *Maid of Pskov*.

But the most pitiless of critics was Tchaikovsky himself, who declared that he always took to his heels during the rehearsals of the third and fourth acts to avoid hearing a bar of the music. " Is it not strange," he writes, " that in process of composition it seemed charming ? But what disenchantment followed the first

THE GREAT OPERA HOUSE, MOSCOW

rehearsals ! It has neither action, style, nor inspiration ! "

Both judgments are too severe. *The Oprichnik* is not exactly popular, but it has never dropped out of the repertory of Russian opera. Many years ago I heard it in St. Petersburg, and noted my impressions. The characters, with the exception of the Boyarinya Morozova, are not strongly delineated ; the subject is lurid, " horror on horror's head accumulates " ; the Russian and Italian elements are incongruously blended ; yet there are saving qualities in the work. Certain moments are charged with the most poignant dramatic feeling. In this opera, even as in the weakest of Tchaikovsky's music, there is something that appeals to our common humanity. The composer himself must have modified his early judgment, since he was actually engaged in remodelling *The Oprichnik* at the time of his death.

In 1872 the Grand Duchess Helenà Pavlovna commissioned Serov to compose an opera on the subject of Gogol's Malo-Russian tale "Christmas Eve Revels." A celebrated poet, Polonsky, had already prepared the libretto, when the death of the Grand Duchess, followed by that of Serov himself, put an end to the scheme. Out of respect to the memory of this generous patron, the Imperial Musical Society resolved to carry out her wishes. A competition was organised for the best setting of Polonsky's text under the title of *Vakoula the Smith*, and Tchaikovsky's score carried off both first and second prizes. In after years he made considerable alterations in this work and renamed it *Cherevichek* ("The Little Shoes"). It is also known in foreign editions as *Le Caprice d'Oxane.* The libretto follows the general lines of the *Christmas Eve Revels*, described in the chapter dealing with Rimsky-Korsakov.

Early in the 'seventies Tchaikovsky came under the ascendency of Balakirev, Stassov, and other representatives of the ultra-national and modern school. *Cherevichek*, like the Second Symphony—which is also Malo-Russian in colouring—and the symphonic poems " Romeo and Juliet " (1870), " The Tempest " (1874), and " Francesca di Rimini " (1876), may be regarded as the outcome of this phase of influence. The originality and captivating local colour, as well as the really poetical lyrics with which the book of this opera is interspersed, no doubt commended it to Tchaikovsky's fancy. Polonsky's libretto is a mere series of episodes, treated however with such art that he has managed to preserve the spirit of Gogol's text in the form of his polished verses. In *Cherevichek* Tchaikovsky makes a palpable effort to break away from conventional Italian forms and to write more in the style of Dargomijsky. But, as Stassov has pointed out, this more modern and realistic style is not so well suited to Tchaikovsky, because he is not at his strongest in declamation and recitative. Nor was he quite in sympathy with Gogol's racy humour which bubbles up under the veneer of Polonsky's elegant manner. Tchaikovsky was not devoid of a certain subdued and whimsical humour, but his laugh is not the boisterous reaction from despair which we find in so many Slav temperaments. *Cherevichek* fell as it were between two stools. The young Russian party, who had partially inspired it, considered it lacking in realism and modern feeling ; while the public, who hoped for something lively, in the style of " Le Domino Noir," found an attempt at serious national opera the thing which, above all others, bored them most.

The want of marked success in opera did not discourage Tchaikovsky. Shortly after his disappointment in *Cherevichek* he requested Stassov to furnish him with a libretto based on Shakespeare's " Othello." Stassov was slow to comply with this demand, for he believed the subject to be ill-suited to Tchaikovsky's genius. At last, however, he yielded to pressure ; but the composer's enthusiasm cooled of its own accord, and he soon abandoned the idea.

During the winter of 1876-1877, he was absorbed in the composition of the Fourth

Symphony, which may partially account for the fact that " Othello " ceased to interest him. By May he had completed three movements of the Symphony, when suddenly the tide of operatic passion came surging back, sweeping everything before it. Friend after friend was consulted in the search for a suitable subject. The celebrated singer Madame Lavrovsky suggested Poushkin's popular novel in verse, " Eugene Oniegin." " The idea," says Tchaikovsky, " struck me as curious. Afterwards, while eating a solitary meal in a restaurant, I turned it over in my mind and it did not seem bad. Reading the poem again, I was fascinated. I spent a sleepless night, the result of which was the *mise en scène* of a charming opera upon Poushkin's poem."

Some of my readers may remember the production of *Eugene Oniegin* in this country, conducted by Henry J. Wood, during Signor Lago's opera season in the autumn of 1892. It was revived in 1906 at Covent Garden, but without any regard for its national setting. Mme. Destinn, with all her charm and talent, did not seem at home in the part of Tatiana ; and to those who had seen the opera given in Russia the performance seemed wholly lacking in the right, intimate spirit. It was interpreted better by the Moody-Manners Opera Company, in the course of the same year.

The subject was in many respects ideally suited to Tchaikovsky—the national colour suggested by a master hand, the delicate realism which Poushkin was the first to introduce into Russian poetry, the elegiac sentiment which pervades the work, and, above all, its intensely subjective character, were qualities which appealed to the composer's temperament.

In May 1877 he wrote to his brother : " I know the opera does not give great scope for musical treatment, but a wealth of poetry, and a deeply interesting tale, more than atone for all its faults." And again, replying to some too-captious critic, he flashes out in its defence : " Let it lack scenic effect, let it be wanting in action ! I am in love with Tatiana, I am under the spell of Poushkin's verse, and I am drawn to compose the music as it were by an irresistible attraction." This was the true mood of inspiration—the only mood for success.

We must judge the opera *Eugene Oniegin* not so much as Tchaikovsky's greatest intellectual, or even emotional, effort, but as the outcome of a passionate, single-hearted impulse. Consequently the sense of joy in creation, of perfect reconciliation with his subject, is conveyed in every bar of the music. As a work of art, *Eugene Oniegin* defies criticism, as do some charming but illusive personalities. It would be a waste of time to pick out its weaknesses,

which are many, and its absurdities, which are
not a few. It answers to no particular standard
of dramatic truth or serious purpose. It is too
human, too lovable, to fulfil any lofty intention.
One might liken it to the embodiment of some
captivating, wayward, female spirit which sub-
jugates all emotional natures, against their
reason, if not against their will. The story is as
obsolete as a last year's fashion-plate. The
hero is the demon-hero of the early romantic
reaction—" a Muscovite masquerading in the
cloak of Childe Harold." His friend Lensky
is an equally romantic being; more blighted
than demoniac, and overshadowed by that
gentle and fatalistic melancholy which endeared
him still more to the heart of Tchaikovsky.
The heroine is a survival of an even earlier
type. Tatiana, with her young-lady-like sensibilities, her superstitions, her girlish gush,
corrected by her primness of propriety, might
have stepped out of one of Richardson's novels.
She is a Russian Pamela, a belated example of
the decorous female, rudely shaken by the
French Revolution, and doomed to final anni-
hilation in the pages of Georges Sand. But in
Russia, where the emancipation of women was
of later date, this virtuous and victimised
personage lingered on into the nineteenth century,
and served as a foil to the Byronic and misan-
thropical heroes of Poushkin and Lermontov.

The music of *Eugene Oniegin* is the child of Tchaikovsky's fancy, born of his passing love for the image of Tatiana, and partaking of her nature—never rising to great heights of passion, nor touching depths of tragic despair, tinged throughout by those moods of romantic melancholy and exquisitely tender sentiment which the composer and his heroine share in common.

The opera was first performed by the students of the Moscow Conservatoire in March, 1879. Perhaps the circumstances were not altogether favourable to its success ; for although the composer's friends were unanimous in their praise, the public did not at first show extraordinary enthusiasm. Apart from the fact that the subject probably struck them as daringly unconventional and lacking in sensational developments, a certain section of purists were shocked at Poushkin's *chef-d'œuvre* being mutilated for the purposes of a libretto, and resented the appearance of the almost canonized figure of Tatiana upon the stage. Gradually, however, *Eugene Oniegin* acquired a complete sway over the public taste and its serious rivals became few in number. There are signs, however, that its popularity is on the wane.

From childhood Tchaikovsky had cherished a romantic devotion for the personality of Joan of Arc, about whom he had written a poem at the age of seven. After the completion of *Eugene Oniegin*, looking round for a fresh operatic subject, his imagination reverted to the heroine of his boyhood. During a visit to Florence, in December, 1878, Tchaikovsky first approached this idea with something like awe and agitation. " My difficulty," he wrote, " does not lie in any lack of inspiration, but rather in its overwhelming force. The idea has taken furious possession of me. For three whole days I have been tormented by the thought that while the material is so vast, human strength and time amount to so little. I want to complete the whole work in an hour, as sometimes happens to one in a dream." From Florence, Tchaikovsky went to Paris for a few days, and by the end of December settled at Clarens, on the Lake of Geneva, to compose his opera in these peaceful surroundings. To his friend and benefactress, Nadejda von Meck, he wrote expressing his satisfaction with his music, but complaining of his difficulty in constructing the libretto. This task he had undertaken himself, using Joukovsky's translation of Schiller's poem as his basis. It is a pity he did not adhere more closely to the original work, instead of substituting for Schiller's ending the gloomy and ineffective last scene, of his own construction, in which Joan is actually represented at the stake surrounded by the leaping flames.

Tchaikovsky worked at *The Maid of Orleans* with extraordinary rapidity. He was enamoured of his subject and convinced of ultimate success. From Clarens he sent a droll letter to his friend and publisher Jurgenson, in Moscow, which refers to his triple identity as critic, composer, and writer of song-words. It is characteristic of the man in his lighter moods :

" There are three celebrities in the world with whom you are well acquainted : the rather poor rhymer ' N. N. ' ; ' B. L., ' formerly musical cricit of the "Viedomosti," and the composer and ex-professor Mr. Tchaikovsky. A few hours ago Mr. T. invited the other two gentlemen to the piano and played them the whole of the second act of *The Maid of Orleans.* Mr. Tchaikovsky is very intimate with these gentlemen, consequently he had no difficulty in conquering his nervousness and played them his new work with spirit and fire. You should have witnessed their delight. . . . Finally the composer, who had long been striving to preserve his modesty intact, went completely off his head, and all three rushed on to the balcony like madmen to soothe their excited nerves in the fresh air."

The Maid of Orleans won little more than a

succès d'estime. There is much that is effective
in this opera, but at the same time it displays
those weaknesses which are most characteristic
of Tchaikovsky's unsettled convictions in the
matter of style. The transition from an opera
so Russian in colouring and so lyrical in sentiment as *Eugene Oniegin* to one so universal and
heroic in character as *The Maid of Orleans*,
seems to have presented difficulties. Just as
the national significance of *The Oprichnik*
suffered from moments of purely Italian influence, so *The Maid of Orleans* contains
incongruous lapses into the Russian style.
What have the minstrels at the court of Charles
VI. in common with a folk-song of Malo-
Russian origin ? Or why is the song of Agnes
Sorel so reminiscent of the land of the steppes
and birch forests ? The gem of the opera is
undoubtedly Joan's farewell to the scenes of
her childhood, which is full of touching, idyllic
sentiment.

In complete contrast to the fervid enthusiasm
which carried him through the creation of *The
Maid of Orleans* was the spirit in which Tchaikovsky started upon his next opera. One of
his earliest references to *Mazeppa* occurs in a
letter to Nadejda von Meck, written in the
spring of 1882. " A year ago," he says,
" Davidov (the 'cellist) sent me the libretto of
Mazeppa, adapted by Bourenin from Poushkin's

poem ' Poltava.' I tried to set one or two
scenes to music, but made no progress. Then
one fine day I read the libretto again and also
Poushkin's poem. I was stirred by some of the
verses, and began to compose the scene between
Maria and Mazeppa. Although I have not
experienced the profound creative joy I felt
while working at *Eugene Oniegin*, I go on with
the opera because I have made a start and in its
way it is a success."

Not one of Tchaikovsky's operas was born to
a more splendid destiny. In August, 1883, a
special meeting was held by the directors of
the Grand Opera in St. Petersburg to discuss
the simultaneous production of the opera in
both capitals. Tchaikovsky was invited to be
present, and was so astonished at the lavishness
of the proposed expenditure that he felt convinced the Emperor himself had expressed a
wish that no expense should be spared in
mounting *Mazeppa*. It is certain the royal
family took a great interest in this opera, which
deals with so stirring a page in Russian history.

The Mazeppa of Poushkin's masterpiece does
not resemble the imaginary hero of Byron's
romantic poem. He is dramatically, but realis-
tically, depicted as the wily and ambitious
soldier of fortune ; a brave leader, at times an
impassioned lover, and an inexorable foe. Tchaikovsky has not given a very powerful musical

presentment of this daring and passionate Cossack, who defied even Peter the Great. But the characterisation of the heroine's father Kochubey, the tool and victim of Mazeppa's ambition, is altogether admirable. The monologue in the fortress of Bielotserkov, where Kochubey is kept a prisoner after Mazeppa has treacherously laid upon him the blame of his own conspiracy, is one of Tchaikovsky's finest pieces of declamation. Most of his critics are agreed that this number, with Tatiana's famous Letter Scene in the second act of *Eugene Oniegin*, are the gems of his operatic works, and display his powers of psychological analysis at their highest.

The character of Maria, the unfortunate heroine of this opera, is also finely conceived. Tchaikovsky is almost always stronger in the delineation of female than of male characters. " In this respect," says Cheshikin, in his volume on Russian Opera, " he is the Tourgeniev of music." Maria has been separated from her first love by the passion with which the fascinating Hetman of Cossacks succeeds in inspiring her. She only awakens from her infatuation when she discovers all his cruelty and treachery towards her father. After the execution of the latter, and the confiscation of his property, the unhappy girl becomes crazed. She wanders—a kind of Russian Ophelia—back

to the old homestead, and arrives just in time to
witness an encounter between Mazeppa and her
first lover, Andrew. Mazeppa wounds Andrew
fatally, and, having now attained his selfish
ends, abandons the poor mad girl to her fate.
Then follows the most pathetic scene in the
opera. Maria does not completely recognise her
old lover, nor does she realise that he is dying.
Taking the young Cossack in her arms, she
speaks to him as to a child, and unconsciously
lulls him into the sleep of death with a graceful,
innocent slumber song. This melody, so remote
from the tragedy of the situation, produces an
effect more poignant than any dirge. *Mazeppa*,
partly because of the unrelieved gloom of the
subject, has never enjoyed the popularity of
Eugene Oniegin. Yet it holds its place in the
repertory of Russian opera, and deservedly, since
it contains some of Tchaikovsky's finest in-
spirations.

Charodeika (" The Enchantress ") followed
Mazeppa in 1887, and was a further step towards
purely dramatic and national opera. Tchaikovsky himself thought highly of this work, and
declared he was attracted to it by a deep-rooted
desire to illustrate in music the saying of
Goethe : " das Ewigweibliche zieht uns hinan,"
and to demonstrate the fatal witchery of
woman's beauty, as Verdi had done in " La
Traviata " and Bizet in " Carmen." *The*

Enchantress was first performed at the Maryinsky Theatre, St. Petersburg, in October 1887. Tchaikovsky himself conducted the first performances, and, having hoped for a success, was deeply mortified when, on the fourth performance, he mounted to the conductor's desk without a sign of applause. For the first time the composer complained bitterly of the attitude of the press, to whom he attributed this failure. As a matter of fact, the criticisms upon *Charodeika* were less hostile than on some previous occasions ; but perhaps for this reason they were none the less damning. It had become something like a pose to misunderstand any effort on Tchaikovsky's part to develop the purely dramatic side of his musical gifts. He was certainly very strongly attracted to lyric opera ; and it was probably as much natural inclination as deference to critical opinion which led him back to this form in *The Queen of Spades* (" Pique-Dame ").

The libretto of this opera, one of the best ever set by the composer, was originally prepared by Modeste Tchaikovsky for a musician who afterwards declined to make use of it. In 1889 the Director of the Opera suggested that the subject would suit Peter Ilich Tchaikovsky. The opera was commissioned, and all arrangements made for its production before a note of it was written. The actual composition was completed in six weeks, during a visit to Florence.

The story of *The Queen of Spades* is borrowed from a celebrated prose-tale of the same name, by the poet Poushkin. The hero is of the romantic type, like Manfred, Réné, Werther, or Lensky in *Eugene Oniegin*—a type which always appealed to Tchaikovsky, whose cast of mind, with the exception of one or two peculiarly Russian qualities, seems far more in harmony with the romantic first than with the realistic second half of the nineteenth century.

Herman, a young lieutenant of hussars, a passionate gambler, falls in love with Lisa, whom he has only met walking in the Summer Garden in St. Petersburg. He discovers that she is the grand-daughter of an old Countess, once well known as " the belle of St. Petersburg," but celebrated in her old age as the most assiduous and fortunate of card-players. On account of her uncanny appearance and reputation she goes by the name of " The Queen of Spades." These two women exercise a kind of occult influence over the impressionable Herman. With Lisa he forgets the gambler's passion in the sincerity of his love ; with the old Countess he finds himself a prey to the most sinister apprehensions and impulses. Rumour has it that the Countess possesses the secret of three cards, the combination of which is accountable for her extraordinary luck at the gaming-table. Herman, who is needy, and knows that without money he can never hope to win Lisa, determines at any cost to discover the Countess's secret. Lisa has just become engaged to the wealthy Prince Yeletsky, but she loves Herman. Under pretext of an assignation with Lisa, he manages to conceal himself in the old lady's bedroom at night. When he suddenly appears, intending to make her divulge her secret, he gives her such a shock that she dies of fright without telling him the names of the cards. Herman goes half-mad with remorse, and is perpetually haunted by the apparition of the Countess. The apparition now shows him the three fatal cards.

The night after her funeral he goes to the gaming-house and plays against his rival Yeletsky. Twice he wins on the cards shown him by the Countess's ghost. On the third card he stakes all he possesses, and turns up—not the expected ace, but the Queen of Spades. At that moment he sees a vision of the Countess, who smiles triumphantly and vanishes. Herman in despair puts an end to his life.

The subject, although somewhat melodramatic, offers plenty of incident and its thrill is enhanced by the introduction of the supernatural element. The work entirely engrossed Tchaikovsky. " I composed this opera with extraordinary joy and fervour," he wrote to the Grand Duke Constantine, " and experienced so vividly in myself all that happens in the tale, that at one time I was actually afraid of the spectre of the Queen of Spades. I can only hope that all my creative fervour, my agitation and my enthusiasm will find an echo in the hearts of my audience." In this he was not disappointed. *The Queen of Spades*, first performed in St. Petersburg in December, 1890, soon took a strong hold on the public, and now vies in popularity with *Eugene Oniegin*. It is strange that this opera has never found its way to the English stage. Less distinctively national than *Eugene Oniegin*, its psychological problem is stronger, its dramatic appeal more direct ; consequently it would have a greater chance of success.

Iolanthe, a lyric opera in one act, was Tchaikovsky's last production for the stage. It was first given in St. Petersburg in December, 1893, shortly after the composer's death. " In *Iolanthe*," says Cheshikin, " Tchaikovsky has added one more tender and inspired creation to his gallery of female portraits . . . a figure reminding us at once of Desdemona and Ophelia." The music of *Iolanthe* is not strong, but it is pervaded by an atmosphere of tender and inconsolable sadness ; by something which seems a faint and weak echo of the profoundly emotional note sounded in the " Pathetic " Symphony.

We may sum up Tchaikovsky's operatic development as follows : Beginning with conventional Italian forms in *The Oprichnik* he passed in *Cherevichek* to more modern methods, to the use of melodic recitative and ariosos ; while *Eugene Oniegin* shows a combination of both these styles. This first operatic period is purely lyrical. Afterwards, in *The Maid of Orleans*, *Mazeppa*, and *Charodeika*, he passed through a second period of dramatic tendency. With *Pique-Dame* he reaches perhaps the height of his operatic development ; but this work is the solitary example of a third period which we may characterise as lyrico-dramatic. In *Iolanthe* he shows a tendency to return to simple lyrical forms.

From the outset of his career he was equally attracted to the dramatic and symphonic elements in music. Of the two, opera had perhaps the greater attraction for him. The very intensity of its fascination seems to have stood in the way of his complete success. Once bitten by an operatic idea, he went blindly and uncritically forward, believing in his subject, in the quality of his work, and in its ultimate triumph, with that kind of undiscerning optimism to which the normally pessimistic sometimes fall unaccountable victims. The history of his operas repeats itself : a passion for some particular subject, feverish haste to embody

his ideas ; certainty of success ; then disenchantment, self-criticism, and the hankering
to remake and remodel which pursued him
through life.

Only a few of Tchaikovsky's operas seem able
to stand the test of time. *Eugene Oniegin* and
The Queen of Spades achieved popular success,
and *The Oprichnik* and *Mazeppa* have kept
their places in the repertory of the opera
houses in St. Petersburg and in the provinces ;
but the rest must be reckoned more or less
as failures. Considering Tchaikovsky's reputation, and the fact that his operas were never
allowed to languish in obscurity, but were all
brought out under the most favourable circumstances, there must be some reason for this
luke-warm attitude on the part of the public, of
which he himself was often painfully aware. The
choice of subjects may have had something to
do with this ; for the books of *The Oprichnik*
and *Mazeppa*, though dramatic, are exceedingly
lugubrious. But Polonsky's charming text to
Cherevichek should at least have pleased a
Russian audience.

I find another reason for the comparative
failure of so many of Tchaikovsky's operas.
It was not so much that the subjects in themselves were poor, as that they did not always
suit the temperament of the composer ; and
he rarely took this fact sufficiently into

consideration. Tchaikovsky's outlook was essentially subjective, individual, particular. He himself knew very well what was requisite for the creation of a great and effective opera : " breadth, simplicity, and an eye to decorative effect," as he says in a letter to Nadejda von Meck. But it was exactly in these qualities, which would have enabled him to treat such subjects as *The Oprichnik, The Maid of Orleans,* and *Mazeppa,* with greater power and freedom, that Tchaikovsky was lacking. In all these operas there are beautiful moments ; but they are almost invariably the moments in which individual emotion is worked up to intensely subjective expression, or phases of elegiac sentiment in which his own temperament could have full play.

Tchaikovsky had great difficulty in escaping from his intensely emotional personality, and in viewing life through any eyes but his own. He reminds us of one of those actors who, with all their power of touching our hearts, never thoroughly conceal themselves under the part they are acting. Opera, above all, cannot be " a one-man piece." For its successful realisation it demands breadth of conception, variety of sentiment and sympathy, powers of subtle adaptability to all kinds of situations and emotions other than our own. In short, opera is the one form of musical art in which the objective outlook is indispensable. Whereas in lyric poetry self-revelation is a virtue ; in the drama self-restraint and breadth of view are absolute conditions of greatness and success. We find the man reflected in Shakespeare's sonnets, but humanity in his plays. Tchaikovsky's nature was undoubtedly too emotional and self-centred for dramatic uses. To say this, is not to deny his genius ; it is merely an attempt to show its qualities and its limitations. Tchaikovsky had genius, as Shelley, as Byron, as Heine, as Lermontov had genius ; not as Shakespeare, as Goethe, as Wagner had it. As Byron could never have conceived " Julius Cæsar " or " Twelfth Night," so Tchaikovsky could never have composed such an opera as " Die Meistersinger." Of Tchaikovsky's operas, the examples which seem destined to live longest are those into which he was able, by the nature of their literary contents, to infuse most of his exclusive temperament and lyrical inspiration.

CHAPTER XIV

CONCLUSION

ALTHOUGH I have now passed in review the leading representatives of Russian opera, my work would be incomplete if I omitted to mention some of the many talented composers—the minor poets of music—who have contributed works, often of great value and originality, to the repertories of the Imperial Theatres and private opera companies in Russia. To make a just and judicious selection is no easy task, for there is an immense increase in the number of composers as compared to five-and-twenty years ago, and the general level of technical culture has steadily risen with the multiplication of provincial opera houses, schools, and orchestras. If we cannot now discern such a galaxy of native geniuses as Russia possessed in the second half of the nineteenth century, we observe at least a very widespread and lively activity in the musical life of the present day. The tendency to work in schools or groups seems to be dying out, and the art of the younger musicians shows a diffusion of influences, and a variety of expression, which make the classification of contemporary composers a matter of considerable difficulty.

In point of seniority, Edward Franzovich Napravnik has probably the first claim on our attention. Born August 12/26, 1839, at Beisht, near Königgratz, in Bohemia, he came to St. Petersburg in 1861 as director of Prince Youssipov's private orchestra. In 1863 he was appointed organist to the Imperial Theatres, and assistant to Liadov, who was then first conductor at the opera. In consequence of the latter's serious illness in 1869, Napravnik was appointed his successor and has held this important post for over fifty years. He came into power at a time when native opera was sadly neglected, and it is to his credit that he continued his predecessor's work of reparation with tact and zeal. The repertory of the Maryinsky Theatre, the home of Russian Opera in St. Petersburg, has been largely compiled on his advice, and although some national operas may have been unduly ignored, Napravnik has effected a steady improvement on the past. Memorable performances of Glinka's *A Life for the Tsar ;* of Tchaikovsky's *Eugene Oniegin, The Oprichnik,* and *The Queen of Spades ;* and of Rimsky-Korsakov's operas, both of his early and late period, have distinguished his reign as a conductor. Under his command the orchestra of the Imperial Opera has come to be regarded as one of the finest and best disciplined in the world. He has also worked indefatigably to raise the social and cultural condition of the musicians.

As a composer Napravnik is not strikingly original. His music has the faults and the qualities generally found side by side in the creative works of men who follow the conductor's vocation. His operas, as might be expected from so experienced a musician, are solidly constructed, written with due consideration for the powers of the soloists, and effective as regards the use of choral masses. On the other hand, they contain much that is purely imitative, and flashes of the highest musical inspiration come at long intervals. His first opera, *The Citizens of Nijny-Novgorod*,[1] was produced at the Maryinsky Theatre in 1868. The libretto by N. Kalashnikov deals with an episode from the same stirring period in Russian history as that of *A Life for the Tsar*, when Minin, the heroic butcher of Nijny-Novgorod, gathered together his fellow townsfolk and marched with the Boyard Pojarsky to the defence of Moscow. The national senti-

[1] *Citizens of the Lower-town* would be a more literal translation of the title, but would convey nothing to foreigners.

ment as expressed in Napravnik's music seems cold and conventional as compared with that of Glinka or Moussorgsky. The choruses are often interesting, especially one in the church style, sung at the wedding of Kouratov and Olga—the hero and heroine of the opera—which, Cheshikin says, is based on a theme borrowed from Bortniansky, and very finely handled. On the whole, the work has suffered, because the nature of its subject brought it into competition with Glinka's great patriotic opera. Tchaikovsky thought highly of it, and considered that it held the attention of the audience from first to last by reason of Napravnik's masterly sense of climax ; while he pronounced the orchestration to be brilliant, but never overpowering.

A more mature work is *Harold*, an opera in five acts, or nine scenes, first performed in St. Petersburg in November, 1886, with every possible advantage in the way of scenery and costumes. Vassilievich, Melnikov and Stravinsky took the leading male parts ; while Pavlovskaya and Slavina created the two chief female characters. The success of the opera was immediate, the audience demanding the repetition of several numbers ; but it must have been to some extent a *succès d'estime*, for the work, which is declamatory rather than lyrical, contains a good deal of monotonous recitative and—because it is more modern and

Wagnerian in form—the fine choral effects which lent interest to Napravnik's first opera are lacking here. In 1888 *Harold* was given in Moscow and Prague. Napravnik's third operatic work, *Doubrovsky*, was produced at the Maryinsky Theatre in 1895, and soon travelled to Moscow, and the round of the provincial opera houses, finding its way to Prague in 1896, and to Leipzig in 1897. The libretto by Modeste Tchaikovsky, brother of the composer, based upon Poushkin's ultra-romantic Byronic tale "Doubrovsky" is not very inspiring. Such dramatic and emotional qualities as the story contains have been ruthlessly deleted in this colourless adaptation for operatic purposes. The musical material matches the book in its facile and reminiscent quality ; but this experienced conductor writes gratefully and skilfully for the singers, the orchestra being carefully subordinated to vocal effects. Interpolated in the opera, by way of a solo for Doubrovsky, is a setting of Coppée's charming words " Ne jamais la voir, ni l'entendre."

Napravnik's fourth opera, *Francesca da Rimini*, is composed to a libretto by E. Ponomariev founded on Stephen Phillip's " Francesca and Paolo." It was first presented to the public in November 1902, the leading parts being created by that gifted pair, Nicholas and Medea Figner. Less popular than *Harold* or *Doubrov-*

sky, the musical value of *Francesca* is incontestably greater. Although the composer cannot altogether free himself from the influence of Wagner's " Tristan und Isolde," the subject has inspired him to write some very expressive and touching music, especially in the scene where the unhappy lovers, reading of Lancelot, seal their own doom with one supreme and guilty kiss ; and in the love duet in the third act. Besides these operas, Napravnik composed a Prologue and six choral numbers for Count Alexis Tolstoy's dramatic poem " Don Juan."

Although not of influential importance, the name of Paul Ivanovich Blaramberg cannot be omitted from a history of Russian opera. The son of a distinguished General of French extraction, he was born in Orenburg, September 14/26, 1841. His first impulsion towards a musical career originated in his acquaintance with Balakirev's circle ; but his relations with the nationalist school must have been fleeting, as some time during the 'sixties he went abroad for a long stay, and on his return to Russia, in 1870, he settled in Moscow, where he divided his time between writing for the *Moscow Viedomosty* and teaching theory in the Philharmonic School. Later on he went to live on an estate belonging to him in the Crimea.

Blaramberg has written five operas in all. *Skomorokhi (The Mummers)*, a comic opera in three acts, based on one of Ostrovsky's comedies, was composed in 1881, and was partly produced by the pupils of the opera class of the Moscow Philharmonic Society, in the Little Theatre, in 1887. The opera is a curious blend, some portions of it being in the declamatory manner of Dargomijsky, without his expressive realism, and others in the conventional style of *opera buffa*, degenerating at times into mere farcical patter-singing. It contains, however, a few successful numbers in the folk-style, especially the love-duet in 5-4 measure, and shows the influence of the national school. The music of *The Roussalka-Maiden* is more cohesive, and written with a clearer sense of form. There are fresh and pleasant pages in this work, in which local colour is used with unaffected simplicity. Blaramberg's third opera, *Mary of Burgundy*, is a more pretentious work, obviously inspired by Meyerbeer. The subject is borrowed from Victor Hugo's drama " Marie Tudor." It was produced at the Imperial Opera House, Moscow, in 1888. In his fourth opera, Blaramberg has not been fortunate in his choice of a libretto, which is based upon one of Ostrovsky's " Dramatic Chronicles," *Toushino*—rather a dull historical play dating from 1606, the period of Boris Godounov's regency. Strong, direct, elementary treatment, such as it might have received at the hands of Moussorgsky, could

alone have invested the subject with dramatic
interest ; whereas Blaramberg has clothed it in
music of rather conventional and insipid character. In common with *Skomorokhi*, however,
the work contains ˎsome admirable touches of
national colour, the composer imitating the
style of the folk-singing with considerable
success. Blaramberg's fifth operatic work, entitled *The Wave (Volna)*, is described as " an
Idyll in two acts," the subject borrowed from
Byron's " Don Juan " : namely, the episode
of Haidée's love for Don Juan, who is cast at her
feet " half-senseless from the sea." Of this
work Cheshikin says : " It consists of a series
of duets and trios, with a set of Eastern dances
and a ballad for bass, thrown in for variety's
sake, but having no real connection with the
plot. The music is reminiscent of Gounod ; the
melody is of the popular order, but not altogether
commonplace, and embellished by Oriental
fiorituri." An atmosphere of Eastern languor
pervades the whole opera, which may be
attributed to the composer's long sojourn in
the Crimea.

A name more distinguished in the annals of
Russian music is that of Anton Stepanovich
Arensky, born in Old Novgorod, in 1861. The
son of a medical man, he received his musical
education at the St. Petersburg Conservatoire,
where he studied under Rimsky-Korsakov. On

leaving this institution, in 1882, he was appointed to a professorship at the Moscow Conservatoire. He was also a member of the Council of the Synodal School of Church Music at Moscow, and conducted the concerts of the Russian choral society for a period of over seven years. In 1894, Balakirev recommended Arensky for the Directorship of the Imperial Chapel at St. Petersburg, a post which he held until 1901. Arensky's first opera *A Dream on the Volga* was produced at the Imperial Opera House, Moscow, in December 1892. The work was not given in St. Petersburg until 1903, when it was performed at the People's Palace. The subject is identical with Ostrovsky's comedy " The Voyevode," which the dramatist himself arranged for Tchaikovsky's use in 1867. Tchaikovsky, as we have seen, destroyed the greater part of the opera which he wrote to this libretto, but the manuscript of the book remained, and in 1882, at Arensky's request, he handed it over to him " with his benediction." Arensky approached the subject in a different spirit to Tchaikovsky, giving to his music greater dramatic force and veracity, and making more of the Russian element contained in the play. The scene entitled " The Voyevode's Dream," in the fourth act, in which the startled, nightmare cries of the guilty old Voyevode are heard in strange contrast to the lullaby sung by the old woman as she rocks the child in the cradle, is highly effective. In his use of the folk-tunes Arensky follows Melgounov's system of the "natural minor," and his handling of national themes is always appropriate and interesting. His harmonisation and elaboration by means of variations of the familiar tune "Down by Mother Volga" is an excellent example of his skill in this respect. Arensky's melody has not the sweeping lines and sustained power of Tchaikovsky's, but his tendency is lyrical and romantic rather than realistic and declamatory, and his use of arioso is marked by breadth and clearness of outline.

Arensky's second opera *Raphael* was composed for the first Congress of Russian Artists held in Moscow ; the occasion probably gives us the clue to his choice of subject. The first production of the opera took place in April 1894, and in the autumn of the following year it was given at the Maryinsky Theatre, St. Petersburg. The part of Raphael, which is written for a female voice, was sung by Slavina, La Fornarina being represented by Mravina. The work consists of a series of small delicately wrought musical cameos. By its tenderness and sweet romantic fancy the music often recalls Tchaikovsky's *Eugene Oniegin ;* but it is more closely united with the text, and greater attention is paid to the natural accentuation of the words. Between

Raphael and his last opera, *Nal and Damyanti*,
Arensky wrote music to Poushkin's poem
" The Fountain of Bakhchisarai," for the com-
memoration of the centenary of the poet's birth.
The analysis of this work does not come within
the scope of my subject, but I mention it because
it was a great advance on any of his previous
vocal works and led up to the increased
maturity shown in *Nal and Damyanti*.

The libretto of this opera was prepared by
Modeste Tchaikovsky from Joukovsky's free
translation of Rückert's poem. *Nal and Damyanti* was first performed at the Moscow Opera
House in January 1904. Some external influences are still apparent in the work, but they
now proceed from Wagner rather than from
Tchaikovsky. The orchestral introduction, an
excellent piece of work, is occasionally heard in
the concert room ; it depicts the strife between
the spirits of light and darkness which forms
the basis of this Oriental poem. This opera is
the most suitable for stage performance of any
of Arensky's works ; the libretto is well written,
the plot holds our attention and the scenic
effects follow in swift succession. Here Arensky has thrown off the tendency to miniature
painting which is more or less perceptible in his
earlier dramatic works, and has produced an
opera altogether on broader and stronger lines.
It is unfortunate, however, that he still shows a

lack of complete musical independence ; as Cheshikin remarks : " from Tchaikovsky to Wagner is rather an abrupt modulation ! "

Perhaps the nearest approach to a recognised " school " now extant in Russia is to be found in Moscow, where the influence of Tchaikovsky lingers among a few of his direct disciples, such as Rachmaninov, Grechyaninov, and Ippolitov-Ivanov.

Sergius Vassilievich Rachmaninov (b. 1873), so well known to us in England as a pianist and composer of instrumental music, was a pupil of the Moscow Conservatoire, where he studied under Taneiev and Arensky. Dramatic music does not seem to exercise much attraction for this composer. His one-act opera *Aleko*, the subject borrowed from Poushkin's poem " The Gipsies," was originally written as a diploma work for his final examination at the Conservatoire in 1872, and had the honour of being produced at the Imperial Opera House, Moscow, in the following season. *Aleko* was given in St. Petersburg, at the Taurida Palace, during the celebration of the Poushkin centenary in 1899, when Shaliapin took part in the performance. It is a blend of the declamatory and lyrical styles, and the music, though not strikingly original, runs a pleasing, sympathetic, and somewhat uneventful course.

Alexander Tikhonovich Grechyaninov, born

October 13/25 1864, in Moscow, entered the Conservatoire of his native city where he made the pianoforte his chief study under the guidance of Vassily Safonov. In 1893 he joined the St. Petersburg Conservatoire in order to learn composition from Rimsky-Korsakov. The following year a quartet by him won the prize at the competition organised by the St. Petersburg Chamber Music Society. He wrote incidental music to Ostrovsky's " Snow Maiden " and to Count Alexis Tolstoy's historical dramas " Tsar Feodor " and " Ivan the Terrible " before attempting to compose the opera *Dobrynia Nikitich* on the subject of one of the ancient *Byliny* or national legends. The introduction and third act of this work was first given in public in February 1903, at one of Count Sheremetiev's popular concerts, and in the following spring it was performed in its entirety at the Imperial Opera House, with Shaliapin in the title rôle. It is a picturesque, wholly lyrical work. Kashkin describes the music as agreeable and flowing, even in those scenes where the nature of the subject demands a more robust and vigorous musical treatment. *Dobrynia Nikitich* obviously owes much to Glinka's *Russlan* and *Liudmilla* and Borodin's *Prince Igor*.

Another musician who is clearly influenced by Tchaikovsky is Michael Ippolitov-Ivanov

SHALIAPIN IN BOÏTO'S "MEFISTOFELE"

(b. 1859), a distinguished pupil of Rimsky-Korsakov at the St. Petersburg Conservatoire. He was afterwards appointed Director of the School of Music, and of the Opera, at Tiflis in the Caucasus, where his first opera *Ruth* was produced in 1887. In 1893 he accepted a professorship at the Moscow Conservatoire, and became conductor of the Private Opera Company. Ippolitov-Ivanov is a great connoisseur of the music of the Caucasian races, and also of the old Hebrew melodies. He makes good use of the latter in *Ruth*, a graceful, idyllic opera, the libretto of which does not keep very strictly to Biblical traditions. In 1900 Ippolitov-Ivanov's second opera *Assya*—the libretto borrowed from Tourgeniev's tale which bears the same title—was produced in Moscow by the Private Opera Company. The tender melancholy sentiment of the music reflects the influence of Tchaikovsky's *Eugene Oniegin;* but by way of contrast there are some lively scenes from German student life.

With the foregoing composers we may link the name of Vassily Sergeivich Kalinnikov (1866-1900), who is known in this country by his Symphonies in G minor and A major. He composed incidental music to Count Alexis Tolstoy's play " Tsar Boris " (Little Theatre, Moscow, 1897) and the Prologue to an opera entitled *The Year* 1812, which was never finished in consequence of the musician's failing health and untimely death. Kalinnikov hardly had time to outgrow his early phase of Tchaikovsky worship.

Another Muscovite composer of widely different temperament to Ippolitov-Ivanov, or Kalinnikov, is Sergius Ivanovich Taneiev,[1] born November 13/25, 1856, in the Government of Vladimir. He studied under Nicholas Rubinstein and Tchaikovsky at the Moscow Conservatoire and made his début as a pianist at one of the concerts of the I. R. M. S. in 1875. He remained Tchaikovsky's friend long after he had ceased to be his pupil, and among the many letters they exchanged in after years there is one published in Tchaikovsky's " Life and Letters," dated January 14/26, 1891, which appears to be a reply to Taneiev's question : " How should Opera be written ? " At this time Taneiev was engaged upon his *Orestes*, the only work of the kind he has ever composed. The libretto, based upon the Aeschylean tragedy, is the work of Benkstern and has considerable literary merit. *Orestes*, although described by Taneiev as a Trilogy, is, in fact, an opera in three acts entitled respectively: (1) Agamemnon, (2) Choephoroe, (3) Eumenides.

---

[1] This composer must not be confused with his nephew A. S. Taneiev, the composer of a rather Frenchified opera entitled " Love's Revenge."

Neither in his choice of subject, nor in his treatment of it, has Taneiev followed the advice given him by Tchaikovsky in the letter mentioned above. Perhaps it was not in his nature to write opera " just as it came to him," or to show much emotional expansiveness. Neither does he attempt to write music which is archaic in style ; on the contrary, *Orestes* is in many respects a purely Wagnerian opera. *Leitmotifs* are used freely, though less systematically than in the later Wagnerian music-dramas. The opera, though somewhat cold and laboured, is not wanting in dignity, and is obviously the work of a highly educated musician. The representative themes, if they are rather short-winded, are often very expressive ; this is the case with the *leitmotif* of the ordeal of Orestes, which stands out prominently in the first part of the work, and also forms the motive of the short introduction to the Trilogy.

Towards the close of last century the new tendencies which are labelled respectively " impressionism " " decadence," and " symbolism," according to the point of view from which they are being discussed, began to make themselves felt in Russian art, resulting in a partial reaction from the vigorous realism of the 'sixties and 'seventies, and also from the academic romanticism which was the prevalent note of the cosmopolitan Russian school. What

Debussy had derived from his study of Moussorgsky and other Russian composers, the Slavs
now began to take back with interest from the
members of the younger French school.   The
flattering tribute of imitation hitherto offered
to Glinka, Tchaikovsky, and Wagner was now
to be transferred to Gabriel Fauré, Debussy,
and Ravel.   In two composers this new current
of thought is clearly observed.

Vladimir Ivanovich Rebikov (b. 1866) re-
ceived   most   of   his   musical   education   in
Berlin and Vienna.   On his return to Russia
he settled for a time at Odessa, where his first
opera *In the Storm* was produced in 1894.   A
few years later he organised a new branch of
the I. R. M. S. at Kishiniev, but in 1901 he
took up his abode permanently in Moscow.
Rebikov has expressed his own musical creed
in the following words : " Music is the language
of the emotions.   Our emotions have neither
starting point, definite form, nor ending : when
we transmit them through music it should be in
conformity with this point of view."[1]   Acting
upon this theory, Rebikov's music, though it
contains a good deal that is original, leaves an
impression of vagueness and formlessness on
the average mind ; not, of course, as compared
with the very latest examples of modernism,

[1] Quoted in the article on this composer in the Russian
edition of Riemann's Musical Dictionary, 1904.

but in comparison with what immediately precedes it in Russian music. In his early opera *In the Storm*, based on Korolenko's legend " The Forest is Murmuring " (*Liess Shoumit*), the influence of Tchaikovsky is still apparent. His second work, *The Christmas Tree*, was produced at the Aquarium Theatre, Moscow, in 1903. Cheshikin says that the libretto is a combination of one of Dostoievsky's tales with Hans Andersen's " The Little Match-Girl " and Hauptmann's "Hannele." The contrast between the sad reality of life and the bright visions of Christmastide lend themselves to scenic effects. The music is interesting by reason of its extreme modern tendencies. The opera contains several orchestral numbers which seem to have escaped the attention of enterprising conductors—a Valse, a March of Gnomes, a Dance of Mummers, and a Dance of Chinese Dolls.

The second composer to whom I referred as showing signs of French impressionist influence is Serge Vassilenko (b. 1872, Moscow). He first came before the public in 1902 with a Cantata, *The Legend of the City of Kitezh*. Like Rachmaninov's *Aleko*, this was also a diploma work. The following year it was given in operatic form by the Private Opera Company in Moscow. Some account of the beautiful mystical legend of the city that was miraculously saved from the Tatars by the fervent prayers of its inhabitants has already been given in the chapter dealing with Rimsky-Korsakov. It remains to be said that Vassilenko's treatment of the subject is in many ways strong and original. He is remarkably successful in reviving the remote, fantastic, rather austere atmosphere of Old Russia, and uses Slavonic and Tatar melodies in effective contrast. The work, which does not appear to have become a repertory opera, is worth the study of those who are interested in folk-music.

There is little satisfaction in presenting my readers with a mere list of names, but space does not permit me to do much more in the case of the following composers :

G. A. Kazachenko (b. 1858), of Malo-Russian origin, has written two operas : *Prince Serebryany* (1892) and *Pan Sotnik* (1902),[1] which have met with some success. A. N. Korestchenko, the composer of *Belshazzar's Feast* (1892), *The Angel of Death* (Lermontov), and *The Ice Palace* (1900). N. R. Kochetov, whose *Terrible Revenge* (Gogol) was produced in St. Petersburg in 1897 ; and Lissenko, sometimes called " the Malo-Russian Glinka," the composer of a whole series of operas that enjoy some popularity in the southern provinces of Russia.

This list is by no means exhaustive, for the

[1] Pan is the title of the Polish gentry, Sotnik, literally a centurion, a military grade.

proportion of Russian composers who have
produced operatic works is a striking fact in
the artistic history of the country—a phenomenon which can only be attributed to the encouragement held out to musicians by the great and
increasing number of theatres scattered over
the vast surface of the Empire.

As we have seen, all the leading representatives of Russian music, whether they belonged
to the nationalist movement or not, occupied
themselves with opera. There are, however,
two distinguished exceptions. Anatol Constantinovich Liadov (b. 1855) and Alexander
Constantinovich Glazounov (b. 1865) were both
members, at any rate for a certain period of their
lives, of the circles of Balakirev and Belaiev,
but neither of them have shared the common
attraction to dramatic music. Glazounov, it is
true, has written some remarkably successful
ballets—" Raymonda " and " The Seasons "—
but shows no inclination to deal with the
problems of operatic style.

The " opera-ballet," which is not—what at the
present moment it is frequently being called—a
new form of operatic art, but merely the revival
of an old one,[1] is engaging the attention of the
followers of Rimsky-Korsakov. At the same

[1] For example, the Court ballets of the sixteenth and
seventeenth centuries were practically opera-ballets, since
they included songs, dances and spoken dialogue.

time it should be observed that the application of this term to *A Night in May* and *The Golden Cock* is not sanctioned by what the composer himself has inscribed upon the title pages.

At the present time the musical world is eagerly expecting the production of Igor Stravinsky's first opera *The Nightingale*. This composer, by his ballets *The Bird of Fire, Petrouchka,* and *The Sacrifice to Spring*, has worked us up through a steady *crescendo* of interest to a climax of curiosity as to what he will produce next. So far, we know him only as the composer of highly original and often brilliant instrumental works. It is difficult to prophesy what his treatment of the vocal element in music may prove to be. The work is in three acts, based upon Hans Andersen's story of the Emperor of China and the Nightingale. The opera was begun several years ago, and we are therefore prepared to find in it some inequality of style ; but the greater part of it, so we are told, bears the stamp of Stravinsky's "advanced" manner, and the fundamental independence and novelty of the score of *The Sacrifice to Spring* leads us to expect in *The Nightingale* a work of no ordinary power.

Russia, from the earliest institution of her opera houses, has always been well served as regards foreign artists. All the great European stars have been attracted there by the princely terms offered for their services. Russian opera, however, had to be contented for a long period with second-rate singers. Gradually the natural talent of the race was cultivated, and native singers appeared upon the scene who were equal in every respect to those imported from abroad. The country has always been rich in bass and baritone voices. One of the most remarkable singers of the last century, O. A. Petrov (1807-1878), was a bass-baritone of a beautiful quality, with a compass extending from B to G sharp. He made his début at the Imperial Opera, St. Petersburg, in 1830, as Zoroaster in " The Magic Flute." Stassov often spoke to me of this great artist, the operatic favourite of his young days. There were few operatic stars, at least at that period, who did not—so Stassov declared—make themselves ridiculous at times. Petrov was the exception. He was a great actor ; his facial play was varied and expressive, without the least exaggeration ; he was picturesque, forcible, graceful, and, above all, absolutely free from conventional pose. His interpretation of the parts of Ivan Sousanin in *A Life for the Tsar*, the Miller in *The Roussalka*, of Leporello in *The Stone Guest*, and, even in his last days, of Varlaam in *Boris Godounov*, were inimitable for their depth of feeling, historic truth, intellectual grasp, and sincerity. Artistically speaking, Petrov begat Shaliapin.

To Petrov succeeded Melnikov, a self-taught singer, who was particularly fine in the parts of Russlan, the Miller, and Boris Godounov. Among true basses Karyakin possessed a phenomenal voice, but not much culture. A critic once aptly compared his notes for power, depth, and roundness to a row of mighty oaken barrels.

Cui, in his " Recollections of the Opera," speaks of the following artists, stars of the Maryinsky Theatre, St. Petersburg, between 1872 and 1885 : Menshikova, who possessed a powerful soprano voice of rare beauty ; Raab, who was musically gifted ; Levitskaya, distinguished for her sympathetic qualities, and Pavlovskaya, a remarkably intelligent and " clever " artist. But his brightest memories of this period centre around Platonova. Her voice was not of exceptional beauty, but she was so naturally gifted, and her impersonation so expressive, that she never failed to make a profound impression. " How she loved Russian art," says Cui, " and with what devotion she was prepared to serve it in comparison with most of the favourite singers of the day ! None of us native composers, old or young, could have dispensed with her. The entire Russian repertory rested on her, and she bore the burden courageously and triumphantly." Her best parts were Antonida in *A Life for the Tsar*, Natasha in *The Roussalka*, Marina in *Boris Godounov*, and Donna Anna in *The Stone Guest*.

Among contraltos, after Leonova's day, Lavrovskaya and Kroutikova were the most popular. The tenors Nikolsky, Orlov, and Vassiliev all had fine voices. Orlov was good as Michael Toucha in *The Maid of Pskov ;* while Vassiliev's best part was the King of Berendei in Rimsky-Korsakov's *Snow Maiden.* Another tenor, whose reputation however was chiefly made abroad, was Andreiev.

Later on, during the 'eighties and 'nineties, Kamenskaya, a fine soprano, was inimitable in the part of Rogneda (Serov), and in Tchaikovsky's *Maid of Orleans.* Dolina, a rich and resonant mezzo-soprano, excelled as Ratmir in Glinka's *Russlan.* Slavina, whose greatest success was in Bizet's " Carmen," and Mravina, a high *coloratura* soprano, were both favourites at this time. To this period also belong the triumphs of the Figners—husband and wife. Medea Figner was perhaps at her best as Carmen, and her husband was an admirable Don José, but it is as the creator of Lensky in *Eugene Oniegin*, and of Herman in *The Queen of Spades* that he will live in the affections of the Russian public.

In Feodor Ivanovich Shaliapin, Russia probably possesses the greatest living operatic artist. Born February 1/13, 1873, in the picturesque old city of Kazan, he is of peasant descent. He had practically no education in childhood, and as regards both his intellectual and musical culture he is, to all intents and purposes, an autodidact. For a time he is said to have worked with a shoe-maker in the same street where Maxim Gorky was toiling in the baker's underground shop, so graphically described in his tale " Twenty-six and One." For a short period Shaliapin sang in the Archbishop's choir, but at seventeen he joined a local operetta company which was almost on the verge of bankruptcy. When no pay was forthcoming, he earned a precarious livelihood by frequenting the railway station and doing the work of an outporter. He was often perilously near starvation. Later on, he went with a travelling company of Malo-Russians to the region of the Caspian and the Caucasus. On this tour he sang—and danced, when occasion demanded. In 1892 he found himself in Tiflis, where his voice and talents attracted the attention of a well-known singer Oussatov, who gave him some lessons and got him engaged at the opera in that town. He made his début at Tiflis in *A Life for the Tsar*. In 1894 he sang in St. Petersburg, at the Summer Theatre in the Aquarium, and also at the Panaevsky Theatre. The following year he was engaged at the Maryinsky Theatre, but the authorities seem

SHALIAPIN AS DON QUIXOTE

to have been blind to the fact that in Shaliapin
they had acquired a second Petrov. His ap-
pearances there were not very frequent. It was
not until 1896, when the lawyer-millionaire
Mamantov paid the fine which released him
from the service of the Imperial Opera House,
and invited him to join the Private Opera
Company at Moscow, that Shaliapin got his
great chance in life. He became at once the
idol of the Muscovites, and admirers journeyed
from St. Petersburg and the provinces to hear
him. When I visited St. Petersburg in 1897,
I found Vladimir Stassov full of enthusiasm for
the genius of Shaliapin. Unluckily for me, the
season of the Private Opera Company had just
come to an end, but I learnt at secondhand to
know and appreciate Shaliapin in all his great
impersonations. By 1899 the Imperial Opera
of Moscow had engaged him at a salary of 60,000
roubles a year. His fame soon spread abroad
and he was in request at Monte Carlo, Buenos
Aires, and Milan ; in the last named city he
married, and installed himself in a house there
for a time. Visits to New York and Paris
followed early in this century, and finally,
through the enterprise of Sir Joseph Beecham,
London had an opportunity of hearing this great
artist during the season of 1913. Speaking to
me of his London experiences, Shaliapin was
evidently deeply moved by, and not a little

astonished at, the enthusiastic welcome accorded to him and to his compatriots. He had, of course, been told that we were a cold and phlegmatic race, but he found in our midst such heart-felt warmth and sincerity as he had never before experienced outside Russia.

Shaliapin's romantic history has proved a congenial soil for the growth of all manner of sensational tales and legends around his life and personality. They make amusing material for newspaper and magazine articles ; but as I am here concerned with history rather than with fiction, I will forbear to repeat more than one anecdote connected with his career. The incident was related to me by a famous Russian musician. I will not, however, vouch for its veracity, but only for its highly picturesque and dramatic qualities. A few years ago the chorus of the Imperial Opera House desired to present a petition to the Emperor. It was arranged that after one of the earlier scenes in *Boris Godounov* the curtain should be rung up again, and the chorus should be discovered kneeling in an attitude of supplication, their faces turned towards the Imperial box, while their chosen representative should offer the petition to the " exalted personage " who was attending the opera that night. When the curtain went up for the second time it disclosed an unrehearsed effect. Shaliapin, who was not aware of the presentation of the petition by the chorus, had not left the stage in time. There, among the crowd of humble petitioners, stood Tsar Boris ; dignified, colossal, the very personification of kingly authority, in his superb robes of cloth of gold, with the crown of Monomakh upon his head. For one thrilling, sensational moment Tsar Boris stood face to face with Tsar Nicholas II. ; then some swift impulse, born of custom, of good taste, or of the innate spirit of loyalty that lurks in every Russian heart, brought the dramatic situation to an end. Tsar Boris dropped on one knee, mingling with the supplicating crowd, and etiquette triumphed, to the inward mortification of a contingent of hot-headed young revolutionists who had hoped to see him defy convention to the last.

In Russia, where some kind of political *leitmotif* is bound to accompany a great personality through life, however much he may wish to disassociate himself from it, attempts have been made to identify Shaliapin with the extreme radical party. It is sufficient, and much nearer the truth, to say that he is a patriot, with all that the word implies of love for one's country as it is, and hope for what its destinies may yet be. Shaliapin could not be otherwise than patriotic, seeing that he is Russian through and through. When we are in his society the two qualities which immediately rivet our attention are his Herculean virility and his *Russian-ness*. He is Russian in his sincerity and candour, in his broad human sympathies, and in a certain child-like simplicity which is particularly engaging in this much-worshipped popular favourite. He is Russian, too, in his extremes of mood, which are reflected so clearly in his facial expression. Silent and in repose, he has the look of almost tragic sadness and patient endurance common in the peasant types of Great Russia. But suddenly his whole face is lit up with a smile which is full of drollery, and his humour is frank and infectious.

As an actor his greatest quality appears to me to be his extraordinary gift of identification with the character he is representing. Shaliapin does not merely throw himself into the part, to use a phrase commonly applied to the histrionic art. He seems to disappear, to empty himself of all personality, that Boris Godounov or Ivan the Terrible may be re-incarnated for us. It might pass for some occult process ; but it is only consummate art. While working out his own conception of a part, unmoved by convention or opinion, Shaliapin neglects no accessory study that can heighten the realism of his interpretation. It is impossible to see him as Ivan the Terrible, or Boris, without realising that he is steeped in the history of those periods, which live again at his will.[1] In the same way he has studied the masterpieces of Russian art to good purpose, as all must agree who have compared the scene of Ivan's frenzied grief over the corpse of Olga, in the last scene of Rimsky-Korsakov's opera, with Repin's terrible picture of the Tsar, clasping in his arms the body of the son whom he has just killed in a fit of insane anger. The agonising remorse and piteous senile grief have been transferred from Repin's canvas to Shaliapin's living picture, without the revolting suggestion of the shambles which mars the painter's work. Sometimes, too, Shaliapin will take a hint from the living model. His dignified make-up as the Old Believer Dositheus, in Moussorgsky's *Khovanstchina*, owes not a little to the personality of Vladimir Stassov.

Here is an appreciation of Shaliapin which will be of special interest to the vocalist :

" One of the most striking features of his technique is the remarkable fidelity of word utterance which removes all sense of artificiality, so frequently associated with operatic singing. His diction floats on a beautiful cantilena, particularly in his *mezzo-voce* singing, which— though one would hardly expect it from a singer endowed with such a noble bass voice—

---

[1] " A singer's mind becomes subtler with every mental excursion into history, sacred or profane."—D. Ffrangcon Davies. " The Singing of the Future." John Lane, The Bodley Head.

is one of the most telling features of his
performance. There is never any striving after
vocal effects, and his voice is always subservient
to the words. This style of singing is surely
that which Wagner so continually demanded
from his interpreters ; but it is the antithesis
of that staccato ' Bayreuth bark ' which a few
years ago so woefully misrepresented the
master's ideal of fine lyric diction. The atmosphere and tone-colour which Shaliapin imparts
to his singing are of such remarkable quality
that one feels his interpretation of Schubert's
' Doppelgänger ' must of necessity be a thing
of genius, unapproachable by other contemporary singers. The range of his voice is extensive,
for though of considerable weight in the lower
parts, his upper register is remarkable in its
conformity to his demands. The sustained
upper E natural with which he finishes that great
song ' When the king went forth to war,' is
uttered with a delicate *pianissimo* that would do
credit to any lyric tenor or soprano. Yet his
technique is of that high order that never
obtrudes itself upon the hearer. It is always
his servant, never his master. His readings are
also his own, and it is his absence of all con-
ventionality that makes his singing of the
' Calunnia ' aria from ' Il Barbiere ' a thing
of delight, so full of humour is its interpretation, and so satisfying to the demands of the

most exacting ' *bel cantist.*'   The reason is not
far to seek, for his method is based upon a
thoroughly sound breath control, which produces
such splendid *cantabile* results.   Every student
should listen to this great singer and profit by
his art." [1]

A few concluding words as to the present
conditions of opera in Russia.   They have
greatly changed during the last thirty years.
In St. Petersburg the Maryinsky Theatre,
erected in 1860, renovated in 1894, and more or
less reorganised in 1900, was for a long time the
only theatre available for Russian opera in the
capital.   In 1900 the People's Palace, with a
theatre that accommodates 1,200 spectators, was
opened with a performance of *A Life for the
Tsar ;* here the masterpieces of national opera
are now given from time to time at popular
prices.   Opera is also given in the great hall
of the Conservatoire, formerly the " Great
Theatre " ; and occasionally in the " Little
Theatre."   In Moscow the " Great Theatre " or
Opera House is the official home of music-
drama.   It now has as rivals, the Zimin Opera
(under the management of S. I. Zimin) and the
National Opera.   In 1897 the Moscow Private
Opera Company was started with the object of

Communicated at my request by my friend, Mr.
Herbert Heyner, who has made a special study of Shaliapin's
art both at the opera and from gramophone records.

producing novelties by Russian composers, and encouraging native opera in general. It was located at first in the Solodovnikov Theatre, under the management of Vinter, and the conductorship of Zeleny. It soon blossomed into a fine organisation when S. Mamantov, a wealthy patron of art, came to its support. Through its palmy days (1897-1900), Ippolitov-Ivanov was the conductor, and a whole series of national operas by Cui, Rimsky-Korsakov, and others were superbly staged. Shaliapin first made his mark at this time.

Numerous private opera companies sprang up in Russia about the close of last century. Cheshikin gives a list of over sixty, mounting opera in the provinces between 1896 and 1903 ; indeed the whole country from Archangel to Astrakhan and from Vilna to Vladivostok seems to have been covered by these enterprising managers ; and the number has doubtless increased in the last ten years. When, in addition to these, we reckon the many centres which boast a state-supported opera house, it would appear that Russians have not much to complain of as regards this form of entertainment. But the surface of the country is vast, and there are still districts where cultivated music, good or bad, is an unknown enjoyment. Nor must we imagine that the standard of these provincial private companies is always an exalted one, or that national operas, if presented at all, are mounted as we are accustomed to see them in Western Europe. We may hope that the case cited by a critic, of a Moscow manager who produced Donizetti's " La Fille du Régiment " under the title of " A Daughter of the Regiment of La Grande Armée," in a Russian version said to have been the work of an English nursery governess, with a picture of the Battle of Marengo as a set background, was altogether exceptional. But indifferent performances do occur, even in a country so highly educated in operatic matters as Russia may fairly claim to be.

As I write the last pages of this book, the comprehensiveness of its title fills me with dismay. " An Introduction to the Study of Russian Opera " would have been more modest and appropriate, since no complete and well-balanced survey of the subject could possibly be contained in a volume of this size. Much that is interesting has been passed over without comment ; and many questions demanded much fuller treatment. One fact, however, I have endeavoured to set forth in these pages in the clearest and most emphatic terms : Russian opera is beyond all question a genuine growth of the Russian soil ; it includes the aroma and flavour of its native land " as the wine must taste of its own grapes." Its roots lie deep in the folk-music, where they have spread and flourished naturally and without effort. So profoundly embedded and so full of vitality are its fibres, that nothing has been able to check their growth and expansion. Discouraged by the Church, its germs still lived on in the music of the people ; neglected by the professional element, it found shelter in the hearts of amateurs ; refused by the Imperial Opera Houses, it flourished in the drawing-rooms of a handful of enthusiasts. It has always existed in some embryonic form as an inherent part of the national life ; and when at last it received official recognition, it quickly absorbed all that was given to it in the way of support and attention, but persisted in throwing out its vigorous branches in whatever direction it pleased. Persecution could not kill it, nor patronage spoil it ; because it is one with the soul of the people. May it long retain its lofty idealism and sane vigour !

INDEX OF OPERAS

INDEX OF NAMES